American Farmers
and
The Rise of Agribusiness

Seeds of Struggle

American Farmers
and
The Rise of Agribusiness

Seeds of Struggle

Advisory Editors

Dan C. McCurry
Richard E. Rubenstein

THE
THIRD POWER

Farmers to the Front

J[ames] A. Everitt

ARNO PRESS
A New York Times Company
New York – 1975

Reprint Edition 1975 by Arno Press Inc.

Reprinted from a copy in
  The Princeton University Library

AMERICAN FARMERS AND THE RISE OF AGRIBUSINESS:
Seeds of Struggle
ISBN for complete set: 0-405-06760-7
See last pages of this volume for titles.

Manufactured in the United States of America

Library of Congress Cataloging in Publication Data

Everitt, James Andrew, 1857-
    The third power.

    (American farmers and the rise of agribusiness)
    Reprint of the 1907 ed. published by Everitt,
Indianapolis.
    1. Agricultural societies--United States.
2. American Society of Equity of North America.
I. Title. II. Series.
HD1485.E7E8 1975   323.44'0973   74-30630
ISBN 0-405-06799-2

THE
THIRD POWER

Farmers to the Front

By J. A. EVERITT

Founder of The American Society of Equity of North America
Indianapolis, U. S. A.

THE FOURTH EDITION

INDIANAPOLIS
J. A. EVERITT, PUBLISHER
1907

Yours to Bring Farmers
to the Front J. H. Curritt

TO

THE LARGEST CLASS

THE MOST DEPENDENT CLASS

THE HARDEST WORKING CLASS

THE POOREST PAID CLASS

OF PEOPLE IN THE WORLD

THE FARMERS

I DEDICATE THIS BOOK

PREFACE

The farmers are under no legal or moral obligation to feed the balance of the world at an unfairly low price.

If there is a place or corner anywhere in the world where the producers of our food and clothing supplies (commonly called farmers) are not ready to revolt against the absolute domination of non-producing classes in pricing their products, I am not aware of it.

That the old and thoroughly bad system can speedily be changed—the producers regulate the marketing of their products and make their own prices—I am thoroughly convinced.

The farmers own the earth. We may safely claim that farming exists by Divine right. The farmers first possess all the food and clothing supplies which are indispensable for the life and comfort of humans and domestic animals; their products constitute the greater portion of traffic for railroads and ships; nearly all the factories work on raw material produced on the farms and the products of the factories are largely consumed by the farmers, or in equipments to handle farm products. It is clear, the important position of the farmer in his relation to all other industries, and how

closely all other industries are interwoven with that
of agriculture. It is the same way all over the
world, in all civilized countries.

If any people, any one class, or any one industry
is entitled to distinction as the preferred business,
or its people "the select of the earth," that business
is agriculture and that people are the farmers. If
any one class should prosper more than another,
this distinction should fall to the farmers. But this
is not an attempt to raise one class over others, it
is not even an attempt to make all equal, but to
equalize conditions so all may have an equal opportunity to secure a fair share of rewards for efforts
put forth.

All movements for the benefit of the masses had
opposition at the start. An idea may be born and
promulgated. The originator of the idea may be
stoned to death or hung, but if the idea is good and
has vital force, it grows and will not down. An
evolution once started never recedes, but develops
into the perfect flower or fruit.

This is an age of organization and co-operation.
The old saying, "Competition is the life of trade,"
is changed to "Co-operation is the life of trade."

An individual would be strong enough if he was
the only individual in the world. However, if he
is one of a large class he is weak and the larger the
class the weaker the individual. The farmer class
is the most numerous, hence, the individual farmer
is the weakest individual when he stands alone. "In
union there is strength." The greater the union
the greater the strength. The farmers united

would be the greatest union—greater than all other unions combined. They would represent a strength and power such as the world never knew before. The farmer power is the third power to assert itself, but it will be the first power in strength and importance.

The bestirring and awakening of this last and greatest power is the most significant event of the present generation. No individual, no matter what his position—professional, industrial or political—can afford to ignore its birth and make calculations on its rise. For, while it is not a power that will contest for mastery by brute force in the fields economic or politic, it will affect all in its demands for equity and the equal rights of man.

The entrance of the American Society of Equity into the economic problems of the world, through which the Third Power will rise, marks an epoch. The awakening of the agricultural classes, the organization of them into national and international co-operative bodies, which is now being accomplished, will remove agriculture from the list of uncertain industries and place it on a basis of certainty for prices equal to that enjoyed by the best regulated manufacturing or commercial enterprises.

The undertaking is great, but since the correct plan has been evolved, the desirable ends, in the ordinary evolution of the times, will work out as surely as the fruit follows the flower. The revolution that will take place in prevailing customs and laws might appal us if it was not for the fact that, in the working out of this stupendous movement everything will be toward betterments—physically, socially, industrially and politically.

* * * * * * * * * * *

The hope of the author is that the soil owners and workers will be aroused to a sense of the true condition of their industry; that agriculture in America and throughout the world will soon occupy the high position to which it is entitled, when it will stand first of all in importance and power.

A fair, equitable, impartial, unprejudiced consideration of the Third Power is asked and your co-operation to quickly make it a real power is solicited. **THE AUTHOR.**

CONTENTS.

CONTENTS—Continued.

THE THIRD POWER

CHAPTER I

A hundred years, and more, ago,
   The farmers rose their rights to take;
They were the first to strike a blow
   For freedom's and for country's sake.

Colonial sires, your path we tread,
   Against oppression's tyrant hand;
Our bloodless battle shall be led,
   Till justice reigns throughout the land.

We battle for the common good,
   Our flag in freedom's cause unfurled,
As when "the embattled farmers stood,
   And fired the shot heard round the world."
                Elma Iona Locke.

RIGHT SHALL PREVAIL.

There is some danger today lest we forget that there are three factors in production—land, labor, and capital. The political economist told us this many years ago, but when we read of the operations of Morgan, Gates, Schwab, and the other great capitalists and promoters, we are sometimes almost convinced that these men are the sole creators of wealth, and that land and labor really have nothing to do with it. Yet the old law is sound, and so it will stand. Mr. Morgan has to stand on the earth, and in this sense at least it is the land that supports him. The Chicago gamblers could not speculate in wheat unless there were such a thing as wheat in existence. Mr. W. B. Leeds's railroad could not last but a little while if it were not for the crops that have to be carried to market. So it is clear that these men do not create, and can not create anything. All that they do is to change the form of wealth, or to make, not to create, new wealth by the application of capital and labor to the products of the land, in one way or the other. If they make money in any other way they do it simply by taking it from some one else. The middleman, who gets between two people who want to trade, and takes toll of them both, adds nothing to the wealth of the country. The subject then is creation, and the relation of the different factors to it.

If it be true that the prosperity and material welfare of a country is dependent on the efficiency of these three instruments, land, labor and capital, it follows that we should do all we can to increase the efficiency of these instruments and maintain them at a high standard. We often seem to act as though we did not believe this to be true. For each class, instead of trying to add to the efficiency of other classes as well as of itself, frequently strives to increase its efficiency at the expense of the other classes. Labor seeks to extract the last dollar from capital, and capital endeavors to force labor to work for the lowest wages possible. Organized capital and organized labor combine to

beat down the price of products from the land until workers on our farms are the poorest paid of
any class of laborers. Yet the intelligent laboring
man knows that the more capital there is in the
country, provided it be wisely and productively employed and carefully managed, the better it is for
him. And the intelligent employer understands that
in order for him to get the best results he must
pay his men enough to enable them to live well and
keep themselves in good mental and physical condition. Perhaps it is safe—at any rate it seems to
be necessary—to allow each of these classes to carry on this warfare for its own good, even though
success costs the rival something, trusting that
good may in the long run come out of the conflict
of interests. With land, however, we all admit the
necessity of keeping the farmers prosperous to insure prosperity to others.

Certain it is that the efficiency of labor and capital has vastly increased in our day, particularly in
our country. The freer use of the credit system,
the more intelligent management of money, the
rapid turning over of capital, the wonderful increase in the use of machinery, and intelligent labor, have all co-operated to enable capital to do
things which it did not even dream of a generation
ago. We build bridges in the Egyptian desert in
half the time and for half the cost that the English can. The Atlas Works in Indianapolis ships
engines all over the world, and sells them in freest
competition with foreign makes. There is hardly a
country on earth that has not heard the scream of

the American locomotive, the click of the American typewriter, and enjoyed the blessings of cheap American bread. The conquests of American capital and the effect of the wonderful resources of this country have been marvelous. Turning to labor we find that here, too, there has been an increase in efficiency. Education, growing intelligence and skill, sobriety, capacity for hard work, ambition to rise out of the labor class and to become a boss, facility in the use of machinery, inventive faculty, have all combined to make our labor the most efficient in the world. But to a certain extent these influences have been at work on the farms as well as in the counting room, the mill and the factory. And our farmers are far in advance of their fathers and grandfathers in ability to turn out results in crops. But there is one great thing which they have not yet fully learned, and that is the power of combination. The laborer has been helped much by his unions, and because of them he can command a wage such as his brethren of other days could not. Through his unions he has made his importance felt, and often has been able to dictate terms to his employer. That employer has also found a great help in combination. By means of corporations and trusts he has been able to carry through large enterprises, to have something to say about wages, to decrease the cost of production while keeping no small part of the saving for himself, and to influence, if not to constitute prices. So we see combinations, co-operation and trusts in almost every branch of industry.

But the farmer has yet to learn the lesson. Others have something to say about the prices at which they will sell their commodities. If they do not fix them, they at least do influence them favorably to themselves. When the market is glutted, the manufacturer or mine-owner can curtail production, or shut down entirely, until the demand catches up with or runs ahead of the supply. The laborer can and does regulate the supply of laborers and does refuse to work except on terms reasonably satisfactory to himself, and the mere fear of a strike often drives the employer to make concessions which he would not otherwise think of making. The worker has a voice in the making of his wages, and the employer passes the tax along by making his prices accordingly.

But the farmer allows others to make prices for him. All he is supposed to know under the present system is how to work many hours a day and the road to market. When he gets there he finds a man who tells him how much his produce is worth, and if he wants to take something home with him he is told the price of that also. He has no organization, and no method of bringing pressure to bear on those who buy of him. Speculators and gamblers on boards of trade tell him what he shall sell his produce for. And he sells at their figures. The board of trade gamblers juggle with the price, and, though the condition of the crops and production and consumption should govern prices, they have very little influence. The prices of the important farm crops are made in organized markets by great

When He Gets There He Finds a Man Who Tells
Him What His Produce is Worth.
See Page 15.

aggregations of corporate capital ruled by unscrupulous human agencies, or by speculators who set prices arbitrarily without any reference to supply demand or equity. This arbitrary fixing of prices destroys the independence of the greatest class of our citizens—the farmers—because the farmers have no part in it. It is more tyrannical than were the taxes imposed by George III. This is because the farmers are unorganized, and usually without a knowledge of the real conditions. Commercial slavery of this degree is as bad as personal slavery. Thus the greatest class in the production of wealth, on which all others depend, is at the mercy of a few. The farmers unorganized are demoralized industrially, and without any influence on the situation at all proportionate to their importance. Comparatively speaking, they are powerless. They grow all the stuff possible and sell it for what they can get—and then wonder why the year's balance sheet does not show a better result.

The agricultural industry of the country is still the victim of the most intensive competition system ever established. Each farmer is in constant warfare against all the others. Each is striving to produce the greatest yields possible—in face of the indisputable fact that the larger the yields the lower the prices—and then he sells the products without the least regard to other producers. In this way the markets are oftentimes glutted and conditions produced for organized speculators and gamblers to perform their perfect work in depressing prices. Notwithstanding that the farmer of today can produce five times as much product as the farmer of a few generations ago, his net earning capacity has not increased to keep pace with the incomes in other lines, but rather decreased. At the same time he is obliged to pay more taxes to meet the extravagances in government and high prices for all he buys. Also his land which then was virgin soil has become in large part exhausted; which item of itself represents probably half the value of his farm as it relates to producing crops, and will require good management, the outlay of much labor and a large cash sum to replace when he is called upon to increase his average yield to keep pace with increasing consumption.

The American farmer of to-day is not living from his investments in farm land, but as a mere laborer, and receives less than half as much pay as the union laborer, yet works harder and longer hours. In short, the farmers of the United States can only continue in business on the present basis by using the cheapest labor on earth, i. e., wife labor, child labor, and labor of their babes. The prices set by speculators and gamblers for the fine grain, vegetables and fruit—the products of God's earth—compel the agriculturist to resort to such unbearable extremities. No hired men can be secured to take their places at wages the farmers can pay. While the nation and states cry against female and child labor in factories, not a word of protest is raised against the toil of the farmer's wife and children.

Why is it so that the farmers, who own the earth, first possess the food and clothing supplies—

wool and cotton—are the creators of nearly all real wealth, the foundation of all our institutions, who are the most numerous and as a class the most wealthy, have become reduced to this condition of slavery?

It is a stupendous problem which, if solved, will mean more for humanity than anything since the Christian era. If the farmers can demand and secure equity in all their business relations with other people it will mean the beginning of a new era for them and through them will make a social and industrial millennium for all humanity.

Let us see what, then, can be done to elevate the agricultural business of this country and of the world and place it on an equality with the best of other professions and industries.

The fact that capitalists and laborers are so effectively organized makes it especially important that the farmers should organize. It is becoming clearer and clearer every day that whatever advantage either the capitalistic or laboring class wins, is won not so much at the expense of the other as at the expense of the great bodies of unorganized people who can not defend themselves. When wages are forced up by a strike the farmer pays a large part of the raise by an increase of price on what he buys. When trusts lift prices simply because they have the power to do so, this increase also is largely made out of the farmers who are the greatest consumers. It must be so. The strife between organizations is bound to hurt the unorganized. When Mr. Mitchell and Mr. Baer agree on an in-

creased scale of wages, Mr. Baer at once shoves up
the price of coal. Or when the government makes
a new law compelling the railroads to spend more
money to give better service they promptly raise
the freight rates and the public pays the bill. I t is
the same way with any organized class or industry
whether the increased cost comes for improvement
or for defense in courts, the public must pay the
bill. The closer the unions and the trusts get together and the more government trials and expensive investigations and defenses, the more certain it
is that the unorganized mob of consumers, of which
the farmers constitute by far the largest element,
will have to pay for whatever gain either wins, or
expense incurred, because they are not in a position
to pass it along.

From every point of view, therefore, it is impera-
tive that the farmers should organize, not for political, but for business reasons. Surely the man
who raises the crops ought to have something to
say about the price he gets for them. He should
also know how much wheat, for instance, is being
raised, so he may know what it is, in equity, worth;
and, let me say, a needful commodity is always
worth, in equity, what it cost to produce it, with a
fair margin for profit added. This margin should
be rated the same as others have set on their goods.
The cost should be found on a basis that allows the
producer a wage equal to what others get, interest
on investment, a sum that will repair waste or overcome depreciation of the plant, with profit added.
Then we have an equitable value. If his market is

in danger of being glutted it should be as easy as it would be quite as justifiable for him to curtail his output or marketing as it is for the manufacturer. He should have it in his power, as the laborer has, to say that he will not work except for fair remuneration. As it is now he is hedged around by the scheming of the shrewdest men in the world who manipulate his market in mysterious ways. Besides this, his business is also subject to other uncertain conditions, such as weather, insects, blight, rust, etc. He can not escape from his thraldom to the natural causes. But he ought, as a freeborn American citizen, to vow that he will break the chains of slavery to the other masters.

The question is simply one of the application of power. The farmer has the power to get whatever he wants, and to make his life what it should be. He must learn how to use it. No power except highly organized power is of any value in these times. The individual man is industrially powerless in the United States to-day. Two things, therefore, seem to be clear. First the farmer must use his power to the end that he may be his own master, and not the slave of others and the burden-bearer of the nation. Second, he must learn that the only way in which he can use the power which is his, is through organization, an organization of his own, controlled by himself, and in his own interest. By doing this he will benefit, not only himself, but all classes of society. It is not proposed that he should wage a war of offense but simply one of defense. He is not to ask privileges, but to insist on his rights—rights which other classes of society now exercise without question from any one, rights which in the farmer's case are Divine. Power applied through organization is the industrial law of the day. The farmer must rule his life by it.

CHAPTER II

There's the wily speculator,
  Who forms his rings of steel,
While the honest man is toiling
  In the hot and scorching field.
He is lying awake and planning,
  You may rightfully suppose,
To cheat the honest farmer
  Out of everything he grows.

THE WILEY SPECULATOR.

In Frank Norris's great novel, "The Pit," is this:
"They call it buying and selling, down there in
La Salle Street. But it is simply betting. Betting
on the condition of the market weeks, even months
in advance. You bet wheat goes up. I bet it goes
down. Those fellows in the pit don't own the wheat;
never even see it. Wouldn't know what to do with
it if they had it. They don't care in the least about
the grain. But there are thousands upon thousands of farmers out in Minnesota and Kansas or
the Dakotas who do, and hundred of thousands of
poor devils in America or Europe who care even
more than the farmer. I mean the fellows who raise
the grain, and the other fellows who eat it. It's
life or death for either of them, and right between
these two comes the Chicago speculator, who raises
or lowers the price out of all reason, for the benefit
of his pocket. Here is what I mean, it's like this.
If we send the price of wheat down too far, the
farmer suffers, the fellow who raises it; if we send
it up too far, the poor man in America or Europe

suffers, the fellow who eats it. * * * The only way to do so that neither the American farmer nor the consumer suffers, is to keep wheat at an average, legitimate value. The moment you inflate, or depress that, somebody suffers right away, and that is just what these gamblers are doing all the time, booming it up, or booming it down. Think of it; the food of hundreds and hundreds of thousands of people, yes millions of them, just at the mercy of a few men down there on the board of trade. They make the price. They say just how much the peasant shall pay for his loaf of bread. If he can't pay the price he simply starves. And as for the farmer, why it's ludicrous. If I build a house and offer it for sale, I put my own price on it, and if the price offered don't suit me I don't sell. But if I go out there in Kansas and raise a crop of wheat, I've got to sell it, whether I want to or not, at the figure named by those fellows in Chicago. And to make themselves rich, they make me sell it at a price that bankrupts me."

That is a true picture of the actual situation. Farmers sometimes talk as though they believed that this gambling in wheat is a good thing for them, but they forget that what they want is a certain definite and steadily maintained price; not a high price that will stimulate over-production, but an equitable price that will always secure the necessaries, comfort and some of the luxuries of life. A good price for a large crop, as well as for a short crop. A steadily maintained price, made by farmers, on the farm, instead of the uncertain price made by the speculators and gamblers on the boards trade in large cities. They may and do make money—a few of them—out of an occasional corner, but the artificially raised price stimulates holdings; the farmers do not sell until the gamblers have had their innings on "ghost" grain, the price breaks and the farmers rush their produce to market, and more often than not the sales are made on a falling market, and at prices as much too low as the corner price was too high.

If the farmers' produce were not a necessity, it would not be chosen for gambling purposes. Men do not gamble with diamonds, for people can get along without them. They do not gamble with air, for every one can get all of it that he needs. Farm products are chosen because everybody uses them, and also because, under present conditions, the farmers do not control them.

Speculators know how prone farmers are to hold on a rising market, and this helps them to accomplish their ends. In other words, the farmer does not control the situation. He simply supplies the chips with which the gamblers play the game, and even when he wins he does so in violation of the principles of equity. There is no design on the part of the gamblers that he should win. The grain pits are a curse to everybody that they touch. They are barnacles that have attached themselves on the produce of the earth. The speculators and gamblers in farm products are sap-sucking, unholy, Godless things that are holding up and gorging themselves on labor's portion as it is created on the farms. Boards of trade now run in the large cities are the Devil's own workshop. where the rewards for honest labor are forged to the profit of the non-

producing class. They are the greatest blight on
the body of industry—a danger that threatens the
very life of the farming industry of America. They
and their imps constitute a bold, fearless, devilish
power, that defies the laws of morality, the state
and nation. There is only one power that can dethrone them. It will be the grand, sweeping, majestic strength of cooperative producers.

Unorganized, the farmers are weak and the
prey of all other strong individuals and organized
classes. Organized, they will become the dominant
power, and their business or profession will become
the preferred on earth. Organized to put prices
on their own products they can remove many of the
uncertainties now attending farming, and elevate
the profession until it will be the equal of manufacturing, banking, merchandising, etc. Farming
is manufacturing, banking and merchandising. To
farm successfully requires a technical knowledge
equaling that demanded by other professions, and
more application and years to attain than most of
the professions. Therefore, the successful farmer
must be a man of attainment and broad business
qualifications. He must be an educated man and
his education must be directed along lines and to
the end that will qualify him for his important position as a farmer and business man, producer and
marketer. This will particularly be true from this
time forward, when more intensive farming must
be practiced to meet the ever increasing demands
brought about by the increasing population and
the multiplying ability to consume.

Farmers can be a power. They represent the greatest invested capital and they are the most numerous. They own the earth from which comes all wealth, the food we eat and the clothing we wear, consequently they can control the industries and the food and clothing supplies. It is clear, in their fundamental position and numerical and financial strength, they hold the key to our entire social, political and industrial system.

It is clear that farmers have within them undoubted great power, but they have been powerless commercially. They can only exert their power through organization and cooperation. There are only two questions before the farmers today, the one is: Do they want to become free, independent and a powerful factor—in fact the most powerful and inflential class in the world? The other is: Will they embrace the only way to accomplish their freedom and independence that will place them at the head in this country and others, socially industrially, and through their power of numbers be able to force a clean, strong, equitable government? Will the farmers answer these questions in the affirmative, or do they prefer to be forever the prey of the gamblers, the transportation companies, and other powers which make whatever rates and prices they please, and discriminate in favor of one class and against other?

To hold that this condition of things must continue is to hold that the farmers, on whom all others depend for their very life, comfort and privilege to do business, must depend on those who are really dependent on them. If the farmers were able to put a value on each of their products the betting in Chicago would stop, for the gamblers would know that they could not settle except on terms made by the farmers. If farmers would control their own products, they could refuse to ship until the railroads gave them fair and equitable rates, and so along the whole line. No man can buy until some other one is ready to sell, and if the farmers of the United States could say through their organization that they would not sell till they got their price, and would back up the declaration, they would get it. They could corner the supply as easily as the Chocago gamblers can, simply by holding on to what is their own—to what no one else has any right to except on payment of the price demanded by the owner, and they would soon come to the farm, or to the farmer's representative—his society—and meet his terms. Only thus can the farmer win his freedom and independence, and he can do it without infringing on the rights of any one else, and to the infinite betterment of all.

These questions seem simple enough, and yet they are apparently giving a good deal of trouble to certain classes of people who are already somewhat disturbed at the thought that perhaps the farmers may decide to control their own business. In a recent number of Harper's Weekly, which is supposed to be dependent on certain Wall Street influences for its existence, there was printed an article entitled, "The Twentieth Century Farmer." It was, as all such articles coming from such sources invariably are, exceedingly flattering. We are assured, not only that the farmer is a good fellow, but that he has things pretty much his own way. "There are, for instance," the writer says, "scores of school districts in the thinly settled portions of the plains where the entire tax is paid by the railroads and eastern corporations, and farmers' children attend the schools so supported." But the school tax is a tax on property, and if railroads and eastern corporations own the land in these districts, is there any reason why they should not pay the taxes assessed against it? How can this be considered a bonus to the farmer? Further, we know—if we know anything about taxation—that corporations shift the burden of taxation whenever they can possibly do so. If, in order to pay this school tax, the railroads raise freight rates, which are paid by the farmers, the farmers after all pay the school tax. At the most our case is simply one in which the farmers had a chance to get even—pass the tax along; there is no gratuity involved in it, yet this movement means more than is yet evident. The tax will not be passed along to the innocent consumers as I will show.

The Harper's Weekly writer speaks of the expense incurred by the general government for irrigation as something wholly for the benefit of the farmer. Surely it is for the benefit of all—of the whole country. Every foot of new territory opened up adds just so much to the wealth of all, and brings down the cost of food. This, certainly, is not to the special advantage of the farmers as a class. They

are precisely the people that would be least benefited by it. Every new farm created out of the present arid region means just so much additional competition of the farmers already engaged in operating farms.

I have opposed this irrigation scheme at every
opportunity and claim that if the government really
is desirous of doing something for the farmers it
can accomplish much more at less expense by helping the present farmers to irrigate their lands. Our
present farms are not producing a third as much as
they can, and must in a comparatively few years,
when the population of the world has doubled again.
Our averages of thirteen bushels of wheat, twenty-
seven of corn, and other crops in proportion are
distressingly low. Consumption has fully caught
up with production, in fact in some lines is ahead
of production. If the flow of the farm products to
market was not hampered and restricted by the selfish interests of speculators and gamblers, and the
uncertainties of values, which enter into every
transaction in agricultural products under the present system, the consumption today of grains, meat,
fabrics, fruit, etc., would be immensely more. Intensive farming that will double, and finally treble
the yields of our farms will be a necessity. It is
not too early to begin now. This means irrigation,
fertilization and scientific cultivation. Instead of
the government, at fabulous expense, opening up
a vast area of land that God did not design for cultivation until the more favored portion of our domain was producing it its maximum, it can more

equitably help the present farmers along the road to prosperity by irrigating the eastern part of our country.

One acre of irrigated land is equal in producing ability to two or three of non-irrigated land in the Mississippi Valley. Therefore, if the government would carry out its irrigation scheme completely in a short time, it would set our present farmers back a generation, and possibly prevent them from realizing their fond hopes of profitable prices for farm products. Our farmers are now just arriving at the point where they can rise above the competition of new territory being opened up for cultivation, and it would be a great calamity to subject them to this artificially created competition.

Let the government encourage irrigation and intensive farming on our present farms. It will result in dividing the large farms into smaller ones; prevent the small ones from being merged into large holdings; furnish new homes for millions of families in sections of the country where the conditions are most favorable for social enjoyment and industrial success. True, this plan may not be of a great benefit to a few railroad corporations and other powerful interests and for that reason may not command the attention of congress, but it would benefit many millions of the common people, and add untold millions to the wealth of our country.

The fact is that there are practically no laws for the benefit of the farmers, and it is the intention of the corporated powers, through the political machines, that there shall not be any. Ours is a government by the people in theory, but by corporations in practice. The people have won their way with little help from the federal government. In the very article under consideration we are reminded of the futile efforts of the farmer to get favoring legislation. "Once in a while," it said, "there is a political insurrection, and a Farmers' Alliance sweeps the boards, sending farmer legislators to frame super-partial laws, which later are blasted by courts." So it is, and so it must ever be until the farmers learn how to exert their strength in practical ways and for practical ends. But we are told that "the settler demands the Indian's land and gets it." "That he demands the ranchman's grazing territory and obtains that." Of course this is true, and it would be true if there were not a government in existence. For the natural evolution is from the savage state to the pastoral state, up to the agricultural state. Nothing could keep the farmer from getting the lands of the Indian and the ranchman. But the moment the farmer attempts to better his condition then we hear a howl from the men who use every power they have, not simply to help theselves, but to persuade or force the government into helping them. So we have this in the article in Harper's Weekly:

"The demagogue devotes a great deal of attention to the farmer. Frequent schemes for uniting the wheat-growers or for forcing up the price of corn are evolved; cooperative plans to make unnecessary the 'middleman' are exploittd—and usually with provision for a salary of commission to some shrewd city promoter who would not know a self-binder from a corn shredder. Every little while the telegraph tells of the probable formation of a mighty union of farmers to reduce or limit the acreage of some crop. It ends in smike—it was the dream of a schemer who hoped to profit by its success."

The threatened combination of the farmers is clearly not looked on with approval by the financial interests. Nothing that would benefit the farmer ever was looked on with approval by those interests. So in this article, the farmer is warned against "demagogues" seeking to make money out of their schemes, as if the very men who sound the warning had not all their lives made their living by "farming the farmers." There are many good texts in this Harper's Weekly article. Here is another:

"There are indications that the farmer does not take these things (proposed organizations) as seriously as he once did. He reads the daily magazines; he understands something of the other side of life. He travels more than in the days of high railway rates; the excursions back east for 'Old Home Week' bring him in touch with people of other states. He is made broader and happier. Most important of all, he is learing to make of his occupation a business, and when that is done, he ceases to consider himself the favorite of fortune. As a result he becomes a business man, and takes rank among the captains of industry—not the commander, for none is supreme in rank, but an equal sharer in the advancement and prosperity of the nation."

Well, if the farmer has become a business man, why should he not act as a business man? Other business men strive to the uttermost to control the market; they form gigantic combinations to limit output, to lift prices, to regulate wages, and to "work" the government. Surely it is not demagogical to urge him to do what other business men are doing in the way of managing their own business. If Mr. Morgan may combine all the steel mills of the country in one great organization, there would seem to be nothing wrong in the farmer attempting to apply the same method to his own business. If he is to be a "captain of industry," he should profit by the examples of other captains of industry as far, of course, as he keeps within the law and the requirements of sound morals. Nor is there any reason why the farmer should not be the "commander," and "supreme." The farming class outnumbers any other class in the country. There are more than 25,000,000 men, women and children engaged in agriculture, and upon them we all depend for our very life. Probably one-half of the people in gainful occupations are either farmers or people closely connected with the cultivation of the soil. Their products constitute the great bulk of our exports, and their crops are the most valuable asset that the country has. We might survive the loss of our steel mills or of many of our great industries, but if our farms were to quit producing the country would go to ruin. Why should not the farmers be supreme? And if they strive at something less than supremacy —namely, mere parity with the rest of our people—ought they not to be encouraged? What is urged here is that the farmer should realize that he is, what Harper's Weekly says he is, "a business man," and govern himself accordingly.   He should play the part which we all agree is his, use business methods, look out for himself and his own interests, and use his vast power for his own good.   Surely there is nothing radical in this.   No line of action is marked out for the farmer which other business men do not follow to their own advantage.   It is no more demagogical to say that the farmer ought to make his own prices and regulate his marketing than it is for a Wall Street promoter to suggest to the steel men that they can make more money by combining for the purpose of controlling the market, regulating wages, and dictating prices.   The cases are precisely parallel.

The real truth is that the critics of such a policy on the part of the farmers know that it would be effective—and they do not want it to be effective. They know further that the plans now proposed— some of them in operation already in a limited way —are marked by none of the weaknesses that characterized the Grange, the Farmers' Alliance, the Farmers' Mutual Benefit Association and the People's Party.   The fruit growers in some sections have already organized, and they have much to do with securing a profitable market for their product. When they find that the market in a certain city is full and in another is bare, they divert the ship- ments from the former to the latter city; and the association keeps its members informed as to the state of the market.   The tobacco growers have or- ganized and have raised their prices three times over.   They have rescued their business from a

poverty producing condition to that of certainty
and sufficient profit. So there are other crops and
some sections where the proposed plan is working
successfully.

There is nothing impracticable about this. If
this limited cooperation is good, who will deny that
complete national cooperation will not do more
good. So when it is proposed to apply the same
great principle of combination, which the Wall
Street people have seen work so well, to the whole
agricultural class, we have a great outcry against
it. They think organization is good for all people
and all classes but the farmers. Some educators
have tried to point out other ways for farmers to
make their business profitable. One of these advised as a means to put wheat to one dollar a bushel,
to "sow less wheat and put the ground in more profitable crops." That's easy; but he stopped too soon.
Why did he not tell what these neglected crops are
that would be more profitable? Another recommends. to cure all the ills of farming and to make it
profitable, to "Always sell at the highest price." A
very simple remedy. We recommend the farmer
who can apply this remedy not to join a co-
operative society. A certain professor of an agricultural college says, "Farm as we do. Our wheat
yields thirty-one bushels per acre, while the average in Indiana this year (1903) is about ten bushels." When I asked him what he thought wheat
would be worth if all raised three times as much
without the ability to fix prices, he said: "Well, I
had not thought of that." Another professor of a

college advised farmers to "have patience and Divine Providence will work out their salvation." And so farmers' teachers have always been referring farmers to God when they knew of no remedy. But I don't think it right to throw the whole work on God. Besides it is written, "God helps those who help themselves." Therefore, can you expect help from Divine Providence if you sit still and won't help yourself? Others say: "Wait for the regeneration of man, and your troubles will disappear." Having waited many hundred years already for this much desired consumation, I can not see much encouragement in this advice for present day farmers.

Organization by farmers is objected to now, simply because they know it will be effective in the light of the twentieth century experience. No better argument in its favor ought to be asked. But why object? Organization of farmers on the plan proposed will not harm, but will benefit every legitimate business, and all people engaged in useful occupations.

CHAPTER III

In the rustle of the cornfields,
  And the plowman's weary tread,
And the fingers of the tassels
  Raised beseechingly o'erhead—
In them all a thousand voices
  Whisper in the listening ear,
"Toil will ne'er possess its products
  Until Equity is here."

In the broad and waving wheatfields,
  A million heads may bow,
And in sunlight gold may glitter,
  Promised fruitage of the plow;
Still the passing breezes whisper
  In the anxious listening ear,
  Toil's just reward will linger
  Until Equity is here."

So with orchard's blushing treasure,
  And with meadow's wealth of hay,
And the lowing in the pastures,
  And the garden's rich array—
All proclaim the same sad warning,
  Toil in vain will seek its own,
For each season's stores will vanish
  Until Equity shall come.
                              —John P. Stelle.

THE THIRD POWER A REAL POWER.

We thus have the three powers—money power, organized labor, and the farmer. And the question is as to the necessity of making the third power— the farmer power—a real power. Let us consider first the relation of these three powers, as things now stand, to the business of government. When a man is elected to congress he finds that the capitalist and the working man are keenly alive to their own interests, and that they are both capable, through organization, of exerting, and as a matter of fact do exert, much influence in Washington and in various state capitals. Their representatives throng the lobby and committee rooms, and press in the most vigorous way on the lawmakers the claims of labor and capital. If a tariff is to be made, abundant opportunity is given to both capital and labor—especially to the former—to be heard, and the opportunity is improved to the uttermost. When a question of subsidy comes up the rich men who want the subsidy do not hesitate to urge the matter on congress, and congress is exceedingly deferential. The workingmen have got their eight-hour law, arbitration statutes, laws regulating the operation of factories and mines, anti-child labor laws, anti-alien laws, weekly wage laws, etc. And all this is taken as a matter of course. But back on the farm, far out on the lonely prairie perhaps, is a man who works with his wife, children and babes, harder than any other class of people on earth. There is no law passed to prevent child labor on the farm. No eight or even ten hour day. He works from sun to sun and then some more, and oftentimes when the year rolls around receive a smaller wage than convicts who are farmed out to corporations. Our new congressman hears little or nothing of him. He does not spend much time in congressional or legislative halls. He is not consulted about tariffs or subsidies. No lobby fights his battles. He is practically forgotten. Congress taxes him for the benefit of the capitalists, and he does not complain—nay, he seems to feel that he has no reason to complain. He has his duty on wheat and a few other crops, to be sure, which in no way affects its price, a duty which is imposed simply for the purpose of making the farmer believe that he is getting some return for the taxes that he is forced to pay for the benefit of other people, and which, in effect, works to the benefit of the speculators and gamblers, by preventing a flow from outside countries when they want to manipulate the markets here. If a farmer goes to Washington he feels so honored and flattered by any little attentions his representative may show him that he never thinks of suggesting that he needs anything in the way of legislation. And when the representative comes back to the district for re-election he talks of the honest farmer and sturdy yeoman, and every one feels that the account is square.

There is no use in getting angry at this, for the fault is wholly with the farmer. The politician knows perfectly well that in dealing with the farmer he is dealing with individuals, or with individuals who are divided into many different classes—even by their own societies, which number about 5,000 distinct organigations—by political and sectional prejudices. But he knows quite well that when a capitalist or a labor leader calls on him at Washington he has back of him a great and powerful organization which is able and ready to punish its foes and reward its friends. He has learned, too, that the farmer can be made to believe that he himself is protected by the very taxes that are levied on him for the benefit of others. But the main point now to be considered is, that the farmers are isolated, and incapable of concert of action. In these days men do not get things unless they go after them. The farmers do not go after them, and so they do not get them. Men in public life have to be coerced or persecuted into doing things. It is so much easier to drift along without doing things, that the statesman, who is always looking for the line of least resistance, is never disposed to champion any cause that demands affirmative action, unless the representatives of that cause force it on his attention. It is easy to ignore and forget the farmer on the lonely and far-distant prairie. It is not easy to ignore the rich lobbyist and his champagne and terrapin, in Washington.

My purpose in all this is, frankly, to make the farmer discontented, not so much with conditions as with himself for allowing them to exist. Discontent that breeds investigation; investigation, knowledge; knowledge causes action and action the remedy. Therefore, I want to make farmers discontented so they will investigate, get wise, and act. Here we have a class of men, the most numerous in the country, who fail to get what they ought to have, simply because they do not combine to get it. Farmers should not have anything to which they are not entitled. And it is not the intention of the writer to array them against their brethren of the capitalistic and labor classes. All that is desired is that the farmer should profit by the example set by these other classes. The demand is for equity and nothing more. And equity for one is equity for all. The farmer can not be truly prosperous without benefiting the whole country. The country can not be prosperous without the farmer is prosperous. Keep the farmer prosperous and we can not have hard times. So the cause of the farmer is the cause of the nation, and of every citizen of the nation. Prosperity begins and ends on the farms. Therefore, keep the farmers prosperous, keep the source of prosperity pure and strong, and it will flow a powerful stream that will invigorate every industry.

Having shown how organization helps the capitalist and the workingman in their relations with the business of government, it is now necessary to show how it helps them in the ordinary conduct of their own private business. The threshermen afford an excellent illustration. Recently in Indiana they have been asking and getting six or seven cents a bushel for threshing wheat. The threshermen have an exceedingly effective organization, and it makes the price for threshing wheat. The farmers have to pay it. The question is not whether or not it is fair, but whether the threshermen can compel their customers to pay it. Feeling that the price was too high, some farmers recently tried to buy threshers and thresh their own grain, but they were told by the manufacturers that they would sell machines only to members of the threshers' association. Thus the farmer is confronted. not only by the threshers' association, but by a partial combination between that and the threshing machine manufacturers. Again it is a case of the organized against the unorganized, and, as always happens, the unorganized lose. They must lose. The farmers pay prices fixed by others, and they sell at prices fixed by others, thus burning their candle at both ends. There is neither equity nor common sense in this, but they are slaves to the system and will be until they can make their own price and pass the expenses imposed by others along.

So the appeal is to the Third Power to become a real power, to the end that it may make itself felt for the good of all the people. If it is right for the thresher to say what he will charge for threshing the farmer's wheat, it is right for the farmer to say what he will charge for his wheat. It is at least not equity for the farmer both to buy and sell at prices made by others. If we admit that it is right for those who sell to the farmer to fix the prices at which they sell, and we don't dispute it, we must also admit that it is right for the farmer to fix the prices at which others shall buy from him. But really it is not a question of right at all—it is a question of power. If the farmer is to free himself from the compulsion to which he is now subjected, he must do so by his own act. And it is better so. A prosperity won by one's own effort is better and more securely based than that created and guaranteed by government. The solution of the problem is not to be found in Washington, but on the farms. There is no need to ask for favors. The politicians can not greatly help, and we don't propose to call on them. The farmers organized, and pricing their own product, will be so strong in the control of the food and clothing of the world, which the other people must have, that they can put any price on them that they want to. Thus they can meet prices, expenses, and taxes, imposed by others. The farmers organized, don't need to care whether there is politics or not, nor how much they are taxed only in so far as they may be interested in another class—the consumers. Nothing should be asked of the politicians except treatment that will make it possible to deal equitably with others.

If my argument is sound it is clear that the farmers need not look to lawmakers, Divine Providence or anywhere but to themselves.

It has been said of the Irish people that they have fought successfully in all battles except their own. This is largely true of the farmers. They have labored, and struggled and paid taxes for others, and upon their intelligence, industry, and thrift, to-day depend the welfare and prosperity of the nation. The farmers in the United States have been the soldiers of civilization. They have reduced a wilderness to subjection, and have made it a fruitful garden. They have endured loneliness, hardship, severe toil, privation and hunger, in order that others might be fed. Our export trade, of which we boast so much, and which has indeed attained tremendous proportions, has been swelled by the fruits of the labors of the husbandman. The factory, the railroad and the mine all live off the farm. We

And Unless the American Farmer Rouses Himself * * * See Page 46.

talk of labor as the source of all wealth, and so it is —but it is the labor of the farmer. And yet we find that, after all these years these men on the firing line of our American civilization, who should be the most independent men in the world, are dependent on the captains of industry, the promoter, the underwriter, the labor leader, and the grain gambler. It is time to end this dependence. And unless the American farmer rouses himself, he will have to always be content to have his business controlled by others, to be called a "jay," a "rube" or "hayseed," and to see himself caricatured in the comic papers and on the stage as the ridiculous victim of the gold-brick swindler and the hay-fork note peddler, and indeed no gold-brick swindle was ever so palpable as that which is inherent in our present industrial organization. The Third Power can end it when it becomes a real power.

CHAPTER IV.

Come shoulder to shoulder,
Ere earth grows older!
The cause spreads over land and sea.
Now the earth shaketh,
And fear awaketh,
But joy at last for you and me.
—William Morris.

WHY OTHERS OPPOSE.

But why, it may be asked, should the speculators and the moneyed men, the bankers, manufacturers, railroad people, etc., object to the organization of the farmers? There are many reasons, each one of which, however, is an argument in favor of the organization when considered from the farmer's point of view. Suppose some fall Mr. Hill, or Mr. Harriman were to back their cars up into the wheat country, after having made every arrangement to transport the crop, and should find that there was no wheat to carry; and suppose the railroad president should find that the farmers had all resolved that they would not let go of their wheat for less than a dollar a bushel. If this resolution were backed by a national organization, the consequences for the railroad and the consumers would not be pleasant. The effect on stocks would be disastrous, and a panic would surely follow. That is, unless concessions were made to the farmer. And, as the capitalists and speculators think they don't want to make concessions to the farmer, they would intensely dislike being put in a position where they would have to make them or suffer ruin.

Every one that has a grip on the farmer, who sells to the farmer at exorbitant prices—all would find that their grip was broken, and that on the contrary the farmer had the upper hand.

The mere shifting of power from the few to the many would be enough to rouse opposition on the part of the few. Oligarchies always hate democracies. The four or five men who now fix railroad freights throughout the country would naturally feel that it was an impertinence for the 10,000,000 farmers to insist on being heard on the subject. They can get along with the Interstate Commerce Commission, but from 10,000,000 organized people, "preserve us!" they exclaim. Those few men may combine to regulate the commerce of a continent, but the farmers may not contrive to regulate their own business and to demand equity from others. They think control by the few is right and proper, but control by the many is a bad thing. The banker might find that, with such a combination, the farmers would have to borrow less money, and that they would have more to say about the rate of interest and the security than they do now. If, when the representatives of the organized manufacturers went to Washington to demand favors at the expense of the people, they found themselves confronted by a lobby of able and intelligent men representing the farmers' organization, the job of pushing through tariffs might be more arduous than it is now. Some of the beggars for tariff might actually be called on to show why they needed them and ought to have them.

As for the speculators, they would not find life wholly pleasant under the proposed conditions. When, to return to Mr. Norris's book, Curtis Jadwin tried to corner the wheat supply, he was beaten by the new crop which came pouring in. Here is how it happened:

"And the avalanche, the undyked ocean of the wheat, leaping to the lash of the hurricane, struck him fairly in the face. He heard it now; he heard nothing else. The wheat had broken from his control. For months he had, by the might of his single arm, held it back; but now it rose like the upbuilding of a collossal billow. It towered, hung poised for an instant, and then with a thunder as of the grind and crash of chaotic worlds, broke upon him, burst through the pit and raced past him, on and on to the eastward and the hungry nations."

What if the farmers had controlled that "undyked ocean of the wheat," and had refused to let any of the ocean get through the dyke? The price would not have broken, and the corner would have won. But with farmers organized there would have been no corner by Jadwin. And what right had he anyhow to control the price of wheat for months? Neither he nor any of his tribe could do it if the farmers would assert their power. It would be the same way with the stock market. As it is now, a few pirates get hold of some great granger road, "merge" it with another, buy the roads by paying for them out of their own treasuries, stock and bond them out of all proportion to their real value, issue "short-time" notes, and then expect them to pay dividends and interest. So rates must go up—and they do go up. They combine to regulate rates, discriminate against non-competing points, and it all comes out of the farmer. The legitimate value of the shares depends on the amount of business that the roads do, and on the price of the stuff they haul. The farmers, I estimate, are responsible for three-fourths of the tonnage hauled by the railroads and stored in warehouses, yet I venture the assertion that not one board of Railroad and Warehouse Commissioners in all the states has a farmer representative. It is on this basis that the speculation proceeds. Who would attempt to bear the market if he knew that the farmers' combination might refuse to send any farm products to market? The value of the shares would, as now, depend on the earning capacity of the properties, but the farmers would have a good deal to say about what that earning capacity should be. And this would be a great dampener on the speculative spirit. Grain and stock gambling would be much less popular than they are now. There would be a new and controlling element in the problem. And it would operate for the good of all. The case of the manufacturer would be much the same. He is, as are we all, interested in selling dear and buying cheap. Backed by the government tariffs, and assisted by his combination, he has it in his power to make, or at least largely to influence prices. With those to whom he sells and

from whom he buys unorganized, he occupies an exceedingly strong position. It would be less strong
were his customers, the farmers, also organized.
They might still have to pay the manufacturer's
price, but they could, if organized, sell at their own
price. The manufacturer, as do all the rest, "looks
with distrust" on any movement looking to an organization of the farmers. This is natural, because
all former farmer organizations were directed to
pull the other person's business down to a level
with unsatisfactory agriculture. But it is different
in this movement as I will show you and there is no
reason why the banker, merchant or manufacturer
should be alarmed. Now it is proposed to build
agriculture up to a level with the best of them.
Therefore these people are needlessly alarmed. In
fact, when the plan to make the Third Power a real
power is understood they will approve and help it.

Nor can the political phase of the question be
disregarded. The tremendous power which organization would clothe the farmers with, could not be
ignored by the government. If the combined agricultural interests of the country should ask the men
at Washington to take off a protective duty—even
though it were for the special benefit of Mr. Morgan's steel trust—that duty would come off. If the
demand were made for special legislation in the interest of the farmer or the consumer of his products,
even though it might injure the manufacturer, or
middleman, that demand would be complied with.
Were the farmers organized, some plan would be
found for checking the aggressions and extortions

of the railroad and food trusts. All this is perfectly
well understood by the minority that now controls
the government, yet, should the farmers think it
worth while to make any demands for legislation it
will be more in the interest of the consumers than
from any necessity on their part. When the farmers co-operate and name prices on their own products they will be so strong in their fundamental
right to price our food and clothing products which
the balance of the world must have that they can
meet all aggressions by others. What matters it if
the railroad charges fifty cents a bushel for transporting grain to market? The farmers' price of this
bushel of grain—when the farmers represent the
Third Power—was made out on the farm before the
transportation company touched it, and was a profitable price. Therefore, I say, if the Third Power concerns itself about legislation, taxes, transportation,
etc., it will be in the interest of the consumers, and
to promote the maximum consumption by preventing the railroads and middlemen from imposing unfair rates. On the whole it is surprising that any
person should oppose the organization of the farmers, and sneer at this plan looking toward that end.

But there is even more in it than this. If there
were resistance on the part of any class to the farmer's demand for fair prices for his products, and if
the farmer should refuse to sell them for less, it is
evident that there would be panic and starvation.
The farmer can live on what he raises, and can
even, as he once did, make his own clothes. But
the men in the banks, the offices and the mills must

have bread, vegetables, fruit and meat. Suppose they could not get them. Pushing the case to this last extremity you can easily appreciate the extent of the farmer's power, the absolute nature of his independence. God rules in Heaven, and the farmers own the earth. All others are suspended somewhere between and are absolutely dependent on the farmers in this world, as on God in the next. The farmer is or may be, if he chooses, wholly self-supporting. No other class of the community can be for all men rely, and must rely, on the farmer to keep them alive. If he should decline to market, on the ground that he was not being paid sufficiently for his service, a crisis would be presented with which the government would have to concern itself. Yet all the while the farmers would be doing nothing that the miners and manufacturers are not doing every day. Indeed, they would be doing only what other men are now doing with the farmer's grain, meat and produce. The only difference is, that the farmer's corner would be more complete, and his control of output and prices, being applied to commodities that are absolute essentials, would be more disastrous in its results. But what would or could the government do? It could hardly confiscate farm products, or compel the farmer to sell them at prices unsatisfactory to himself. Surely it could not compel those men who failed or refused to put in crops lest there should be overproduction, to cultivate their farms against their will.

The arbitration question here presented, if it is a question at all, would be one far more difficult than that between the anthracite miners and operators which President Roosevelt arranged for, and practically compelled. The government could not destroy the farmers' organization and continue to permit capitalists and workingmen to organize.

The difficulty would in all probability be adjusted either by fair compromise, or by a complete yielding to the demands of the farmers. But the problem would not be solved. On the contrary, the government would have had such a warning as would drive it into the adoption of a just policy. Theoretically we have the most just government in the world. The preamble of the constitution reads thus:

"We, the people of the United States, in order to form a more perfect union, **establish justice,** insure domestic tranquility, provide for the common defense, promote the general welfare, and secure the blessmings of libery to ourselves and our posterity, do ordain and establish this constitution for the United States of America."

"To establish justice"—this is one of the purposes which our forefathers had in view in adopting the constitution. If it is found that justice has not been established, it must be either that the constitution is defective, or else that we have been false to its principles. It makes no difference which of these alternatives is true, the fact remains that our government at the present time is not conducted in accordance with justice and equity. It has too many favorites, and among those favorites the farmer is not found. He is taxed, not only for the support of the government, but for the benefit of others of his fellow citizens, who are not taxed for his benefit. As taxes are levied on land and as land can not be hidden from the taxgatherers, it follows that he pays proportionately more taxes than do those whose wealth is in money or stocks or bonds, which can be hidden. Under our constitution has grown up a system of laws which favor the corporations and trusts at the expense of the individual. And it has come to pass that our government is weaker than its citizens. The combination of politicians, speculators and corporations controls the government— nay, is the government.

To illustrate: The powerlessness of the central authority would be brought home to all men in such a struggle as that between those wanting to buy farm products (food and clothing) and those refusing to sell them. The people would demand that their government should at least be as strong as its most powerful citizens, or as the most powerful combination of citizens. Then it would be able to do equal justice to all. And we should all realize that justice pays—indeed that it is essential to the perpetuity of our institutions. So, without doing one illegal thing, or making a single demand on the government, the farmers could, were they organized, work such a radical and wholesome reform as would transform our whole social order. All the people—and that is what the government ought to be, and in theory is—might conclude to fix a minimum price for the necessaries of life, and say that no one should be compelled to sell for less than that price, or that, if the crisis were grave, any one who offered that price should get the commodities. At least the government would realize that it could not afford to be unjust to the farmers, the most numerous class in the country. If we are to have a class government at all, and this ought not to be, we should have a government of the largest and most influential class. If we are to have favoritism, it should be favoritism, not for the minority, but for the majority. If it be said that the scheme involves socialism, the answer is that socialism for the many would be better than socialism for the few. If the government helps the manufacturer to make prices which are often exorbitant—as it does by imposing tariff taxes—it surely might help the farmer make prices that are fair and just. So the result of the effort of the farmers to organize to control their own business might easily have the effect of forcing reforms all along the line, and I predict it will have. Hence, hasten the farmers' organization—the Third Power—the equitable government.

CHAPTER V.

UNITE, O LOYAL FARMERS

Unite, O loyal farmers,
  Beneath the banner true
Of equity and justice,
  That shall thy foes subdue.
Cooperate with others,
  And helped by numbers' might,
Go forward into battle
  For liberty and right.

Unite, O loyal farmers,
  Fear not the active foe;
The right shall ever conquer
  For those who reap and sow.
Fair Justice, ever smiling,
  Holds out her hands to all
Who follow in her footsteps,
  In answer to her call.

Unite, O loyal farmers,
  Waste not your time in rest,
Nor talk of mighty efforts
  If money you possessed;
But seek for higher prices,
  Reward for toil and care,
Let nothing you discourage,
  But all things do and dare.

Unite, O loyal farmers,
  And in one happy band
Press onward for the conquest
  Of this, your native land.
O let your watchword ever
  Be Equity for all;
Unite and quickly level
  Oppression's mighty wall.

Unite, O loyal farmers,
  Press on—press on to-day;

The time is ripe for action,
  Let nothing you dismay;
For victory is coming,
  To those who brave the wrong
And push with earnest vigor
  The cause of truth along.
                    —Effie Stevens.

NO GOOD REASON FOR OPPOSITION.

It has been said, and it is not surprising, that those who are now more or less in partnership with the government, should oppose and sneer at this effort to organize the farmers. And yet there is no good or honest reason why they should not welcome it and cooperate with it. For its purpose is not to help any one class at the expense of the others, but by helping one class, which is now neglected, to help all, and to improve the general social and business conditions. It has been said that the country could not prosper unless the farmers prosper, and that the farmers could not prosper without benefiting all other classes. Neither of the statements can be denied or doubted. So the real reason why this movement is opposed is, that the men who oppose it are getting special privileges from the government, and they know that these would be taken from them when the Third Power compelled an equitable government. The fear is, not that the farmers would be unjust, but that they would insist on equal and exact justice to all. And justice is the last thing that the corporation trust magnates, graft gatherers and the tariff-pampered manufacturers want under the present system. Many men in this country at the present time thrive on inequity, and so they do not want the present arrangement disturbed.

The man who both buys and sells grain or other produce at prices made, not by the owners but by himself, knows well enough that he would have no just cause for complaint if the farmer made the prices on the farm. But he does not want this, because he thinks it would interfere with his own game, and would curtail or destroy his profits. But he may be mistaken, as a certain profit would be better than an uncertain one. So the protected manufacturer, who buys in a free trade market and sells in a protected one, thinks he does not care to have the farmer share in that advantage. To his mind there is nothing wrong in compelling the farmer to pay tariff-raised prices on all that he uses, and to sell his products at free trade prices, and in competition with the whole world. The banker favors cooperation between himself and the farmer which shall enable the banker to fix the rate of interest which the farmer shall pay, but he thinks he would not like to have the farmers cooperate with one another so that they might become their own bankers or put themselves in condition that they don't need to borrow. The combined railroads, which, subject to the slight restraints imposed by the Interstate Commerce Commission, fix the rates on farm produce, will no doubt object to a combination among the farmers to secure profitable rates, a fair price for their crops and regulate their movement to market. Even the trade-unions, which vociferously, and often violently, assert the right of

Many Men in This Country at the Present Time
Thrive on Inequity. See Page 58.

their members to say what wages they shall be paid, and who subject the country to great inconvenience and even suffering in the struggle to carry their point, might be disposed to deny the farmers the right to combine for their own protection and independence, on the ground that it might advance the price of living. Always this desire to secure an unfair advantage, or an advantage at the expense of some one else, develops opposition to an organization among the farmers.

But, as has been said, there is no good honest ground for any such objection. For the farmers propose to demand nothing that is unfair, unjust or dishonorable, nothing that it would not benefit all classes, for them to have. To illustrate: If farmers organize and put profitable prices on their crops,, they will have more money to spend for labor and will buy every necessity and many of the luxuries of life. It is only the profit that may safely be spent. Therefore, more profit—margin—to the farmers will benefit the country merchant, bankers, professional men, etc. To give a clear illustration of the benefits, we will assume a condition like the following, and it has been true many times in every community:

Surrounding the town of L is a wheat growing county. There was raised in 1906, 750,000 bushels of wheat. This wheat should have sold for $1.00 a bushel or $700,000. But the speculators put a price on it of 70 cents a bushel and it sold for $525,-000, or a difference of $225,000. In other words, through lack of power of the farmers to get the price they should have had, that community is poorer by \$225,000 than it would have been and this on only one crop. Every farmer, banker, business man, woman and child, in short every man in the town of L and surrounding country would have been benefited by this additional sum.

Farmers intend to put such a price on their products that they can hire the best help in the country. Thus the demand for union labor will be increased by millions.

The illustration might be carried out indefinitely; but what the use? If unfair advantages are cut off, or other classes built up to a level, though the class enjoying them would lose something, it would lose nothing to which it was entitled, and everybody would be benefited. This government can not continue half just and half unjust, any more than it can be half slave and half free. Indeed, injustice involves slavery, for the man who is the victim of injustice is the slave of him who profits by it. Thus the question is one of emnacipation quite as much as it was forty years ago.

So it is proposed to raise up this Third Power as the defender and champion of liberty. The man who is forced to pay one dollar more for an article than it is fairly worth, or to sell it for a dollar less than it is worth, is to the extent of that dollar a slave. The toil represented in that extra dollar is as truly slave labor as was the toil of the black man forty year; ago, or that of the miserable peon in the Alabama cotton-fields, or the Kentucky tobacco fields a few years ago. And how can the

American farmer, who is grandiloquently spoken of by campaign orators as the freest man on earth, be free at all, in any proper sense, when he is compelled to market the fruits of his hard labor at prices made by some one else, who frequently enjoys, at the hands of the government, an advantage that the farmer does not enjoy? Many fantastic schemes have been devised for the emancipation of the American farmer, but they have all had one or two fundamental defects in that they looked in the first instance to the government instead of the farmer himself, or to the enslaving of all, so there would be, comparatively, no slavery. No people was ever freed except by its own exertions.

"Who would be free themselves must strike the blow."

So this appeal is not to the government, not to the politicians, not even to the law, but to the farmers themselves. If they show themselves worthy of the blessings which they crave, they can get them. The demand is not for government warehouses. free silver, unlimited issues of paper money, loans from the treasury on crops or land, duties on farm products, or even for the destruction of trusts and corporations, but simply for the use of the power which the farmers have to help themselves. The question is whether they are patriotic enough, intelligent enough, self-restrained enough, determined enough, and wisely selfish enough, simply to put out their hands and pluck the fruit which hangs within easy reach of their grasp. They, in the beginning at least, need no help from any one. Governments are like God in one particular, in that they help those who help themselves. When people generally, and the politicians in particular, see that the farmers are in earnest about this business they will promptly co-operate and the farmers will find that they have as many real friends as they now have pretended ones. Success will bring unexpected allies, and will uncover and discomfit secret enemies.

Would the American colonies ever have won their freedom if they had waited for France to begin the struggle? Nay, rather did not France withhold her aid till she was convinced that the colonists could win their freedom even without her aid? The Cuban patriots battled for a generation before our great republic, at last convinced that there could be no peace till Spain was driven from the island, intervened in behalf of Cuban freedom and independence. English liberties are the product of centuries of toil and fight, and it was the French people that won liberty for France and maintained it against combined Europe. So the American farmer must not whine, and beg, and supplicate, must not rely on politics and politicians, nor even on Divine Providence wholly, but must do as others have done, fight his own battles. The victory is sure. And when it is won, as won it will be, it will be found that all will be benefited. So it is true that no American freeman, able and willing to support himself without bonuses or subsidies from the government, and without the protection of unfair and unjust laws, loving justice and fair play, and asking for nothing more than is of right his—an honest reward for honest toil—need have the slightest apprehension about this movement for the organization of farmers. The beggars, the preyers on other men's wealth, the parasites, the government pets, the grafters, the boodlers, and all who look on government as an instrumentality for their own enrichment, may well be disturbed. But there is no warfare to be waged against the rights even of these. We want to take the broad and manly view of this movement. It is not a grab for privileges, or a war of reprisal, but simply a firm and resolute stand for justice and equity. The farmers are not going to ask any one to give them something. They are merely going to take what is theirs. The Third Power, representing the divinely established business of agriculture, when it is organized, will not need to ask favors; it will only have to insist on rights. Favors it does not want or expect. Rights it will have.

CHAPTER VI

A NEW REBELLION

One hundred years and more ago, when America was
    young,
And writhing 'neath the tyrant's chain, the cruel oppres-
    sor's wrong;
Her gallant sons for freedom's sake went at the country's
    call,
And faced the Cannon's shot and shell to bravely fight or
    fall.

They fought and bled for liberty, that this fair land of ours,
Might throw the tyrant's shackles by, yield but to higher
    powers.
They fought the fight, in God's good time they won the
    victory,
They laid the gory saber down and called their children
    free.

But are we free? Does the sun in Heav'n look down on
    men today,
Freed from all bonds of slavery, who own no tyrant's
    sway?
Do they tread America's standard soil all equals in her
    sight,
All sharers in her bounty under Equity and right?

Go ask the busy farmer there, who toils from sun to sun,
If he enjoys that liberty, the right of such an one.
He'll tell you that there still remains injustice in the land,
That foul oppression grinds the sons of toil on every hand.

The farmer knows no liberty, for Power holds the reins;
He has to take the leavings after others count their gains.
His fruits of labor are controlled by grinding Capital,
And he is deemed a servant who, in fact, is king of all.

To arms, to arms! then men of brawn, you won the battle
    once,

Gird on your shining armor now and rally to the front!
Take freedom for your battle-cry, your watchword Equity,
And make the tyrant tremble when your ready sword they
    see!

Fear not though you have tried and failed for lack of
    Union strong,
Cooperation will succeed and right will conquer wrong.
Think you that our forefathers quailed when foemen
    charged the field?
They bravely met each sharp attack and would not, did
    not yield.

Then, farmers, rise in all your might and strike for liberty;
Demand your rights in unity, then call this nation free.
Put forth your earnest efforts in this grand and glorious
    fight,
Associate, then work and pray, and God will guard the
    right.
                              —Maude E. Smith Hymers.

AN EQUITY SOCIETY

A little further elaboration of the general helpfulness of the proposed plan may lead to a better
understanding of it. It has been said that the farmers could not be prosperous without benefiting all
classes, and that the prosperity of the country depends on the prosperity of the farmer. No one
doubts the truth of these statements. They have
a very important bearing on this argument. For,
if they are true, as they are, it must follow that a
movement to better the condition of the farmers will
be in the intersts of all. And this is precisely the
point that I desire to emphasize. For, unless it is
made clear, the impression may prevail that we are
making war on other classes and trying to seek an
advantage at their expense. The further we get

into the case the more obvious will it become that this is not the purpose at all.

What do the stock speculators mean when they say that the prosperity of the country depends on the well-being of the agricultural class? Simply that that class is the largest in the community, that all others depend on it, that our farm produce is our greatest national asset, and that a bad crop or a bad condition here is a national calamity. Foreign trade, railroad earnings, the price of stocks, bank deposits, wages, and of course the welfare of all the industries directly dependent on the farm, are all affected by the condition of agriculture. Prices are largely regulated by the ability of the farmers to buy. Thus, all our business and industry are based on the farm—it is the foundation on which the whole structure rests. Is it not clear that it is to the interest of all that that foundation should be solid and substantial?

Look at the matter in another way. The farming class is the greatest consuming class in the country. When it, through stress of circumstances, is driven to rigid economy, sales fall off, stocks accumulate in factory and store, prices decline, collections are bad, there is le : available capital to loan, money gets tight just when it is most needed, and we all feel the pinch. Luxuries are dispensed with. There are fewer pianos and organs in the houses of the farmers, fewer pictures on the wall, fewer books and newspapers bought. The farmer and his family make the clothes do for another year instead of buying new ones. Farms are allowed to run down,

either because their owners can not afford to keep
them up, or because they do not think it worth
while. Improvements are not made; less machines
are bought, and fewer hands employed, and finally
the gains of former years are wiped out. Then
comes the mortgage, and the whole process of re-
construction has to be gone through with again.
We have seen it several times. It is all the result
of a diminished consumption on the part of the
farmers, brought about by low prices. With the
farmer out of the market, or in it only to a limited
extent, the market is bound to suffer, and all industries be harmed.

The first thing that the merchant wants to know,
when he sends his commercial travelers out to the
smaller towns, is whether the farmers are buying,
and whether they are paying their bills promptly.
The credit to be extended to the local merchant depends largely on the financial condition of the farmers. If they are buying liberally, and paying their
bills with reasonable promptness, the city merchant
knows that he can afford to sell larger bills of goods
to the local dealer, and give him better terms than
he could do under other circumstances. All this is
elementary, and yet we often forget it. We seem
to feel that prosperity is maintained solely by the
buying of the rich people in the cities who are so
lavish with their money. But it is not so. The
farmers are the great consumers, and when they
cease to buy, or curtail their expenditures, they not
only limit the market by just that much, but they
lessen the power of people in the cities to buy.

Smaller stocks in the stores mean a smaller output from the mills and factories, and that means reduction of wages and of the labor force. So the working man consumes less. So, too, less freight is hauled, earnings and wages fall off in the railroad industry, and consumption again suffers. Thus the farmer is inextricably bound up with all other classes of society.

Looking at the question, therefore, from the non-farmer point of view, we see that it is one of maintaining and increasing the consuming power of the farmer, which is equivalent to the maintaining and increasing of the general consuming power. And that is a result which all are interested in bringing about. Thus this movement is not for the good of the farmer alone, but for the good of all—the good of the whole country. To regard it in any other way would be singularly to misapprehend it.

The name of the organization which is now in process of forming, and which will make the Third Power a real power is **The American Society of Equity.** It is not a farmers' society only, but an American society—that is, for all good Americans who want to see better conditions prevail on the farm. It is not a benefit society, but an equity society. Benefits are always for an individual or class, while equity is for all. Indeed, it can not be equitable unless it is for all. Equity for one and not for another is not equity, but inequity. It is a society that knows no state bounds; one that reaches from one side of the agricultural region to the other, and it is for all crops; one that every farmer can join,and be the better for joining. So when we propose to organize and secure fair prices for the farmer, it is not simply that he may be benefitted, but that all may be benefited, and it has been shown that all would be benefited. To demand more than a fair price would be inequitable, and so that is not to be thought of. Fair wages for a fair day's work, fair profits for the manufacturer, fair interest for the capitalist, fair prices to the consumers, and fair values for the products of the farm —this is equity.

It is important that this should be thoroughly understood. For the attempt will be made, indeed it has already been made, to make it appear that the farmer is proposing to rob others for his own enrichment. This has been the method used by other classes, and it is not surprising that those who have practiced it should think that the farmers are going to adopt it. In fact, unfairness is so prevalent in commercial enterprises that every movement is looked upon with suspicion. The outsiders begin to look for the hooks that will catch them. The golden rule, "Do unto others as you would have them do unto you," is interpreted today, "Do him before he has a chance to do you." But it is not so with this society. The name and purpose of the society alike forbid it. It is an old maxim that those who seek equity should do equity.

Farmers are fortunate in being in such a position that nothing can benefit or help them which will not help and benefit all others. So they are not subjected to the temptation to prey on others to which other classes have yielded. If they would put their prices too high they would curtail consumption. Hence, how reasonable then that they will do everything possible to secure the maximum market. In fact, this is one of the leading reasons for organizing and one of the princpal objects of the society. If the Third Power controls the other powers it will be only because it is the biggest and most essential to the national welfare, and so ought to control. But it will be ruled by equity, and in and by seeking its own good it will, even admitting that it may not mean to do so, seek the good of others. Therefore, there is no reason why it should be antagonized and feared by any legitimate interest or industry. Rather it should have the cordial and friendly co-operation of all who want to see freedom and independence, peace and happiness, truth and equity, religion and piety established among the people of the earth.

CHAPTER VII

CLEAR THE WAY

Men of thought! be up and stirring night and day!
Sow the seed! withdraw the curtain! clear the way!
　　There's a fount about to stream;
　　There's a light about to beam;
　　There's a warmth about to glow;
　　There's a flower about to blow;
There's a midnight darkness changing into gray.
Men of thought, and men of action, clear the way!

Once the welcome light has broken, who shall say
What the unimagined glories of the day?
What the evils that shall perish in its ray?
　　Aid the daring, tongue and pen!
　　Aid it, hope of honest men!
　　Aid it, paper! aid it, type!
　　Aid it, for the hour is ripe!
And our efforts must not slacken into play.
Men of thought, and men of action, clear the way!

Lo, a cloud's about to vanish from the day!
Lo, the right's about to conquer; clear the way!
And a broken wrong to crumble into clay.
　　With that right shall many more
　　Enter smiling at the door.
　　With that giant wrong shall fall
　　Many others, great and small,
That for ages long have held us for their prey.
Men of thought, men of action, clear the way!
　　　　　　　　　　　　—Charles Mackay.

SUPPLY AND DEMAND.

It is, of course, obvious to all that the price of
farm products bears little or no relation to the cost
of producing them. Wheat may range in price

from $0.50 to $1.00 a bushel, and yet it costs the
farmers as much to raise it in years of low as in
years of high prices. Fifty-cent wheat may even
cost more to produce than dollar wheat. For the
lower price indicates an abundant crop, and this
means that the demand for labor is great, and that
consequently wages of farm laborers are high; but
the point is that there is no fixed and established
relation between the cost of production and price.
Surely there should be. The consumption of farm
products is reasonably uniform from year to year,
and there is not often any great decline in consumption that would account for low prices. There is
little or no fluctuation in demand, no real surplus,
and the cost of production is a fairly constant
quantity. Yet prices have a wide range.

Of course, it will be said that they are regulated
by supply and demand—and how often have we
heard that phrase; it is used very glibly by many
men who have no knowledge whatever of its meaning. Let us try and find out what it does mean.
Demand and supply are really the same thing—or
at least they are the two faces of the same fact.
Money in the hands of the man wanting wheat is
supply, while wheat is what he demands. The
farmer, on the other hand, demands money and supplies wheat. This would be clear if there were no
money in the world, and if all trade were carried on
by barter. Then all the goods in the country would
be both supply and demand. It is only when we
measure goods against money that we come to look
on money as demand and goods as supply. So the

farmer demands money and supplies wheat, while
the miller demands wheat and supplies money. So
the law of supply and demand describes the working of a force that is not so simple and easily understood as we may at first think.

Again, we talk of demand equaling supply, or of
supply equaling demand. This means absolutely
nothing unless we take into account the question of
price. An increase of price will affect both supply
and demand, increasing the former and lessening
the latter. And this brings us to the main point
to be noted in this connection, and that is, that the
force under consideration is not a great natural
force above and beyond the power of man to regulate or control. We may say that the price of harvesters is regulated by the law of supply and demand, and so it is. But the men who make them
control the supply and manufacture no more of
them than they think can be disposed of at a good
profit. Further, by raising or lowering the price
they can, and do, temporarily influence the demand
for harvesters. And here is the thing to be borne
in mind. We may admit that the price of farm products is, or should be regulated by supply and demand, or, better still, by production and consumption, but still it is true that the farmer has—or may
and should have—the power to say what the supply
shall be. A controlled supply is as much within his
power as it is in the power of the manufacturer.
So when the amateur political economist talks to
you learnedly about the law of supply and demand,
tell him that you propose to make that law work

for you instead of against you. Coal is mined and marketed under the law of supply and demand, but when the anthracite barons think that the demand is not sufficient to absorb their coal at the right price, although there are millions of tons down in the mines, they shut off the supply. If the price is too low they raise it at the rate of fifty cents a ton a month. The farmers may do the same thing, if they will. Supply and demand, certainly,—but they can make the supply large or small at pleasure, or withold it altogether. And you may play upon demand by raising or lowering the price of your products as you see fit. Yet, always bear in mind that as much food and clothing will be consumed at a fair price as at an unduly low price.

So the man can not be left out of the problem. And that is something that you must never forget. There would be no supply of farm products at all except for the intelligent work of the farmers. From their partnership with the earth flow these assets that we all value so highly. Supply is a human product, not a natural growth like breadfruit. It must be adjusted and regulated at all times to the demand, but only at a price that is fair to both parties to the trade, not a temporary over-supply at times to force prices down, nor a scarcity at others to force prices up. The plea is that these adjustments should be made by the farmers, inasmuch as the supply is theirs, and they are the only ones that can make the adjustment in a way to benefit all. And in making it they must consider, first of all, the cost of production—that is, what they pay for corn,

The Farmers May Do the Same Thing if They
Will. See Page 76.

wheat, cotton, fruit, vegetables, dairy and poultry products, etc., in investments, toil, pain, abstinence and self-sacrifice. We see how it is in other departments of industry. Wages are regulated, we may say, by the law of supply and demand. Yet trade-unions control, to no small extent, the number of laborers—thus regulating the supply. And they strain themselves to the uttermost to keep the supply of laborers small enough to insure good wages. The capitalist, on the other hand, determines to a considerable extent the amount of capital available for the payment of wages, and endeavors to lessen the competition for laborers. Both these classes influence, in a marked degree, both supply and demand. Why should not the farmer do the same?

So do not allow yourselves to be deceived by the talk about supply and demand. What you have to decide is whether you are getting prices properly proportionate to the cost of production. It is clear that often you do not. Indeed, cost of production is the last thing that you, and those who buy from you, take into account. If wheat at one dollar only sufficiently compensates you, it is evident that wheat at fifty cents does not. There is no natural or economic reason for such fluctuations. They have a bad effect in many ways. Who can make any definite calculation on such a basis as this? Here is the secret of the failure of many farmers to make needed improvements. The owner is afraid to undertake improvements for fear prices will fail, and he may not be able to pay for them. What would you think of a manufacturer who sold plows this year for fifteen dollars, but who was haunted by the fear that, the cost of production remaining precisely the same, he might have to sell plows next year for ten dollars? The business simply could not go on. It would be impossible for the proprietor to figure on prices, wages or raw material. Profits would be as uncertain and problematical as they now are in the farming business It is so in farming, which, after all, is manufacturing. The farmer is capitalist, laborer, manufacturer, scientist and landowner, so that all the forces of production are combined in him. Now, with all these qualifications we want him to become a business man. The earth is his factory, the plant food his raw material, the plant his machine, and the crop his finished product. Yet, though he is the supreme producer, and though all the forces of production center in him, he is, under present conditions, the most powerless of all producers, and the only one who takes no account of the cost of production. Is it not time that he asserted himself? He must quit increasing the supply extravagantly and to his own hurt, and insist that the price at which he sells shall be such as to earn him a fair profit, year in and year out, over and above the cost of production. He can not do this by himself. So here, again, organization is absolutely necessary.

To illustrate more forcibly the need of regulating prices, we will say that, always, the larger the crops the lower the prices. Frequently the largest crops sell for the least bulk money, and vice versa, the smallest crops bring the farmers the most money. This is proven in the corn crop of 1901. It was the smallest this country raised for many years, yet it brought to the farmers more money than any other corn crop except the one of 1902. This latter crop was the largest ever raised; it had the advantage of high price established by the preceding shortest crop, yet sold for comparatively little more than the short one. This condition is also illustrated by potatoes. In 1895 this country raised the largest crop in its history, and they sold for only about half the money as did the crop of 1901, which was the smallest for many years. The same is true of wheat, oats, cotton, fruit and other crops. An enterprise which is subject to such wide and violent irregularities can not be healthy, and a system which makes them possible is bad and vicious. Any person who will take the trouble to study the crop statistics will be convinced that something is wrong. It is clear from this showing that it is the large crops and low prices that are a menace to the farmers—consequently to the nation's prosperity. Short crops will make good prices for themselves, as then the buyers go to the farm seeking them, and the farmers can price them.

By organization and co-operation the temporary surplus of any crop can be controlled—held on the farm or in the farmers' warehouses—and the same conditions produced as when the crop is small. All that is necessary to do to make prices on the farm is to control that part, which, at times, overstocks the market, and which fixes prices on all. In other words, to keep the market in a seeking condition. We claim that as much of our food products will be consumed at a fair price to the farmer as at an unfairly low price. The cities are fairly reveling in prosperity. Labor is better paid now than ever before; manufactured goods sell higher than ever before. Therefore, the consumers off of the farm should pay a fair price for their food, even though it leaves them a little less for luxuries; but we don't believe it will be necessary for the consumer to pay more. The advent of the Third Power will benefiicially affect distribution of farm products, eliminate some of the toll gates, and cut down the mountains of profits realized by unfair middlemen between the producers and consumers. The success of the farmers' movement will guarantee an equitable price to the farmers, a fair margin to the middleman, lower prices to the consumer, and a larger market for all farm products. By removing the uncertainties of prices, encouraging free buying and selling on certain and legitimate margins, greater consumption will result, again benefiting the farmers.

This matter of making prices on farm products is the most important problem before the people of the world. It directly affects the entire population of our country, and many millions of people in Europe and other countries. As the United States is the great surplus producing country, it can make prices on food products for the world. It has done it in the past, and has set the price too low. The result has been, our farmers are the poorest paid of all laborers in this country, and the European and Argentina farmers except where protected by tariffs are paupers. Through the Third Power operating through the American Society of Equity prices can be set on an equitable pasis, the American farmer will rise to an equality with the best business men of the nation, his profession will be above any other, and the European farmers will rise proportionally.

CHAPTER VIII.

MARCH OF EQUITY

Face about aud turn to freedom,
  Shout our blessings o'er the land!
Lift our flag of Equity,
  Show the emblem's triumph band!
Convert foes or turn them under,
  Here is Equity for all;
Let the light of this transcription
  Conquer prices to our call!

Free our farmers, free our farmers,
  From the harmers of their price;
We are striving, merchants thriving—
  Now we want our proper slice!
We will break it, we will break it,
  With the wise man as our guide;
Star is over Power the rover,
  Now we'll conquer ev'ry side!
              —Pearl Udilla Davis.

NECESSITY OF ORGANIZATION.

Perhaps it has not been made sufficiently clear
that organization is necessary to accomplish the results desired. It has been shown that the farmers
ought to organize, and that organization is the law
of the industrial and commercial world, and that in
other industries organization has been found to be
necessary. Further it has been argued that farming
is a business quite as truly as manufacturing, and
that the same laws govern both. It has been insisted, too, that unorganized power has little chance
in the world at the present time, and that unity of
action is necessary to make power felt. Yet some

may ask whether it may not be possible, admitting
that organization is desirable, for the farmers to better their condition, in the ways indicated, by their
own individual efforts. This, at least, raises the
question as to the scope of organization, for few will
maintain that anything could be done without some
combination. How extensive should it be? If you
will stop to thing about the matter you will see that
if the farmers of one county, or even of one state or
section should agree to market only at a fair price
they not only would fail to accomplish much, but
they would put themselves in great peril. What
would it profit the Indiana farmers to adopt this
course while the farmers of other states were rushing their crops to market to be sold at whatever
price was offered?

Suppose there were two stores in your town, and
that the proprietor of one of them should make up
his mind that the price of dry goods was too low,
and that he would not sell to any one except at an
advance of 50 per cent., and suppose that the proprietor of the other store should keep on selling at
the old price. Obviously the latter man would get
all the trade, and the former would have to meet
his price or go out of business. If the anthracite
coal men were in a combination, would it be possible for any one of them to raise the price of coal as
long as one kept on selling steadily at the old price?
Clearly not. The lowest price asked for a commodity must be the prevailing price, for the reason that
the buyers will pay no higher price than the lowest
at which goods can be secured.

It is precisely so with the farmers. Recently the announcement was made that the farmers of Indiana seemed to be holding on to their wheat, and the question was asked whether attempts to organize them under the banner of "dollar wheat" were meeting with successs. One of the millers said:

"It is a simple proposition which Indiana farmers will face if they withhold their wheat from the market. Other producers will supply the urgent demand and the holders will be glad to get what they can for their wheat after the others have sold out. The question resolves itself into the old one of supply and demand."

The supply and demand question has already been discussed, but on the main point the miller is right.

A combination of Indiana farmers can not fight against freely sold wheat in other sections of the country. Another miller said that he had no doubt that there was a combined effort on the part of Indiana farmers to withhold their wheat, but he said, and truly, "Indiana farmers can not control the market here as long as we can buy elsewhere at the same price." But suppose they could not buy elsewhere? And this was the condition they met, but they did not want to admit it: Farmers were holding to a great extent in all the states, yet without sufficient organization and cooperative ability to force the price to the dollar mark quickly. The millers, however, would not admit it, and the statements made were calculated to stampede the farmers and cause them to market more freely. This occurred in August, 1903, and the farmers did produce a condition that fully justified dollar wheat by withholding supplies and decreasing the visible to the lowest point in many years. The speculators, however, were determined to hold the price down and defeat the farmers. Every bear argument that could be found, real or imaginary, was brought to bear. Another reason why prices were so strenuously held down was the fact that the 1903 wheat crop was sold out by the speculators around sixty-five cents a bushel in the spring when prospects were so flattering and a nine-hundred-million-bushel crop was predicted; also millers contracted flour that would keep their mills grinding for months. It was to the interest of these speculators and millers to keep the price down as low as possible until they could fill their contracts. The obvious conclusion, therefore, is that the combination, to be effective, must include a large number of farmers. The temporary surplus of any crop must be controlled; that is, a surplus must not appear at any time. I estimate that one million farmers will be sufficient. This is only a comparatively small portion of them, but this number cooperating through one central head can, I believe, fully control the surplus of any crop this country produces, and fix the price equitably for all farmers in this country, and on staples like wheat, corn, oats, cotton and meat, set the price for the world.

The Grange and Alliance had millions of members; therefore, if farmers organized before, they can again, if there is a good reason for it. The reason is more urgent now than ever before, also, the plan is so much more practical and the objects so much better, that I contend if the farmers will organize once more, they will realize such great benefit that they will never disorganize. And it is such an organization as this that it is proposed to form. Also, we expect, after the million members are secured for the American Society of Equity, other millions will come, until its growth will be stopped because there is no more material to grow upon.

The farmers' organization must be strong enough and general enough to regulate the marketing. The question is not one of holding products, but of selling them. The proposition is that they shall be held only for the purpose of securing a fair price. In a word, the farmers must make a seeking market, instead of dumping their fine, valuable products without system, like in the case of bankrupt stocks.

Incidentally, something may be said about the ability of the United States to control prices of agricultural products. It is a fact, that, do the best they can, the other producing countries of the world of bread grains never have enough to supply the demand. Every year Europe requires many millions of bushels of wheat from this country. Without this, bread prices in the thickly populated countries of Europe would probably rise to fabulous prices, and we predict famines would be frequent. Claims may be made that production in other countries can be greatly increased. In some cases this is true, but at the same time population and consumption will be increasing. Consumption has been increasing for a few years, faster than production. Figures clearly prove that consumption has been greater than production, even when production was unprecedentedly large. W can not hope to keep up the recent rate of production of bread grain except through more intensive farming or the opening of new territory. This letter is problematic. But suppose the area could be ougmented by another empire equal in size and productive ability to our Mississippi valley. This great region has been put under cultivation within the memory of present men, and has not the world consumed the products? Are we likely to have such an increase in producing area in the next generation? I say no. In short, to supply the food for future generations, will require intensive farming. This means organization, co-operation and better prices, so our present farms can be brought up in fertility to in time produce double or triple the present low averages.

To talk of foreign countries exporting wheat or other products to this country in view of our 25 cents a bushel protective tariff is absurd, even though prices were kept unusually high here. The more likely result, in fact the inevitable result, will be for foreign farmers to put their prices up to meet those of the United States. European farmers are more for co-operation than are the American farmers, and they will be glad to embrace the first opportunity to get rid of the competition of this country, in setting cheap prices. Besides, it is proposed to organize this society in all foreign countries.

Thus, we will have the Russian Society of Equity, the German Society of Equity, etc.

But suppose it was not possible to retain the foreign market on wheat—our principal export grain—and our farmers were confined to the home market. This country consumes enough wheat to make the crop profitable and farmers can well afford to quit raising for foreign markets. If farmers will organize and get a profitable price for all their crops, they can also regulate the production by regulating acreage. With profitable prices assured, farmers would not need to put out as large crops as in the past. With farming removed from the old system when labor was the only factor that earned anything and the person who worked the hardest and the most hours in the fierce competitive struggle was the one who made the most, the tendency will be to not work so hard, and cut down the acreage. At all events, a short crop at a profitable price is always better than a bumper crop at a losing price.

This country produces nearly all the corn of the world, and is the only one that has the soil and climate to grow the crop successfully on a large scale. On this crop we can surely dictate to the world.

But there need be no fear about our market. The world needs—must have—our surplus and will pay a fair price for it when it learns that it can not get it at an unfair price, nor will the Argentine or Russian exporters be able to beat the American farmers, when the farmers in these countries are also organized in the Equity society.

Do you not begin to see how powerful and beneficent this organization will be? Already the Chicago speculators have been heard crying for wheat. They can have all they want, but after the farmers' organization is completed, only at prices made by it. And the work has only begun. You are asked simply to conduct your business as other business is conducted at the present time.

It has been said that the twentieth century farmer is a business man. It is for him to show it. The opportunity will be offered to him. A definite aim—dollar wheat and fair prices for all other crops—will be placed before him. We are to see whether he, like other busines men, is able to get what he goes after. To say that he can not do this is to impeach his intelligence. Other men have no difficulty in seeing what is for their own good, nor will the farmer have. If others can organize, he can organize—and he can be true to his organization, especiallly when he would injure himself by being false to it. There will, of course, be predictions of failure, as there have been already, but they will come from the enemies of the farmers—from those who flatter him by telling him he is a business man and yet want him to act as though he were a child or a fool. But such criticisms are the surest indications of success. If the movement were hopeless or weak there would be no objections to it. The fact that there are objections to it on the part of those interested in defeating it, proves that it is practical and powerful. The people at large, who love fair play, will support the movement when they fulllly understand it.

CHAPTER IX

THE FARMERS' FUTURE

The dawn of light is breaking
  To quiet farmers' fears;
The sons of toil are awaking
  To enjoy peaceful, happy years.

Then all that want protection,
  Here is the way, you plainly see:
Don't continue competition,
  But join the A. S. of E.
                    —W. R. Freeman, Woodville, Mich.

CONDITIONS FAVOR ORGANIZATION.

Undoubtedly one great, and probably unsurmountable, obstacle that has hitherto stood in the way of any effective and lasting organization of farmers by any of the plans tried, has been the isolation of the agricultural class. When towns were few and widely scattered, means of communication meager, and when the nearest neighbor was dozens, or even scores, of miles away and without any means in the organization for frequent communication, the farmer could, in the nature of things, know little of what was going on in the world, could have few or no relations with other farmers. Lacking knowledge of the lives of others, he lacked sympathy. There was no sense of relationship or interdependence. Men in the same county were farther apart than are men now in widely severed states.

Now, organization implies some closeness of touch.
Men must know something of one another; care
something for one another; have common interests
and also a realization of the fact that their interests
are the same.

A few illustrations will serve. Capital can combine easily because capital moves freely from one
point to another. It can be, and is, handled in large
masses. A dollar in Indiana is as close of kin to a
dollar in New York as is the closest neighbor of the
New York dollar. Laboring men even yet find it
difficult to migrate from one section to another, but
capital flows freely to the place where there is the
greatest demand for it. Distance is no barrier—the
ocean is no barrier. A man may live in Kansas and
have his capital working for him in the Philippines
or in Wall Street. The natural tendency of capital
is toward combination. And it knows nothing of
isolation. Turning to labor we find that labor combinations are easily effected because laboring men
live in cities, and close together. Thousands of
them work in the same factory or on the same railroad. They meet constantly and talk over things
affecting their condition. It is natural and easy for
them to co-operate; indeed, they can hardly help
doing so. Each man feels—and he would feel it
whether there were an organization or not—that
he is a member of a vast body, and he gets the
daily encouragement of touching elbows constantly
with his fellow-soldiers. Thus there is this sense
of unity independent of the organization itself. He
knows that others are interested in him as he is in

others. Combination and concert of action could not but come. And it was easy because the laboring men were close together.

It has been different on the farm. The farmer, to be sure, knew that there were millions of others engaged in the same occupation as his, but he never saw them, knew nothing about them, and he could hardly help feeling that he was a lone skirmisher, not certain whether he would be supported by the main body or not. He worked for himself as others did for themselves, and, as a consequence, each was subjected to the severest competition from the others. Community of interest was not thought of. combination for industrial betterment seemed unnatural, and so, impossible. The conditions implied division and separation. Isolation was the bar to organization. But now all this is changed, and henceforth the tendency will be strong in the direction of combination. The rural delivery, the telephone, the interurban trolley, good roads, the wider diffusion of books and papers, the growth of cities and towns throughout the rural region, have all served, and will increasingly serve, to bring the farmers closer together. The farmer can get to town every day now, where twenty-five years ago he could not, or did not do so once a week or once a month. Formerly he depended on the government or the speculators for reporting his crops, and they came so late as well as were so unreliable that they were of no value to him at all, but a positive injury. In his own business organization, with all members connected up by telephones down through the local, county and section unions to the National Union he will have a crop report of all marketable supply each twenty-four hours and can have a complete report of acreage conditions or yield of any crop whenever called for in an equally short time. Will there be an opportunity for speculators to ply their trade under such conditions? He meets his neighbors in societies and institutes, where they discuss subjects of interest to all. He, too, feels the touch of the elbow on each side of him, and knows that millions of others are fighting the same battle that he has to fight, and that they can fight it best by combining forces. Rural America is today one vast neighborhood with interests in common from ocean to ocean, and the American Society of Equity is specially constructed to promote good fellowship and co-operative industrial development.

So we hear from all sides talk of organization. This means that organization is felt to be both a necessity and a possibility. When men—at least when Americans—are brought together the first thing they think of is organzation. No people that ever lived had such a capacity as the Americans have for concerted action. In the present case, I have not proposed to organize the farmers simply because I saw that conditions invited organization. This is the way in which great and successful movements always come. Prophets and seers may dream of wonderful things, but if they are in advance of their time, they try to accomplish them and fail, or, desparing of success, they attempt nothing. The centuries roll by, and at last, in the fulness of time, the man and the hour coincide and then the world takes a tremendous step in advance. Only the other day a man wrote a book on submarine navigation. He showed that inventors had been busy with the problem for centuries, and that one boat had been built three hundred years ago, which actually did travel a short distance under water under propulsion of oars. But the writer said that this inventor could do little simply because he had outstripped the possibilities of the science of his day. Steam navigation was then two hundred years in the future. Even thirty years ago submarine boats were looked on as impracticable—Jules Verne writing fancifully of a trip under the sea as he did of a journey to the moon or the center of the earth. Now the problem is solved not because the men of our day first thought of solving it, but because science had advanced sufficiently to enable them to solve it—had given them the materials to work with. Much the same thing is true of aerial navigation. It is so of reform movements. Even the Christian religion could not have spread so rapidly had it not been that the world was prepared for it. The Romans had built the roads over which missionaries traveled, had welded mankind together, had established peace, law and order throughout the civilized world, and created a system of government that was marvelous for its efficiency.

The moral is plain. Every influence that can be named is operating to bind the farmers together. Railroads, the telegraph, the wonderful extension of the telephone service, the rural mail service, the

trolley roads, the growth of towns in proximity to
the farm, the spread of education, the development
of the scientific side of farming, the multiplication
of agricultural schools and farm journals, the work
of the agricultural department of the government,
the settling up of the country, and, above all **the
right plan hos been devised.** And these will combine to knit the farmers closely together, to destroy
the old isolation, and to make the farmers themselves see that organization is as natural and easy
in their case as in the case of the city laborers,
manufacturers and others. And now, with every
condition favoring, the **American Society of Equity**
has arrived. Those who have dreamed of an organization of the farmers may now see their dream
realized. The new society is not an artificial thing
imposed on a civilization not ready for it. On the
contrary, it is the outgrowth of the very same influences which have wrought such marvelous
changes in the condition of the farmer. As the
close association which the working men have with
one another inevitably suggested organization, so
organization will be suggested to the farmer by the
closer associations that now exist between him and
his fellow farmers. Isolation will yield, as it has
done already to some extent, more and more to
combination, and the farmers, united and acting together for the good of each and all, will no longer
be conquered in detail by other classes. Instead of
ignorantly and unconsiciously carrying on a guerrilla warfare against one another, they will henceforth co-operate loyally and effectively for the im-

I've Got to Sell It Whether I Want to or Not, at
the Figure Named by Some Fellows in
Chicago. See Page 24.

provement of the agricultural situation, because
they can and because it will be profitable to do so.

Who dare predict that farmers can not and will
not stand by each other in a great national body for
business benefits? He might as well attempt to
deny that milions of farmers have not been loyal
to the great political parties, Republican and Democratic, these many years. If the farmers will rally
to the support of their party in politics as often as
called upon will they not be faithful to themselves
in a business body? The farmers united in the
great American Society of Equity will each find a
brother at his elbow on the right and on the left
who is wearing the badge, "For Profitable Prices."
They all have common interests. When they are
called upon by headquarters to express themselves
on any matter it will appeal to them even more than
politics. The appeal will not be ambiguous. What
they will be asked to do will be for their benefit.
Their self-interests will be appealed to and why
should they do otherwise than cast their vote in favor of their own interests? If the farmers are told
to ask a fair price for cotton, wool, wheat, corn,
oats, potatoes, eggs, milk, butter, tobacco, vegetables, fruit, hogs, cattle, etc., and each farmer knows
that the word goes to the millions of other farmers
all over the broad land, do you suppose they would
do the contrary thing? Or if we will admit that all
will not obey,—some because they can not stop marketing,—there will still be enough in this great body
to control the marketing and the price. All that will
be necessary is to stop marketing, whenever the

buyers will not pay the price. In other words, to supply the goods as the markets need them, and not dump them in uncertain quantities at uncertair times. The system of marketing the bulk of a crop soon after it is produced results in creating a large **visible supply**, which is used as a club ever after to beat down prices for the balance of the year. Speculators understand this to perfection. The clubs of "visible supply" and "daily receipts" are the bears' leading arguments. The farmers can prevent a large visible supply by keeping the produce back on the farm and let it come forward graduallly during twelve months. And if they will sell only when they get the agreed price the buyers will look out for the daily receipts. When considering this matter of prices and marketing, farmers should always keep in mind this fact: That the world will consume as much of their products at a fair, profitable price as at an unprofitable price.

CHAPTER X

THE LIGHT IS BREAKING.

The dawn of light is breaking,
  The darkness disappears,
The sons of toil are waking
  To drive away their fears
Let all be up and working
  With all their might and main,
To make our union lasting
  And all the youths to train.

The work is now before us,
  Let's up and at it strong.
Let not a member falter
  To push the work along.
Let every one unite
  With shoulder to the wheel,
And carry the heavy load aright
  That all may happy feel.

When to our homes we do return,
  Our hearts are light and free
To know we have our honors earned
  And made our brothers free.
Come brothers, sisters, all,
  United now we stand.
Come heed our leaders' call
  And make a firm, strong band.

PRODUCING AND MARKETING.

Something has been said of the influence of agricultural schools and papers, which is undoubtedly good as far as it goes. But it does not go far enough, and there is need here for reform. The whole purpose of those who teach agriculture as a science is, of course, to develop the scientific side of the business, and to teach the farmers how to make their land as productive as possible. This is well, but it must be remembered that what the farmer wants to produce is not crops, but money—or crops as a means of getting money. His aim is, or should be, to make his farm productive, but productive of money. To this end he should practice the economies that other business men practice. Making extensive use of machinery, keeping his soil in good condition, studying the question of crops and their rotation, observing the markets; in short, trying to raise as big crops as possible are commendable, but, after all these are done, there is something more important. It is the profitable market. It is one that, in justice to the farmer, ought not to be overlooked by any of the teachers, speakers or experimenters.

The only people who profit more from a large crop than a small one are the consumers, railroad men, middlemen, and the speculators. The railroads charge as much for hauling a cheap bushel as a dear one, and the more bushels there are the better it is for them. The same way with the speculator and middleman. Cheap and abundant wheat is quite as profitable for speculative purposes as dear and scarce wheat. The farmer's prosperity, on the other hand, depends on both the price and the quantity. As the freight is the same on the cheap as on the dear bushel, it is evident that a larger proportion of the price goes to the railroads in the former than in the latter case, to the reduction of the farmer's profit.

So the question is much more complex than it seems to be on its face.

Suppose by the application of improved methods the average of wheat per acre could be raised from twelve to thirty bushels, and this is exactly what a professor of the Indiana Agricultural Experiment Station said the farmers could and should do, by coming to them and learning how. This on the same acreage as now would mean a yield of more than 2,000,000,000 bushels instead of 700,000,000. Under present conditions the effect on price would be most depressing. No one can say how far the price would fall, but it is certain that the farmer would get less profit for the large crop than he now gets, even at the present moderate price, for the smaller one. While it is not possible to increase any of our crops so enormously as in this illustration, it will serve to show the folly of the farmers' institutions, teaching how to raise large crops without the ability to put profitable prices on them. Better devote their efforts to teaching them how to raise less; as under present systems, if each farm would raise uniformly less, so as to always make a hungry market, our farmers would revel in prosperity. Better yet would be to join in the educational work and teach them how to get a good price for a large crop as well as for a small one, or give a balanced education.

The farmer is more interested in the question of price now than in quantity of crop. However, with the ability to fix profitable prices on the farm, and prevent a surplus from appearing on the market at any one time, it will be practically impossible to raise a surpuls of any of our crops for many years. As we have shown, profitable prices will curtail production at first, rather than stimulate it, while population and consumption will go on increasing. Those who advise the farmer to raise larger crops and to make his land more fruitful, without the ability to fix prices, are, therefore, unsafe advisers, and unconsiously have been playing into the hands of the transportation companies, middlemen, and speculators.

By all means the farmer should adopt scientific, up-to-date methods, but he should apply them to the marketing of his crops, as well as to the raising of them. Scientific business as well as scientific agriculture is needed. The crop in which the farmer is most interested is the crop of money. It is for that that he works. He does not want to raise crops simply for the sake of raising them. He raises them to sell. The money that he gets for them is his living. The bigger the crop the better, of course, provided the price is right. But, and here is the point, the bigger the crop, the greater is the necessity that the farmer should control the sale of it. Under the present free competitive system, a big crop may be, and frequently is, anything but a blessing to the man that grows it. When the crop is small it, in a measure, takes care of itself, even as things are today. It is when the fields are most fruitful and the conditions most favorable that the farmer is likely to find himself swamped by the very plenteousness of his yield. I have made the assertion that the short crops of 1901 were responsible directly and indirectly for bringing more prosperity to the farmers than any other crops they ever raised. Really they, the farmers, get their blessings in disguise.

Thus it apears that the very instruction that is being given by the Department of Agriculture, at our agricultural schools, experiment stations, farmers' institutes and by farm papers makes further instruction necessary. When you teach a man how to grow the largest possible crop on a given acreage, and press on him the necessity of doing so, you put yourself under obligation to show him how he may best deal with the products which he has raised in such abundance. Without this latter instruction the former may be worse than useless—nay, may be positively harmful. This is a subject to which our schools and papers ought to give their attention. Certainly the farmers should think about it very seriously. When you increase largely the output, you, of necessity—other conditions remaining the same—depress the price, unless you can control the marketing. A community or country will, however, consume as much at a fair price as at a low price. A fair price appears to add dignity to a commodity, and makes it more desired. Besides, if we can keep the farmers prosperous by giving them good prices, we can keep the world prosperous, thus stimulating consumption.

The present average yield of wheat is in the neighborhood of thirteen bushels an acre, and at that average the country can produce about 650,-000,000 bushels. That is enough at the present time to supply the needs of our people, and to furnish a quantity for export. Whether it would pay the farmer to raise more under the old conditions, depends entirely on the price he could get for it. A short crop at a high price might bring him more money than a large crop at low prices. This condition has frequently prevailed. In fact it is the rule that the smallest crops sell for more money than the largest ones.

So the question is whether the price of the large crop, though lower than that received for the small crop, is still high enough to enable the farmer to make at least as much money net on his investment. If it is not, he loses. This question of the ratio between quantity and price is of vital importance, and the ratio is one that is easily disturbed and thrown out of joint. He would be a bold man who, understanding the matter, tells the farmer that he ought to raise more than he is now raising, and the farmer who will listen to such teaching without a protest does not deserve a better fate than has been his portion in the past. Yet the whole object of so-called scientific instruction in farming is to induce the farmer to do just that thing.

But the farmer will not forget the question of price. The American Society of Equity is not going to let him forget it. This is the first and great object of the society. It is the stepping-stone to the accomplishment of the Third Power. The society is willing to co-operate with the schools by showing the farmer how to market and by helping him to market profitably the larger crops which he is being taught to raise. The two things—up-to-date farming and up-to-date business—must go together. No sane manufacturer makes more goods than he thinks he can sell profitably, or increases his facilities beyond what he believes to be the power of his customers or possible customers to consume. He does not put in new and elaborate machinery simply that he may increase his output—whether ne does that depends on the condition of the market, and his ability to control prices—but that he may produce more cheaply and thus, if need be, to sell more cheaply, yet make more money. It should be so with the farmer. He must never forget the question of price, and must ever remember that the product which he is after is not corn or wheat or cotton, or pork or beef, but **gold**. He who gets the most gold out of his grounds is the most successful, up-to-date and scientific farmer.

Good prices for farm products means increased prosperity, and increased prosperity means greater consumption. The element of waste alone of food and clothing when people are prosperous is a great item, and will have an important bearing on the farmers' market and prices.

CHAPTER XI

All hail the cause of Equity!
  Let all the nations ring
With glad huzzas from wakened hearts,
  That blithsome tribute bring.
In honor of the dawn of truth,
  Of justice, fair and right;
For farmers who so patiently
  · Have waited for the light.

That light is swiftly coming now;
  It spreads along the way,
And brightens all the world about
  With its hope-giving ray.
Soon, soon the day of right will glow,
  In ·splendor through the land,
When every farmer lad shall march
  In Equity's fair band.

CAN FARMERS CONTROL MARKETING?

Such are some of the needs of the farmer? It has been shown that they can be satisfied only through organization, and it must now be enquired whether **The American Society of Equity** is the sort of an organization that the situation demands. A consideration of the subjects that it proposes to accomplish will at least prove that its founder intends it to do the work which it has been said must be done, if the farmer is to weild the power that he should wield. The objects that it aims at are precisely the ones that have already been put before the reader, the very first thing proposed is, that the farmer

should obtain profitable prices for all farm products, including grain, fruit, vegetables, stock, cot-
tion, etc., and their equivalents. It has been shown
that the farmers oftimes do not obtain fair prices for
these products, and that such prices can not be obtained without organization among the farmers.
This is the theory on which the **American Society
of Equity** is based. That organization can do this
it has been the purpose of this argument to demonstrate. That the **American Society of Equity** can do
it follows necessarily, if the argument already made
is sound, for it is based on principles that have been
set forth in the preceding pages.

But there are certain details connected with this
question of price that need further exposition. In
order to get a fair price it has to be proved that the
farmers are under no necessity of selling their crops
at irregular intervals and in uncertain quantities,
and this involves two questions: First, Have the
farmers the facilities for holding them? and second,
Can they hold them? It is insisted that few
farmers are driven to the necessity of selling their
crops to the first purchaser that offers, for the farmers are even now the most completely self-supporting class in the country. Many of them have been
asked, "Why do you sell your crop now?" and the
answer almost invariably is, "I have found from
experience that the price is about as high now as it
will be at any time, so I let it go." That is, they do
not sell because they have to, but because they are
disgusted with former results when they held. They
exercise a free choice, and they choose to sell be-

cause they think they can make as much money by
selling as by holding. Undoubtedly this is the true
reason in the majority of cases for their haste to get
rid of their crops. The farmers think that the price,
though not good, is as good as they can hope to get,
and they fear that they may get caught in a decline.
So they let go and then complain that farming does
not pay. But do you stop to consider that somebody holds these crops—your wheat, oats, corn, potatoes, poultry, butter, eggs, fruit, tobacco, cotton,
meat, etc. The world don't consume them—gulp
them down—as soon as you let go of them. They
go into elevators, cold storage houses, packing
houses, etc. There they are held by comparatively
a few individuals until the hungry consumer wants
them, when they come forth with profits added. The
present system of marketing by farmers is similar
to that of throwing bankrupt stocks on the market.
And the farmers adhere to it, not because they like
it, but because they have no better way. The purpose of the American Society of Equity is to point
to and provide a better way. And as the farmers are
free agents, they can tread that way if they choose
to do so.

The other question is as to the ability of the farmers to hold their crops. This, too, is answered by
the American Society of Equity. For another of its
objects is "to secure equitable rates of transportation, and to provide for storage in warehouses."
There has always been more or less strife between
the farmers and the railroads and the elevator interests, and in that strife the farmers usually lose. Of

late co-operative societies have been formed in the western and northwestern states, the object of which is to enable the farmers to store and ship their own grain. As a rule they have been successful and profitable. These associations can easily affiliate with the American Society of Equity, and with the ability to control prices, as well as to save the grain trusts' profit and get equitable rates of transportation, they will be in a very enviable position. Without the ability to make equitable—profitable—prices, they will still be at the mercy of the trusts, speculators and gamblers. And without the power to hold the grain, prices can not be fixed. Thus the two things must go together. I claim the best place to hold grain is on the farm in a good, safe, vermin-proof granary. The farmer then has no elevator charges to pay, which in public elevators is about one cent a month and eight cents a year. This is a heavy tax, and is about sufficient to build an elevator, if used to its capacity, in a year. The next best way is to have a community elevator. Several local unions of the A. S. of E. will join together and erect it. And beyond this it is the design of the society to have large elevators in the leading market cities, where grain will be stored for members at lowest rates. Cold storage houses will serve a similar purpose and on the same system for perishable products. Individual members can store their fruit, poultry, or dairy products, meat, etc., in the local union line of storage houses, or consignments from local unions or large individual producers will be received in the National Union storage houses. In this way the produce can be taken care of, the market supplied regularly with what it needs, and uniformity of prices maintained throughout the summer and winter. The producers will be benefited by higher prices and the consumers benefited by lower prices, because the mountains of greedy profits that are now added by unfair middlemen aid trusts will be cut out.

But you mak ask, how are the poor farmers to be provided for?

In the first place it will not be necessary to hold all crops at any time, and those who do hold will make a better price for those who cannot hold. Also our farmers and farms need the "rest cure," and will not work so hard with profitable prices in sight, thus reducing the crops.

Second, with the farmers organized and fixing a minimum (lowest) price dealers will see that they can not buy any cheaper, and there is a possibility that prices will be higher. Therefore, they will all want to buy all they can at the low price, and will put all their capital in the commodity when the poor producer must sell.

Third, the society will provide for those farmers who hold their grain and other produce a rising market each month. This may be one-fourth or one-half, or one cent per bushel or hundredweight, depending on the commodity, kind of crop and the market. The advance will be sufficient to offset shrinkage, interest, etc. If there is a tendency to market too freely this monthly advance can be increased to make it profitable to hold. It is reasonable to believe that farmers will hold on to their crops if there is a certainty of making money by doing so. This monthly advance should be adjusted to a nicety, so it will not allow loss nor make a profit, but the inducement will be to maintain prices, which will result when twelve months' requirements are filled, by marketing one-twelfth of the annual crop each month.

Fourth, grain in a granary or elevator, produce in a storage house or property anyhere in evidence, establishes credit. If cash is wanted for pressing needs it can easily be raised on warehouse reseipts, or on personal notes, at any financial institution.

Let me say right here that the American Society of Equity does not propose to loan money to its members unless it engages in the banking business later. Also we want to effectually explode the theory of maintaining profitable prices for farm products **by the use of money.** No individual, society, corporation, nor United States government can make and maintain profitable prices for farm products by the use of money. It would be possible to keep prices up for a while by the use of money, but remember, when a price is paid for a commodity that you cannot consume yourself, you must find another party who will take it off your hands **at a higher price,** and here is where the trouble comes. If the farmers' society would supply the money to take their crops at profitable prices it would be a great thing for the members as long as it lasted. They—the members—would not need to concern themselves about anything but to go bock to the farm and raise as large crops as possible and turn them into their soicety, which must not only pay them a profitable price but find some other person to take them at a higher price. This is a sure way to run up an unwieldy surplus. The only way to handle this problem is to make each individual producer responsible for production and markets. If he produces too much he must take a lower price or hoid it over to a season of less production. In this way he pays the penalty for his indiscretion. Also, if farmers will not sell at the equitable minimum price and foolishly hold out for a higher price, prevent the crops from going into consumption and run up a large surplus, the board of directors must declare a lower price, and thus they will suffer again for their stubbornness. The American Society of Equity does not stand for high prices but for equitable prices, believing that as large consumption will result at a profitable price to the producer as at an unprofitable price. It will as strenuously oppose holding for unfairly high prices at it opposes selling for unprofitably low prices.

How will the society secure money to build warehouses, etc., may be asked?

Farmers can do anything they want to do, or what they in equity should do, if they will organize and co-operate to put profitable prices on their products. Suppose they would want to build or buy elevators, cold storage houses, stock yards, telegraph systems, railroads, ship lines, make good country roads, etc., they could do all these things and not issue a bond, mortgage their property nor pay a cent out of their own pockets.

Suppose they would add a little extra to each principal crop they raise and cut it out of the middleman's and trusts' profits. We have an illustration like the following:

Barley—119,000,000 bu. at 10c per bu..........$ 11,000,000
Buckwheat—10,000,000 bu. at 10c per bu...... 1,000,000
Corn—2,666,000,000 bu. at 10c per bu.......... 266,600,000
Oats—943,000,000 bu. at 10c per bu........... 94,300,000
Rye—25,000,000 bu. at 10c per bu........... 2,500,000
Wheat—658,000,000 bu. at 10c per bu.......... 65,800,000
Potatoes—273,000,000 bu. at 10c per bu........ 27,300,000
Flaxseed—19,000,000 bu. at 10c per bu........ 1,900,000
Apples—175,000,000 bu. at 10c per bu......... 17,500,000
Hay—84,000,000 tons at $2.00 per ton......... 168,000,000
Cotton—4,717,000,000 lbs. at 2c per lb......... 94,340,000
Tobacco—868,000,000 lbs. at 5c per lb......... 43,400,000
Swine—10,500,000,000 lbs. at 2c per lb......... 210,000,000
Eggs—1,293,000,000 doz. at 5c per doz......... 54,650,000
Dairy Products—218,600,000 dollars at 10 per
                       cent. increase 28,160,000

Total $1,086,450,000

This, as you will allow, does not near cover all the sources of income to the farmers, and a like appreciation of value in other products would add additional millions to the total. Suppose this amount was to be expended for a few years, the farmer could own all the facilities for reporting their crops and markets, holding for advantageous prices and transporting them to markets.

Another way:

If it was not desired to raise money by an assessment on the crops, each member, when he is getting benefits such as this society will give, will willingly pay a few dollars a year to provide facilities for handling his business. With a membership of five million, an assessment of $10 each will raise a fund of fifty million dolars. If this amount is expended each year for five or ten years all the necessary facilities will be provided. It is not, however, proposed to decide on the way to do these things now. But rather to organize and put the farmers in condition to do whatever they want to do when the time comes. Thus with no compulsion to sell, with facilities to store, with power to make prices, the farmers will be what they ought to be and now are in theory, viz; independent.

But it is proposed to use this power fairly and honorably. It is not proposed to favor a high price, but simply a profitable price. And every one is entitled to a profitable price if he can get it. The question is how to get it. By the plan of the A. S. of E. no hardship will be imposed on any one, and the consumers of farm products have nothing to fear. Indeed, it has already been shown that the whole country is interested in having the farmer get profitable prices. There need be no conflict of interest here.

What difference would it make to the consumer whether the price of wheat is eighty cents or a dollar a bushel? The average consumption of wheat is about five bushels per capita, or twenty cents increase per bushel is one dollar increase a year. This will be eight and one-third cents a month, or less than one-third cent a day. For a family of four persons a little more than one cent a day. It is proposed to reduce the price of so many commodities when this society is in operation—notably meat—that the average will clearly be in favor of the consumer.

But suppose the establishment of the farmers' society and the Third Power would result in a slight advance of food. Wages have been increased out of all proportion to any advance that can result here. Also by giving the farmers a lift now along with the general industrial elevation we will be increasing his consuming powers for all manufactured goods, and for everything he can consume on the farm and in his family, thus benefiting the laborers in prospect of continued high wages. Also if we put the farmers in a position where each of them will keep one or more hired men at union wages, the year around which is what this movement means, we make a market for labor such as was never before dreamed of.

Is it necessary to illustrate this further? Is it not clear that if marketing was done systematically and the existing demand supplied, and no more, that prices can be maintained at equitable rates? The American Society of Equity, through its board of directors, will be the head or clearing house to the entire agricultural industry. Through the official paper and the press of the country this head will speak to every member weekly and give news about crops and crop prospects; advice about market and marketing. All the millions of farmers will have the same advice at the same time about the same things from an authentic head quite in contrast with the blind guessing as at present. All will thus be pos-

sessed of the same knowledge, influenced by the
same motives, and they may act as one man—in
short, co-operate—for the single purpose of securing
the equitable minimum price.

The plan of the American Society of Equity is
broad enough and comprehensive enough to care
for every branch of agricultural effort—the grain
grower, the stock feeder, the dairyman, the poultry
man, the cotton grower, the tobacco grower, the
fruit grower, etc. As soon as it is in operation it
will benefit the largest operator, no difference in
what line nor where situated, and also the owner of
a few rods of ground, by securing stability of price,
which means stability of prosperity.

The plan is to recommend a minimum price at
which staple crops shall be sold in leading or base
markets. For instance, grain prices will be based
on Chicago, cotton on New York or New Orleans,
beans on Detroit, etc. Other markets and the farm
prices will then be regulated by the base market.
The farm price will be the base market price less
transportation and cost of handling. Farmers, whose
produce does not go to the base market, can calculate the freight from the principal market that receives their crops. This minimum value will be
named each year when the crop is produced and will
be equitable on the basis of production and consumption, lower in years of large crops than in years
of small crops, but always a price that will protect
the farmer. If speculators force the price over the
minimum price the farmers may, of course, take it.
Farmers will be expected, however, to stop market-

ing when the market will not take more at the minimum price. The minimum price will be the safety valve which will regulate the supply to the demand.

It must be understood that there has not been a genuine surplus of any farm crop produced in many years. All have gone into consumption. It is the tempory surplus that is responsible for low prices, and it is this temporary surplus that the farmers are expected to control in the American Society of Equity. We see illustrations nearly every day in the market reports, when the visible supply of any crop increases considerably from free marketing the price goes down. When farmers stop marketing, prices go up. This is clearly shown in the cattle markets. We reproduce from the Chicago Live Stock World as follows:

"Country shippers are surely not hurting cattle buyers by sending in little runs of cattle on days when more could be used at steady prices and piling up a glut on one or two days when prices go off ten to twenty-five cents and oftentimes worse.

"Here is the way it looks on paper:

Monday Receipts......36,010, prices 10 @ 15c lower
Tuesday receipts...... 7,081, prices steady
Wednesday receipts... 25,174, prices steady
Thursday receipts.....11,472, prices 10 @ 15c higher
Friday receipts........ 2,990, prices 10 @ 10c higher
Monday again.........36,000, prices 10 @ 15c lower

"It ought not to be hard to figure out who gets the worst of this sort of a distribution of cattle."

But there are those who think that the farmers are getting fair prices now—and of course they do get

fair prices sometimes. However, let us consider the
case of wheat as typical. Is $1 too much? For
fourteen years, from 1888 to 1902, the average price
of wheat in Chicago was 76 2-3 cents. The average
yield is less than thirteen bushels an acre. Taking
thirteen bushels as a liberal average, it appears that
during this time the farmer has realized $9.95 off
each acre planted in wheat. This is for the use of an
acre for one year, and must cover the cost of labor,
of seed, of sowing, of care, of harvesting, of twine,
of threshing and of marketing. From this must
further be deducted interst on investment, loss of
fertility in the soil, wear and tear of machinery and
operator's profit. It is such a price as this that is
responisible for the farm laborer earning only
twenty-six cents a day and that has put farmers in
the very lowest class of laborers. Surely even those
who hold that $1 is too high must admit that 76 2-3
cents is too low.

Thus it is that question of price is fundamental.
We are all interested, not simply in the farmer, but
in his land—which, in a sense, belongs to all of us.
Rudyard Kipling, writing of the American, says:

> "An easy unswept hearth he lends
> From Labrador to Guadeloupe;
> Till elbowed out by sloven friends,
> He camps, at sufferance, on the stoop."

It is so. We have been prodigal with our national domain, and we have invited people from all
over the world to come here, take up land, and compete with those already in possession. And now we
find that many of our farms are in an improverished

condition from long cropping, and the return from grain and other farm products is not sufficient to justify the expense of restoring the fertility. Farmers have truly sold their birthright for a mess of pottage. This is obviously a very serious matter, and it can only be dealt with by securing equitable prices for all farm products. The farmer should have not less than $1 for wheat any year, and a proportionate price for all his other products. He can get these prices through the American Society of Equity, which is the organized Third Power.

CHAPTER XII

In council there is wisdom,
  In union there is strength,
And by co-operation
  We will succeed at length.
With a bold, united effort
  We are sure to win the day,
When Equity shall triumph
  And producers have their way.

Now this is our condition,
  Though a shameful tale to tell;
The speculator prices
  The things we have to sell;
And when we want to purchase
  Our purchases come high,
For the speculator prices
  The things we have to buy.

FARMERS' AND OTHERS' EARNINGS COMPARED.

Having spoken of the present dependence of other classes on the farmer, and having shown the effect of low prices on his consuming power, and also on his land, it seems necessary, before leaving this question of prices, to say a few words about the earnings of the farmer and present additional comparisons. There are many who tell him of his happiness, prosperity and independence. While there is no intention to make things appear worse than they are it is intended to put the exact truth before the farmer. The census of 1900 shows that, taking

all the farmers together, the average income per
family during the census year was only $643, or only
a little over $2 a day, counting 300 working days to
the year. The average income of the families of
other laborers was $1,146, or $4 a day. Two and
a third million of farmers' families had a yearly income of less than $200, while 4,000,000 families had
an income of less than $400 each. Only one family
in eight had an income of more than $800. If these
figures are wrong then the census returns are wrong.

Are farm prices equitable when two-thirds of the
families on the farm are limited to an income of less
than $400 a year each? For this they must work
longer hours at the most exacting and wearisome
labor, oftentimes under the most disagreeable conditions, while the laborers in towns and cities, who
are largely engaged in producing the goods that the
farmers buy, work short hours, under pleasant conditions, and receive three times the reward. Brad-
streets has figured that manufacturers, with an investment of ten billion dollars, produce thirteen billions of products, while the farmer, with an investment of twenty billions, produces only five billions
of products. In other words, the dollar of the manufacturer returns him $1.30 of products, while the
dollar of the farmer returns him only 25 cents of
products. Where is the equity when a dollar invested in one form of manufacturing returns five
times as much as in another. Is not James J. Hill,
the railroad magnate, right when he says: "The
time has come when the United States should take
steps to strengthen the backbone of the country—

the farming class," and James Wilson, our secretary
of agriculture, when he says: "We can not do too
much for our farmers"? Prices of farm products
will never be maintained at profitable rates by the
government, nor by the buyers, nor by the consumers. Uncertainty of values of farm products will
never be at an end until, through national co-operation, farmers make their own prices on the farm.

When we consider the slight reward that the
farmer gets for his labor we can understand why rural America is today largely the reflection of wasted
efforts and hopes not realized. It should be a paradise of prosperous farms, beautiful homes, and happy, contented families. An equitable distribution of
rewards will make it all this. A bushel of wheat,
for which the farmer may receive 72 cents in the
Indianapolis market, will make forty pounds of
flour, sixteen pounds of bran and four pounds of
waste. The consumer pays 3 cents a pound for the
flour, or $1.20 and the farmer buys the bran back
at $22 a ton, or 19 cents. Here is a total of $1.39
produced from an original value of 72 cents. It is
thus seen that the farmer's wheat has doubled in
price by the time it reaches the consumer. By the
route of the bakery 50 to 100 per cent. more will be
added. It is the same way with the farmer's meat,
butter, eggs, fruit, vegetables, cotton, etc. The
farmers are not responsible for the price consumers
pay. They are not now and never were responsible
for the high cost of living. And the consumers
should rejoice at the thought that the farmers soon
will be in a position, through the help of the Ameri-

The Reflection of Wasted Efforts and Hopes Not
Realized. See Page 123.

can Society of Equity, to cut out the mountains of profit that have been raised between the producers and the consumers.

In the meantime it is important that the American people should know that both the prices that the farmer gets and the prices the consumer pays are made by organized speculators, trusts, middlemen and manufacturers. They say that prices are made by the law of supply and demand—which is the merest subterfuge. That law, under present conditions, is a myth and a fraud. It may be better called a machine erected by the boards of trade to work in an organized market, and directed against an unorganized source of supply. The machine is equipped with numerous levers, wheels and spigots. As you pull a lever of frosts, floods or drought, you reduce the supply, and prices go up. Turn the wheel of increased visible supply or open a spigot of favorable weather in the Argentine or elsewhere, and prices go down. And there are men who put in all their days and nights pulling levers, turning wheels and opening spigots. And thus it is that the farmers and the consumers alike are squeezed and robbed.

We have seen that the farmer does not get high prices, that his annual average income is pitifully small, that the returns on his investment are meager, and that, not getting high prices for himself, he is not responsible for the high prices the consumer pays. And yet, confronting such a situation as this, all that the farmer asks is equity. Shall he not have it? Ought any man, with a proper sense of obligation to himself, to his family and to his country, to be satisfied with anything less than equity? Is it not what we all pretend to want for ourselves, and profess to be willing and eager to grant to others? The American farmer is very patient—proverbially so. He has been compared to Issachar, of whom we have this record in the Bible:

"Issachar is a strong ass crouching down between two burdens, and he saw that rest was good and the land that it was pleasant, and bowed his shoulder to bear, and became a servant unto tribute."

Rest may be good, and the land may be pleasant, but he who consents to become "a servant unto tribute" will know little of what is good or pleasant. It is on the patience and docility of the farmer that the capitalists and politicians have traded. And even now they are predicting the failure of the American Society of Equity, because, as they say, the farmer is contented and happy, and don't need it. Are they right? It is for the farmers themselves to say. If they want "rest" and would enjoy "pleasant" country that they have made their own, they must make up their minds that they will have to free themselves from "tribute," assert their rights as American citizens, and at the same time show that moderation of which we all boast by demanding only what is equitable. So the American Society of Equity offers them the means by which they can demand and secure fair prices.

The need of some such agency as this has been shown, and so far it appears that the American Society of Equity is thoroughly adapted to meet the emergency, inasmuch as its aims, as thus far pointed out, are just what those of the farmer should be. It will be shown as we proceed that the other objects in view are quite as important as those already described. For the present we have the assurance that the society proposes to secure, or enable the farmers to secure, a fair price for their products, and to co-operate with them in securing facilities for holding or marketing products and in getting equity from those with whom they deal.

CHAPTER XIII.

Then awake ye honest farmers,
  Producers one and all,
And let us be united,
  For divided we must fall.
Now a better day is dawning,
  When producers will be free,
For Equity is coming
  Through our grand A. S. of E.

Through Equity we'll conquer,
  No other way we can,
For in Equity we acknowledge
  The brotherhood of man.
In Equity there's justice,
  True principle of right;
Then let us work together,
  And work with all our might.

EVER VICTORIOUS ARMY.

There is not one thing that the American Society of Equity proposes to do that does not bear directly on the question of price. As we have seen, it is intended to secure equitable rates for transportation. The price the farmer is to ask is the minimum price that he may decide is fair in some selected market, and then deduct from that the fair cost of transporting and handling the products. When the minimum price is decided upon then the smaller the amount he has to deduct on this account the more will there be left for him. With reasonable rates, and with his crops stored in elevators or ware houses owned by the American Society of Equity, or local unions of the same, so much larger will be the profits of the farmer. So the plan is to increase his income both by raising prices and by lowering the cost of moving, handling and marketing the crops. This latter, however, is more in the interest of the consumer. It cannot matter much to the farmer whether the middlemen or railroads charge ten cents a bushels or seventy-five cents a cwt. for carrying his produce to market. In his fundamental position he puts his price on the absolutely necessary articles of food and clothing before any other person or corporation can touch them. Therefore, he takes his profit—all that he wants or in equity should have—first. You can not fail to realize the strength of position of the farmer, when organized, by this illustration. Therefore, it is mainly to protect the consumer and secure the maximum markets that he, through his society, will interest himself in the elevator charges, railroad rates, taxes, insurance and a thousand other things. None of these things can hurt the farmer or prevent him from making a profit when organized, but through his strength he can prevent them from working injury to others.

It has been shown already what an influence the farmer could have on the railroads by simply putting himself in a position where he could refuse to ship unless the prices and freights were satisfactory to him. The railroads can not exist unless they have stuff to haul and plenty of it. They are dependent, directly or indirectly, on the farmer, and they can easily be made to feel their dependence. This ques-

tion of transportation is a very large and important
one, in that it involves the future development and
settling up of the country. Indeed, the whole history of the march of men across this continent is a
history of transportation. It has been said by some
supposedly wise men that our people have moved
westward along parallels of latitude. But it is not
so. They moved along the water courses, first down-
stream, and then up-stream. Always the effort was
to make transportation as easy as possible. And the
railroads have contributed powerfully to the making
of the country. We must give them full credit.
Still when it comes to carrying the farmer's produce they have not always been reasonable in their
charge.

And it seems to be probable that they are going to
be more unreasonable as time goes on. While there
was fierce competition competing points at least got
the benefit of low rates, though non-competing
points suffered severely. The railroads taxed the
latter to make up for the low rates of necessity
granted to the former. Certain sections have been
discriminated against, and powerful individuals or
companies forced the railroads to give them special
rates sometimes too low which were offset by charging weak individuals and companies rates too high.
All rates have often been too high, and some rates
have always been too high. But it has been suggested that the situation may get worse for the
farmer. If the tendency toward railroad consolida-
tion goes on we may see an end to competition. It
is certain that the purpose of combination is to

check and control competition. If it succeeds the
farmer will be forced to look out for his own interests. He should be in a position to say that he will
not ship at all unless he can be sure of a fair net
price on the farm for the products of his toil. And
a fair price to the consumer so his markets will be
large.

The farmer is often told that the railroads are his
friends. He himself need not be an enemy to the
railroads in order to realize that there are no friend-
ships in the business world. That world is a world
of struggle and conquest. In that struggle the
strongest win. Under present conditions the railroads will be as fair to the farmer as it pays them
to be. Under the conditions which it is proposed to
create they will be as fair as the farmer can compel
them to be. Other men use the power that they
possess, often in illegal and criminal ways, to coerce
the railroads into favoring them. It is not intended
that the farmers shall do anything illegal or criminal, but it is meant that they should realize that any
unfair concessions are paid for by less powerful and
favorable shippers, the farmers among them. So it
is important that these latter should stand up for
their own rights. If all shippers were treated
equally there is reason to believe that freight rates
could be reduced considerably, to the great benefit
of the whole country.

Further, in the vast reorganization schemes of
which we have heard so much, some of the railroads
have been over-capitalized just as other industries
have. And the farmer has to pay enough to enable

these railroads to pay interest and make dividends
on their vast issues of bonds and stocks that don't
represent real value. He may well question the fairness of this arrangement. At any rate, the American Society of Equity when established will give
some attention to this vital question of transportation. The individual farmer can not fight the railroads, but he can make a good showing as a member of a great and powerful organization numbering
a million or more, made up of farmers all over the
country determined to get their rights. Mr. John
D. Rockefeller, who knows something of the virtues
of combination, and who has recently been engaged
in an effort to secure control of large systems of
railroads, says:

"To fight the battle alone is to be lost. Association with others is an absolute necessity if we would
be successful. In union there is strength and success. We can see this illustration every day in the
business world."

Mr. Rockefeller is right. Especially is organization necessary for the farmers who are at the present
moment unorganized themselves, fighting organizations in practically every branch of industry. Mr.
Rockefeller's reference to the "business world" does
not at present include the farmers. Everybody
knows that they are not considered business people.
But is it not time for them to get into the business
world? .What is good for one class of people who
produce, manufacture and sell, is good for others.
If "in union there is strength and success" for
Rockefeller and his associates, why would it not

mean strength and success for the farmer? A good many years ago the Chinese were oppressed and harried by the civilized nations of the world very much as they are today. The people of China could make no headway against the trained soldiers of Europe. Finally a formidable rebellion broke out in the empire, and the authorities secured the services of that great Christian soldier, Charles George Gordon, who organized his Ever Victorious Army, and with it suppressed the rebellion without losing a single battle. No better army followed a gallant leader to victory. Precisely the thing that the Chinese lacked was the power of organization and co-operation. But when they did act together it was with decisive results.

It can be so with the American farmers. They, too, have been oppressed and harried by highly organized bands of marauders, and they have been unable to protect themselves simply because they have not acted together. What we want to see is an Ever Victorious Army of American Farmers, which shall fight, not for conquest, but in righteous defense of their rights, their families and themselves. Their victory, which will be sure, will redound to their own honor and prosperity and to the welfare of the whole country. We want a victorious army, a new declaration of independence and a new independence day. God grant that they will come speedily.

CHAPTER XIV

Thus the syndicates and bankers
  Always crying out for bonds,
With both feet on the neck of labor,
  While they're clipping their coupons.
With their palace cars and banquets
  They can pass their time away,
And you old honest farmers
  Will have their banquet bill to pay.

There are many corporations
  That's no better now than knaves;
For they pay starvation wages
  And make men and women slaves;
And they work the little children
  In their sweat-shops day by day,
And to fill the rich man's coffers
  They must wear their life away.

FARMERS NOT INDEPENDENT.

In the daily papers a few years ago was this interesting item:

"An increase of $4,500,00 in the capital stock of Deere & Co. was announced here today. The present capital of the concern is $1,500,000, and the stockholders have voted to increase this to $6,000,-000. The additional capital is to provide for the remarkable growth and expansion of the business during the past few years and the further increase that is assured. It has all been subscribed by the present owners."

Of course this meant that the farmers will have to

pay the dividends on this quadrupled stock in the price of agricultural implements made by this firm. And this brings to the front another one of the objects of the American Society of Equity, which is to enable the farmer to buy advantageously. It is a fact that the farmers frequently pay much more for their farm supplies than is necessary to insure a fair profit to the manufacturer and the merchant. As I write a letter comes from a member in Oklahoma. He says: "I am paying 2 per cent. per month for money to meet current expenses so I can hold my wheat for $1." Must such sacrifice and determination go unrewarded? Would any banker dare charge a farmer 24 per cent. a year if they were thoroughly organized? Besides, the margin of profit placed on goods sold to the farmers is often much greater than that added to goods sold to the people of the towns and cities. The reason is clear. In trading, the farmer is not an independent person. He does business as the merchant or manufacturer dictates. He is usually a debtor to the implement dealer and the storekeeper, whereas if he had cash to pay for his supplies he could buy more cheaply in any market in the country. Wherever the farmer turns to make his purchases he finds himself face to face with a trust or union. He is worsted in the encounter and loses some of the legitimate results of his work when he puts his unorganized skill and labor against the organized efforts of the union laborer. He loses again in the encounter with the organized miners who mine the steel—or, rather, the iron from which the steel is made—which enters into his implements. He loses when he meets the woodworkers, the wagonmakers, the furniture makers, the implement makers, the horseshoers, the threshermen, the milk handlers, the carpenters, the masons who build his buildings, the armies who manufacture the household articles and the clothing, the army of leather workers, and behind them the army of tanners, the armies which run the railroads, and the armies which run the trains over the roads to haul to market the product of the farmer. The farmer does not drive a nail, use a pin, lift a hoe or spade, coil a rope, or turn a furrow but he pays tribute to some one of these numerous armies arrayed against him. Day and night, night and day, he is being taxed for the support of these armies, and because he is meeting them single-handed he can not resist their encroachments, nor pass the tax along. Plainly he needs help to enable him to buy advantageously, which will be, largely again, in the interest of the consumer.

And this it is hoped to give him. Considering the great number of farmers who will be members of the American Society of Equity, and the fact that they will soon have a good cash balance as the result of selling at profitable prices, there can be no doubt that they will be able to purchase for cash and at the lowest prevailing prices. Even if the farmer buys his supplies with his own produce, his ability to put a price on it will enable him to turn it in at higher figure than is now possible. He will no longer be under the necessity of asking for long credit, and whatever credit he may need he will get on the same favorable terms that other business men receive. Mention has already been made of the combination among the threshing men, which enables them to charge seven cents a bushel for threshing. If a farmer were able to say to the thresher that he would pay five or four cents, and that no farmer in the United States would pay a cent more, and if this was an equitable price, he would get his threshing done for four or five cents. This is the position in which the American Society of Equity would place every farmer in the country with reference to buying. While it is not probable that as much money is lost to the farmer by exorbitant prices which he has to pay as by the inadequate prices which he is compelled to take, yet it is a very great factor. He loses in both directions. It is time to stop the loss. The farmers can do it if they will, for they have the power, and their interest demands that they should use it. If they apply it properly, that is, through organization, the result can not be doubted.

In seeking to buy at fair prices the farmer, through the American Society of Equity, will help all the people. Economically the struggle of man is for cheapness. Men, in trying to satisfy their wants, always endeavor to do so as cheaply as possible. The call for cheapness by the farmer has, in the past, been of necessity, and this necessity has been of such a degree that they not only got cheapness but nastiness—low grade. Witness the volume of trade to some catalogue houses, where the chief recommendation is cheapness. The success of the American Society of Equity will benefit the home

Would Find   *   *   *   That on the Contrary
the Farmer Had the Upper Hand.
See Page 48.

dealer who will keep a high grade of goods and sell at equitable prices. We look for a turning from the cheap, low grades, to high grade goods at equitable prices.

We have seen how the price of farm products has been influenced by this tendency, and also how manufacturers combine to resist the tendency. Every new invention, every new process, every application of a newly discovered force, and every improved application of a well-known force, contributes to bring about cheapness. The old force of competition works toward the end. But recently we have had a great advance of prices with no effective effort to resist the advance.

The farmers propose to take the field in a campaign for lower prices on the things they buy where lower prices should prevail, and they are going to use a force the opposition of which will be irresistible. It is not so much a high price or a low price, but an equitable price all around that is demanded. The entrance of the Third Power through the American Society of Equity into the economic problems of the world marks an epoch in the history of the race. Although the last of the great powers to be organized, it is yet the fundamental or first power or force which will dominate all others. The development of this society and the power it will represent and wield may be compared with the development of the force, electricity, which has revolutionized the industrial world. The awakening of the agricultural classes, the organization of them into a great national and international co-operative body, which is now being accomplished, will make possible the control by them of practically all the material that enters into the manufacturing and commerce of the world, and on which human and animal life depend. Such a revolution might appall us were it not for the fact that in working out this stupendous movement everything will be in the direction of improvement and better conditions for everybody and for every legitimate enterprise.

It will be so in the matter of prices. There will not be one price for the farmer and another for the working man and professional man. Whatever conquests the farmers win in this direction will be for the benefit of all. What the farmer gets, all will get. In fighting his own battle the farmer will fight the battle of every American citizen. It will be impossible to charge the farmer a fair price and to charge other classes an unfair price. So the American Society of Equity does not come to oppress or enslave any class, but to give liberty and independence to all others—not to destroy or cripple any institution, but to benefit and strengthen all institutions, including the government itself. Heretofore farmers thought when organizing they must fight every institution on earth to get their right. This we admit is human nature, but also a relic of barbarism. There are too many such relics remaining. The farmers really have **no fight** against anybody or anything; all they need is equity, and this they can take, regardless of the disposition of other parties.

Many schemes have been devised, and many more

suggested, for the regulation and control of trusts. The law does something, and more stringent legal enactments might do more. But no curb can be as effectual as an organization of American citizens **greater** and **stronger** than the trusts themselves. Through this and through this alone can trust extortion be prevented, and fair treatment be secured for all. The people can do it. And the trust magnates understand this. With the help of shrewd and unscrupulous attorneys they can usually find a way to evade the most formidable statute, and to organize so as to get within the letter of the law. But they could make little headway with the people organized against them, and when the farmers are organized the people will be organized. How could the cotton or woolen manufacturers get along without the farmers's cotton or wool, or the packers without his cattle? This but indicates the power which the farmer could exert as a member of the American Society of Equity. He could oppose his trust—if you choose to call it so—to the manufacturing trusts, and in such a contest the farmer must, of necessity, win. This is a force—this new force, this Third Power—which the industrial trusts would understand and respect. Thus organized, the farmers could meet their enemies and oppressors on their own ground, and overthrow them, if necessary, for the common good. The trust problem would be solved, and solved in such a way as to benefit all. And the farmer, enabled to both buy and sell advantageously, would enjoy a prosperity and freedom such as he has never known, and that prosperity and freedom would be shared by all our people. The world has been waiting long for this Third Power. Now it is at hand.

CHAPTER XV

If farmers were only half as persistent
As politicians are wholly inconsistent,
    What a different footstool!
They walk up to the secret voting booths,
The aged and younger and hopeful youths,
And vote for men that others may choose
    Over them to rule.

The farmer produces the wealth of the land;
In framing the laws he should take a hand—
    Insist upon his rights.
He feeds the whole world by sweat and toil,
Forces great crops from the resisting soil,
From famine a safe and shielding foil,
    And no wrong incites.

INFLUENCE ON POLITICS.

Something has been said of the influence that the farmer can exert through organization on the politics of the country. One of the purposes of the American Society of Equity is to enable him to exert such influence. Here, again, it is not because the farmers, organized, need to look to politics for relief or strength on their account, but for the general welfare of humanity. The farmers, through their society, not only intend to do equity, but to get equity; not only to give equity, but to demand equity. It is not the object of the society to become a political party. But it is intended to secure, through existing parties, laws in the interest of agriculture. Though legislation is not the first thing sought, nor the most important thing, legislation is nevertheless needed. The reason that it has not been secured is that the politicians, though prolific in promises, when seeking election, forget all about the farmers when they get to Washington. They quickly fall under other influences. Moreover, they know that the farmers are easily put off; that they do not persist in the pursuit of their aims, and that when election day comes round again they may be trusted to support the party, readily accepting excuses and trusting to new promises. Nor are the farmers adequately represented in Congress by men of their own class. Thus they are largely without influence in shaping legislation. Until they are in a position, through co-operation, to secure what they want, progress will be slow. With the American Society of Equity a success, all these things can be rapidly accomplished.

It is not necessary to set out here all that the country needs in the way of legislation. But some things may be mentioned. Possibly the first and most important thing is some lightening of the burden of taxation; and this also implies less extravagance with the people's money, less graft, rake-offs and boodle, or, in short, the money wisely and economically expended, when we will see greater results with less tax. The farmer is taxed on everything he buys and yet is protected on scarcely anything he sells. This is an evil that must be righted, and it can be righted, but only by the combined efforts of the farmers. Until there are such efforts nothing will be done. As long as there are a few

people who can control the taxing power of the government, and many people who are content to have
that power so used, it is idle to hope for relief. The
few will control as long as the many allow them to
control—and not one moment longer. Even the
slightest measure of relief is denied at the present
time. Opportunities have long been presented for
making reciprocal commercial treaties with foreign
nations that would have had the effect of making a
much larger market for farm products, but they
have invariably been put aside at the dictation of
selfish interests demanding protection. Treaty after
treaty of this sort has been killed or allowed to die
in the Senate, which has been indifferent to the welfare of the farmer if only the protected industries
were allowed to have a monopoly of the home market. Rather than remove or lower the duty on one
article manufactured in New England, our Congress
has preferred to allow the farmer to get along as
best he could—to find his own market. Yet when
protection hurts a certain corporation, Congress is
quick to grant a rebate of the tax on any product
that goes into a manufactured article when that
article is exported. But nothing is done for the
farmer.

Yet there are many millions of foreigners who
would eat meats produced on our American
farms, if an earnest and well-directed effort
were made to open and cultivate foreign
markets. Lower taxes and wider markets could
thus both be secured by legislation, and the
American Society of Equity will work for such

legislation, bringing directly to bear on Congress the influence of over 10,000,000 American voters who now play little part in the business of lawmaking. This constant failure of the efforts to secure reciprocity has another bad effect on the farmer, for it provokes retaliation on the part of other countries from which the farmer even now suffers, and will suffer still more. Our fruits, cattle and meat products have been made the subjects of discriminating taxes and vexatious inspection imposed and resorted to by foreign governments in retaliation for exorbitant duties levied by our government on their exports to this country. There are threats of further retaliation, and we even hear talk of a European combination to save the European markets from so-called American invasion. Yet we go on in the same old way, and our manufacturers get even for the low prices at which they must sell abroad, by charging the home consumer greatly higher prices. Thus the farmers are kept out of the foreign markets that they ought to have, and the manufacturers plunder the home market by charging the farmers excessive prices.

Such arrangements as these are plainly not the work of farmers or of the friends of the farmer. They were devised by men who understood perfectly that the agricultural class is docile, patient, and most easily fleeced. The farmer is not interested in paying taxes for the benefit of people who never seek to benefit him, in narrowing the market for farm products, or in provoking retaliation from foreign governments. What he wants is freedom, equity, fair play to all, markets as wide as the world, low taxes—and not one of these things is his at the present time. With all these and with the American Society of Equity at work in his behalf, he probably would need little else from the government. But whatever he needed, he would get. For the politicians, who now so quickly forget the farmer, would realize that it was dangerous to do so, if they were aware that they were dealing with a great organization acting as a unit—an organization that refused to accept promises as legal tender, but that insisted on a redemption of those promises in honesty and good faith. Thus may the farmers make their influence felt in the condition of affairs which is rightfully theirs. The Third Power can easily defeat the first, second or third house. The farmers will be ignored as long as it is safe to ignore them, and no longer. The thing to do is to make it unsafe. The American Society of Equity is the means to bring that result to pass.

CHAPTER XVI

Of all the modern ideas,
  In the North, South, East or West,
The justice bringing idea
  Of Equity is best.
It can harm no human calling,
  And can boost none o'er the rest;
But brings equal chances to all of them,
  And therefore it's the best.

CROP REPORTING AND ADVICE.

Manifestly it will be imposssible for the farmers to co-operate unless they are kept thoroughly informed of what is going on in every part of the country, and indeed of the world. It would be foolish, to take a simple case, to attempt to fix and maintain a price on farm products unless each member knew what that price was. This information, at least, must be regularly furnished. It will be conveyed to the various members of the society through their official paper, which is a part of the plan. This official organ is printed weekly and there can be little doubt that with this plan in operation the recommended price will be printed by all the other daily and weekly papers as regularly as the markets are reporter now. The price agreed upon by the society will have to be printed by all newspapers having a market department, for it will be the market price.

With the knowledge obtained from the official paper concert of action will be easy. For every member of the society will have the same price and the same advice about the same crop at the same time, and, feeling sure that purchasers can not get those products from any one else for less than they can get them of him, he will be under no temptation to sell for less himself. Without this knowledge it would be wholly impossible to make the scheme work. But further than this, it is felt that the members of the society should have information that would convince them that prices agreed on are fair and reasonable—and attainable. So it is proposed, through the local unions or members, to carry on a system of crop reporting that will surpass anything ever before accomplished, or even attempted. Every member will be a crop reporter. The present system, or lack of system, of reporting crops is the source of great loss to the farmers. Take wheat, for instance: The harvest begins in Texas in May and ends in the Dakotas about September. Yet, as a matter of fact, crops are maturing and harvests are in progress in some part of the world every day in the year. From the beginning to the end of the harvest in this country, and more or less every day in the year, false crop reports are circulated, the yields are exaggerated, damage from weather, insects, etc., is emphasized, and all manner of frauds and deceptions are practiced. The result is that the market fluctuates every day, until the poor bewildered farmer sells rather than holds against uncertainties. The government reports, from the very conditions under which they are obtained, can not be more than reasonably good guesses, and consequently they are not held in good repute. So much discredit has sometimes been placed upon them that the market has been known to have acted in exactly the opposite way from that in which the reports should have influenced it.

So, the American Society of Equity will see to it that the farmers have full and accurate reports of conditions and crops. The size of the yield, and the character of the product; the nature of the season, whether favorable or unfavorable—all this will the members of the society get. Each member will be in a position to report the exact condition of growing crops on his own farm, and also yields, quantity on hand, and more important than all, the quantity he has ready for market can be reported by telephone daily. He can also give a correct report of his neighbor's crop, if that neighbor does not belong to the society. These reports will be given to the secretary at each meeting, to be forwarded, or will be sent to headquarters, direct by members, where they will be tabulated by statisticians, and in this way more accurate results will be secured than could be obtained in any other way. The crop reports and market conditions will be sent to each member, and thus all will be able to co-operate in asking and obtaining uniform prices. This is not only one of the strongest features of the proposed plan—it is an absolutely essential feature. With such trustworthy information, prices can be adjusted in such a way as to be equitable to both producer and consumer. Without this information such adjustment would be impossible.

But correct knowledge of the yields of the crops

and a price known to all farmers would avail little if the possessors of the crops were not able to hold them—control them—for the price.

Here the society again performs an important function, or makes it possible of performance. The organized farmers can pool their crops, store them and get advances in cash on them to meet their financial obligations. This is being practiced already in many places and for various crops by the organized farmers, but would not be practicable for the individual farmer operating on a small scale.

Thus, with a known minimum price which is a profitable price, the ability to hold the crops and still get the money to meet pressing obligations, the power to control production, if necessary, which will come with organization and the knowledge that the consumers always needed all the crops and not only a part of them, the last excuse of dumping for a lower, and less profitable price will be removed.

But other information of an educational sort will be furnished by the American Society of Equity. Reference has already been made to the work of agricultural schools and colleges, but valuable as this work is, it does not meet the requirements. The time has arrived when more intensive farming must be practiced, and conditions will soon be such that our farms must produce two or three times as much as they do now, if they are to supply the ever-increasing demands of the world. It is a fact that the average of our staple crops can be raised to three times the present average. This has been done in European countries, and what is done there can be duplicated here. Intensive farming implies more intelligent farming. To farm intelligently, the people must be educated in the mysteries of the science. To educate them schools must be established and maintained. There are, at present, many agricultural schools and colleges, but they are not sufficient for the almost universal education of the young people from the farms which will be required when the American Society of Equity is in successful operation. Nor do they fully meet the requirements of the advanced agriculture that must be practiced in the near future. The schools and other institutions which it is proposed to establish should be the meeting-places of farmers within the neighborhood, and they should be looked to for enlightenment on the intricate matters related to seed, soil, fertilizers and cultivation. Each farm should be plotted; there should be a chart giving the analysis of the soil in each field, or parts of fields; and recommendations should be made regarding the plant food needed to produce 40 bushels of wheat, 80 bushels of oats, 100 bushels of corn and 250 bushels of potatoes, etc., to the acre. Such an institution could be of vast help in giving instruction concerning drainage, irrigation, breeding stock, grain, fruits, vegetables, etc.; it could help in stamping out disease, fighting insects and blight, analyzing seeds for impurities, and guarding against and eradicating weeds. It could, and should, award prizes and medals for the best stock, the most successful crops, and in many ways it would guard and promote farmers' interests in the highest degree. The education which the sons and daughters of the farmer would get at these schools, at a merely nominal expense, would be of the greatest value, in that it would greatly increase their efficiency, and what is even more important, would give them a pride in and make them content with their lot in life. A membership of 5,000 for each such institution, and annual dues of $5, would afford a revenue of $25,000, from which enormous benefits would flow. And as agriculture is the foundation of our national prosperity, we should strive to promote the most intelligent conditions on the farms to the end that our material prosperity may be large and perpetual.

Yet the qualification that has already been made must not be forgotten. All this education, as far as it involves the raising of larger crops, and an increase in productiveness of the land, would be calamitous unless the farmer also had the power to fix the price of his products. But with this power assured, and the American Society of Equity will assure it, the more education and the larger the average yields, the better will it be for all. The two things work together. The farmer must control the present supply before he devotes himself to the work of increasing it. And the greater his success in increasing it, the greater is the necessity that he should have the situation wholly within his own control.

CHAPTER XVII

The cause of Equity is good;
  It seeks not it's own gain,
Against the weak ones of the earth,
  Who toil mid want and pain;
It welcomes all within its band,
  The strong as well as weak;
Its motto is, "Cooperate,"
  Each other's good to seek.

The cause of Equity is just;
  It lends a helping hand
In lifting up a mighty force—
  The Third Power in our land.
That is the struggle it may win
  Against foes unafraid,
Who wish to cause its overthrow,
  It needs each farmer's aid.

FARMERS, FELLOW-HELPERS.

All this means, what co-operation must ever mean, unity and solidarity among the people co-operating. The farmers, instead of being strangers to one another and rivals and competitors of one another, will be friends and fellow helpers. This will be a great gain, and in many ways. Every person will be the better for knowing that he is working for the good of all. He will know that while he is working for others, others are working for him, and that out of the combined effort good must come to the whole agricultural class, and indeed to all classes. There will be such an incentive to work and sacrifice as the American farmer has never known. The very sense of unity will be a great stimulus. Other men have found it so. They all have their organizations—manufacturers, working men, lawyers and physicians, etc., and these minister to their pride in their calling, and help to make that calling honorable and profitable. The farmers should learn from the experience of other workers unity, combination, co-operation, mutual helpfulness, each for all and all for each, instead of the fierce guerrilla warfare of competition—these are along the lines of present-day tendencies, and are the products of what we may truthfully call natural forces.

And it all strengthens the influences which make for self-help. There are many things that the farmers can do in combination that they never can do under the present individualistic system. It would be difficult to show, for instance, why farmers should not carry their own insurance. It has been abundantly demonstrated that fire risks on farm properties exclusively can be written at only a small fraction of what the old companies now charge. The hazard is slight, and of course it would be slighter still if each farmer were interested as a stockholder in the company which would have to pay for losses. Already there are farmers' insurance companies operating in various parts of the country, to the great satisfaction of their members. But whether it be through local companies or through one central company, the farmers certainly ought to carry their own fire insurance. It is the same with life insurance. For instance, if limited to the agricultural class, can easily be offered at a lower rate than that charged by companies that take all classes of risks up to the extra hazardous. And with improved conditions on the farm, which it is intended to secure, life will be prolonged, and the farmer will become an even more desirable risk that he is now. Also, because of this movement it becomes possible, and will become desirable as well as practicable to insure crops. These are incidental, and are not involved in the main plan, but they are important as being among the many things which the farmers may, and should, do for themselves. They even might, as has been suggested, in time, become their own bankers.

Viewed in this way the field of the American Society of Equity is almost limitless. It is remarkable how everything that is suggested contributes to solidarity. For example, the society will exert its influence to secure the improvement of the highways, toward which something has already been done. The amount of money that the farmers lose each year by bad and impassable roads is almost incalculable. The light loads which they are often compelled to haul, the wear on wagons and stock, the often enforced loss of a favorable opportunity to sell through the inability to get to town at all—all this is costly and wasteful. We all realize what the railroads have done for the farmer in the way of opening up markets, and we know that if the railroads were allowed to get out of repair they would be of much less service. Insufficient or worn-out rolling stock, broken-down locomotives, unsafe

He Worked for Himself as Others Did for Themselves.   See Page 93.

tracks, weakened bridges, poor terminal facilities
or none at all, would cost the farmer millions of dollars. It is precisely so in the case of wagon roads.
When these are good and easy to be traveled every
day in the year, there is just so much added to the
value of the farm. When they are impassable, the
value of the farm is lessened by just that much.

But this is not the whole story, one of the terrors
of the farm is isolation and loneliness. Against
these the American Society of Equity proposes to
wage war by improving or compelling the improvement of the highways, in order that, among other
things, there may be an increased social intercourse
among the farmers. Good roads and human rela-
tionships alike tend to bind men together. Present
conditions, on many American farms, have been
beautifully and truthfully described by Meredith
Nicholson in his poem, "Watching the World Go
By.":

Swift as a meteor and as quickly gone
   A train of cars darts swiftly through the night;
Scorning the wood and field it hurries on,
   A thing of wrathful might.

There, from the farmer's home a woman's eyes,
   Roused from the sudden jar and passing flare,
Follow the speeding phantom till it dies,—
   An echo on the air.

Narrow the life that has always been hers,
   The evening brings a longing to her breast;
Deep in her heart some aspiration stirs,
   And mocks her soul's unrest.

Her tasks are mean and endless as the days,
   And sometimes love can not repay all things;
An instrument that rudely touched obeys,

Become discordant strings.

The train that followed in the headlight's glare,
    Bound for the city and a larger world,
Made emphasis on her poor life of care,
    As from her sight it whirled.

Thus from all lonely hearts the great earth rolls,
    Indifferent though one women grieve and die,
Along its iron track are many souls
    That watch the world go by.

And another poem contributed by B. H. Van Bremen to Up-to-Date Farming, as I was revising this work as follows:

THE FARMER'S WIFE.

The farmer came in from the field one day;
    His languid step and his weary way,
    His bended brow, his sinewy hand,
All showed his work for the good of the land;
            For he sows,
            And he hoes,
            And he mows,
All for the good of the land.

By the kitchen fire stood his patient wife,
Light of his home and joy of his life.
With face all aglow and busy hand,
Preparing the meal for the husband's band;
            For she must boil,
            And she must broil,
            And she must toil,
All for the good of the home.

The bright sun shines when the farmer goes out,
The birds sing sweet songs, the lambs frisk about;
The brook babbles softly in the glen,
While he works so bravely for the good of men;
            For he sows,
            And he mows,
            And he hoes,
All for the good of the land.

How briskly the wife steps about within,

The dishes to wash, and the milk to skim;
The fire goes out, flies buzz about—
For the dear ones at home her heart is kept stout.
   There are pies to make,
   There is bread to bake,
   And steps to take,
All for the sake of home.

When the day is o'er, and the evening is come,
The creatures are fed, the milking is done,
He takes his rest 'neath the old shade tree,
From the labor of the land his thoughts are free;
   Though he sows,
   And he hoes,
   And he mows,
He rests from the work of the land.

But the faithful wife, from sun to sun,
Takes her burden up that's never done;
There is no rest, there is no play.
For the good of the house she must work away:
   For to mend the frock,
   And to knit the sock,
   And the cradle to rock,
All for the good of the home.

When autumn is here, and its chilling blast,
The farmer gathers his crops at last;
His barns are full, his fields are bare,
For the good of the land he ne'er hath care,
   While it blows,
   And it snows,
   Till winter goes,
He rests from the work of the land.

But the willing wife, till life's closing day,
Is the children's guide, the husband's stay;
From day to day she has done her best,
Until death alone can give her rest,
   For after the test,
   Comes the rest,
   With the blest,
In the farmer's heavenly home.

Is it not so? There is a spiritual side to this question of life on the farm that we can not safely ig-

nore. And the man who is not deeply interested in making farm life all that it should be, and can be, is not fit to be an American citizen. We may not be able to bring the farm to the world, but we can take something of the world, its life, its virtues, its beauty and its intelectual stimulus to the farm. Something of this has been done already, as has been shown, but more remains to be done. We can not cure human discontent and dissatisfaction, but we can, and must, as far as possible, destroy those conditions which give discontent and dissatisfaction a reason for being.

CHAPTER XVIII

The time has surely now come to pass
When farmers should rise in solid mass
    And throttle wrong.
They are the ordained rulers of the earth,
So intended from the day of creation's birth.
Without their help what'd our land be worth?
    Arise, be strong!

SOME OF THE BENEFITS.

General irrigation of the farms, the prevention of food adulteration, the settling of disputes without recourse to the courts, and the organization in other surplus-producing countries of societies similar to the American Society of Equity, are all within the scope of this movement; and they all have a direct bearing on the problem to be solved. With a constantly fertile and productive soil, freed from the wrongful competition of base and fraudulent products, relieved from the vexations and delays of litigation, and bound together with his fellows all over the world in a society seeking the good of all, the American farmer will be his own master, and will enjoy a peace, prosperity and dignity such as he never before knew.

Such will be the general result. Particulaly, the farmer will find that the value of his land will increase from 25 to 100 per cent. Producing more value, the farms will, of course, be worth more. It has been said that the capital invested in farming amounts to twenty billions of dollars, most of which is, of course, in land. This could easily be doubled, by making the farms more productive of money. Reference has been made to the action of a certain corporation in quadrupling its stock. This is common in the commercial world. Is it not in order for the farmers to declare their farms and plants worth four times the old value? It is quite the style for manufacturers of agricultural implements to quadruple their fortunes by the simple act of making a declaration to that effect, and then to put the price of their goods on a basis that will enable them to pay dividends on the increased capitalization. If the farmers must pay prices for their plows, cultivators and other machinery that makes such things possible for the manufacturers, why not put up the price of grain and farm produce so that the earning capacity of farms will be increased to such an extent that farmers also may declare their capital stock to be four times as great as it was?

But this would not be a case of simple "marking up," for the real value of the farms would be increased. With fair prices, close and intelligent cultivation, equitable laws for all, wide foreign markets, good roads, irrigation, information as to actual crop and market conditions, ability to direct produce to the best markets, systematic marketing and organization, farm lands would rise in value greatly, and every farmer and the whole country would be the richer. On such a firmly established basis as this our national prosperity could hardly be shaken. As has been pointed out, the farmer could and would spend more money for improvements, more for education, and more for both necessities and luxuries. Indeed, things that are now luxuries would speedly become necessities. The certainty of the business, as contrasted with the present uncertainty, would put a new life and spirit into the farmers. They would be proud of their occupation, and happy and contented in it. Travel, books, pictures, better clothes, better house furnishings, more amusements, and a wider and fuller life, would all be in reach of the farmers. There would be no need of pinching economy in the good years to insure against distress in the bad years. Having a certain profit from their products, they would spend it freely, and every industry in the country would be benefited—even beyond the dreams of the past—thus benefiting every man, woman and child. The improvements that the farmer would feel that it was worth while to make would further increase the value of the farms, and thus in every possible material way the improvement would be tremendous. The men on the farms would not have to work as hard as they do now, and they could shorten their working day, thus gaining time for other things. With a larger margin of profit, they would not be driven to raise the largest possible crops in order to make a bare living. There would be less drudgery and more rational enjoyment, and thus rural life would take a charm which it so sadly lacks under present conditions. There would be more

money, fewer notes in bank, possibly no mortgages,
and with it a general ease and security which present uncertainty and anxiety make quite impossible.
The farmer is the last man who should feel any
anxiety, and yet anxiety seems to be almost his
special foe. It grows out of the uncertainty he feels
in regard to his income from year to year, the inevitable result of uncertainty of weather, yields and
prices and his sense of helplessness. It is from
these things that he is asked to emancipate himself.
Think for a moment of the effect that freedom of
this sort has on the minds of men. They at once
begin to feel that many things are worth while
which never seemed to be so before. Even life itself becomes more worth while. This freedom
would encourage the farmer to improve his property, to make his home more pleasant and attractive, would increase his pride in his occupation,
keep his interest up to the mark and his mind on the
alert, and would make his life the joy that it ought
to be. To sum up: The effect of the American
Society of Equity will be to benefit the farmers of
the United States and of all the world and all other
businesses as well, for they are all dependent on the
farm. It will mean higher education, better citizen-
ship, less poverty, misery and crime, lower taxes,
fewer saloons, more schools and more innocent
places of amusement. Present uncertainties as to
price will be removed, farm values will increase,
thus adding billions of dollars to the wealth of the
country. Business everywhere will be stimulated,
and there will be more equal distribution of wealth,

a much larger proportion of it remaining in the country. Speculation in the products of the farm will be done away with, and all its evil effects on those products and on the people who watch the board and ticker will vanish. The success of the American Society of Equity will make it possible for the farmers whose tastes run in that direction to have comfortable and even luxurious homes, and will make of the country a veritable paradise. And prosperity will be general and permanent because based on the prosperity of that industry on which all other industries depend. An ambitious program surely, but it can be carried out if the farmers will but loyally and intelligently co-operate. This is no dream—or, if it is, it is one that can be easily realized. The farmers of the United States can make it come true. The future of the United States of America is the future of agriculture; mark this prediction. So the appeal is to the patriotic as well as to the selfish motives of the farmers. Through their salvation the salvation of the country must be worked out.

CHAPTER XIX

Cooperate! Cooperate!
  If you would keep the boys
Contented with the farmer's lot,
  A sharer of his joys.
Lift them above the path that you
  Of old were wont to walk,
A humdrum round of drudgery,
  Where wolves of want close stalk.

Cooperate! Cooperate!
  The good wife needs a rest,
For she has shared your burdens long,
  Your true friend and your best.
Through countless tasks and thankless toil
  Her youth was gladly spent,
But now the load too heavy lies
  Upon her shoulders bent.

FARMERS' PROBLEMS SOLVED.

There are many problems that are troubling our wise men a good deal that will be solved by the successful operation of this plan. A few of them may well claim our attention. We have all read the mournful lamentation over the unwillingness of young men to remain on the farms. The tendency of population is, we are told, constantly toward the cities. And the tendency is growing stronger all the while. The percentage of the city to the total population is larger than it was ten years ago, it being 41 per cent. in 1890, and 47 per cent., counting in towns of 1,000 population and over, in 1900.

The growth of cities in the United States is one of the most marked features in our American life. That the cities will continue to grow may be taken for granted, but there is no reason why they should grow so largely at the expense of the country and country towns.

A writer, discussing this question a short time ago, said that the reason the sons of farmers sought the cities was that city life was so much more complex than life on the farm, and that the whole tendency of our civilization was toward complexity. This may be the philosophy of it, and it is undoubtedly true that our people demand excitement and variety. Dullness and monotony are to most of us intolerable. So there is a shrinking from the uneventful farm life, and also a longing for the more stirring life of the large city. But this is not the whole of the question. What the American youth whether he be country or city bred, wants above everything else is a career—an opportunity. The city offers a thousand chances to one offered by the farm. The chance of failure is greater in the city than on the farm, when a mere living is considered, but so is the chance of success. And Americans were ever drawn by risk. They will play for high stakes, and they do not as a rule grumble if they lose, provided they have had a fair chance to win.

So the young man wants his career. He considers the case of his father, perhaps, and sees that he has worked drudgingly all his life for the most contemptible reward. Long hours, severe and heartbreaking toil, anxiety, pinching economy, self-denial and sacrifice, and finally old age, with, it may be, little to show for it all—what is there in the picture that is alluring to the high-spirited young man? The young man loves his home, and if he loves it he remembers it with affection, but still he knows that the life is narrow, that the hardships are many, and that the return was slight. Apparently there is nothing more in the life for him than there was for his father, and so he escapes to the city, where there is at least a chance for him to win his spurs. People may have theories and write learnedly on this subject, but there is no way of keeping the young man on the farm if we allow things to remain as they are. Our wise, good and honest men may deplore the tendency toward the city, but they can not honestly quarrel with the young man's choice. Nor can they forbid him to make his choice.

There is only one thing to be done, and that is to make farm life more attractive, and equip it with good possibilities. We can not exclude men from the cities or chain them to the farms, but we can allure, attract and keep them to the farms. And this is what we propose to do through the American Society of Equity. If the farmer's son could feel sure that he would get good prices for his products, that he would be able to control his business, that he would not, as now, be neglected by the government, be ridiculed by his acquaintances, and that all the capacity he possesses and all the education he might acquire would find abundant scope for exercise on the farm with the certainty of liberal reward, he would think long before migrating to

the city. Give the farmer as many of the comforts
of the city as he cares to possess, a fair chance at
the city's amusements, plenty of books and papers
and an education that would fit him to enjoy them,
and he will, with a sure chance for a career, be
quite content to remain a tiller of the soil. But if
he is to be a mere drudge, a hewer of wood and
drawer of water for others, we have no right to be
surprised that agriculture has slight charm for the
young man.

It is admitted that it is a bad thing both for the
city and the country to have the young men in such
large numbers leave the latter for the former. The
professions are crowded; there are more clerks and
bookkeepers than are needed, and the farm needs
laborers more now than ever before, and it is besides dangerous when there is a large element of
the population living in boarding-houses without
any of the restraints and safeguards of home. This
congestion of population is getting worse. And
with it the chance of the individual is growing
slighter all the time. Yet all the while there is a
clamor for workers on the farms. Would the average young man run away from a good chance on the
farm to a desperate struggle in the city with thousands of others perhaps better equipped for it then he
is? This is not likely. The farms need the young
men, and it is to the interest of the nation that they
should stay on the farm. There would be more than
enough work for all if the conditions were right and
if the workers could only be assured that it would
pay to farm to the limit. With larger profits the

farmer could afford to pay better wages and to grant a shorter working day to the men employed by him, and so those toilers who are now stranded in the city would be drawn to the farm, to the great advantage both of agriculture and themselves.

The possibilities in this direction are very great, and they should be attractive. Nothing is more needed in this country than a redistribution of the population wisely and judiciously made. To secure this we must make farming as attractive as it was meant to be by God when He created a garden and put a man in to to dress it. The poet Cowley writes: "God the first garden made, and the first city Cain," and Cowper assures us that "God made the country, and man made the town." True to his nature man has done what he could to spoil the country, God's handiwork. It can be, to some extent at least, restored to its lost estate. And it is fortunate that much is already being done to accomplish this. We have only to co-operate intelligently with forces already at work in order to keep the country from being depopulated and the city from being overcrowded. In some other countries rural life is popular. It can be made so with us. Indeed, the popular taste is already turning in that direction. There is no business that demands more brains than agriculture if it is properly carried on. But in these days brains must be liberally paid. The competition for talent is severe, and the farm must be prepared to meet it. If there were assurance of adequate reward for farming even the present isolation and loneliness and other unsatisfactory conditions would not repel. Men go to the Klondike and live there simply that they may make their fortunes. They will brave anything for the sake of a chance to make their way in the world and to find free scope for the talent they feel stirring within them. The frozen north, the burning tropics, the islands of the sea, aye, the most barbarous and dangerous life—all of these call to our young men, and they do not call in vain. Yet they turn their backs with something like contempt on the farm. Is it not strange? And does not the fact condemn us as a people? Surely we can do better than this. The American Society of Equity offers the chance. It would make farming attractive, and would again clothe it with the old seductiveness that it once had for our people in those days when every American citizen wanted to become a landowner. A shame it is that that charm has been lost. But it need not be lost permanently. Even as it is the life has a charm which the shriekers on the floor of the stock exchange and in the wheat pit know nothing of. For the farmer does produce something, and he at least has the satisfaction of knowing that he is of some use in the world.

The problem, then, is to develop the life on the farm up to the full measure of its great possibilities. We must make farming a career in the sense that other honorable occupations are careers, assure the farmer of a fair return for his labor, develop in him a pride in his work, make him see that it is worth while for him to put into it all the brains he possesses and that scientific farming pays, and give him that intellectual stimulus which comes from a larger and freer life. We must elevate the farmer's business until it is on an equality with the best business in the country, and when farming as a profession is the best profession on earth. When we have done all this, when the Third Power at last asserts itself, there will be no difficulty in keeping the boys on the farm, and other boys will want to come. Is not the experiment worth trying? Do not the farmers see that they owe it to their profession, to exert themselves to the utmost to give it that standing in the eyes of the world that it ought to have and once did have? And can not all our people be made to understand that anything which contributes to the accomplishment of all these results is worthy of their cordial and enthusiastic support? There is nothing here suggested that may not be done. The question is, Will the farmers do it?

CHAPTER XX

Who, then's, more entitled to inspire the laws,
Who'd take more interest in the common cause,
    Than he with good at heart?
As barnacles on the great ship of state,
Politicians decrease its fast sailing rate
And have no cares for its final fate;
    They know no chart.

INTIMATE CONNECTION WITH POLITICS.

It is, of course, quite impossible to consider this question apart from politics. Few questions in this country can be considered in this detached way. In this case it happens that there is a very direct and intimate connection between the reform proposed and politics—not party politics, but politics in the larger and more scientific sense. The air is full of talk about political reform. The abuses, injustices and oppressions incident to the business of government in this country are dwelt on with much emphasis. All know that corruption abounds on every hand, that graft is almost the law of our political life, that extravagance is the rule, that favoritism is prevalent, and that those with the strongest "pull" get the greatest consideration. There is discrimination everywhere, and it is in favor of the strong and against the weak. The law itself is too often the mere agent of the rich and powerful for carrying out their doubtful schemes.

Why is all this true in a country in which the people are supposed to govern? None of us can be made to believe that the people are corrupt or that they deliberately prefer bad to good government. The people are not corrupt, and so far from preferring bad government it is they who chiefly suffer from it. The trouble is that the people do not govern. Nominally a democracy, this government is the oligarchy controlled by a comparatively small class in its own interest. The people simply take what is given to them. Thus we have turned our system upside down and are false to the fundamental law of our political being. When a scoundrel in the postoffice department is caught with money in his hands that does not belong there we all know that it is the people's money that he has stolen. When a rascally law is enacted taxing the people for the benefit of a few greedy and grasping individuals, it is they that are oppressed. Divided into parties, the respectable and decent men of our cities are powerless to checkmate the rogues who prey on all alike, no matter what party they may belong to. The combination between men in office and corporations seeking franchises and favors is a combination in the interest of the politicians and the corporations and against the interest of the people. The people everywhere suffer, not because they govern, but because they are governed, and really without their consent. Pulls, influence, money, party trickery, corporate corruption in politics practised by our leading citizens—these be our rulers. And to this perversion of our government from its true aim and purpose are due all the ills from which we suffer.

And it is only those who make something out of

government who have any constant and effective influence in public affairs. President Hadley, of Yale University, writes:

"Except in those grave crises when a wave of patriotism sweeps over the community the support on which a democratic government relies is spasmodic and accidental. No man except the professionel politician feels that the government is being run in his particular interest. On none, therefore, except the professional politician can it rely for continuous activity in giving effect to its decrees."

We all understand this perfectly well. Who are the men directly and keenly and continuously interested in politics if not those who work simply that they may get something out of the game? The men who speak in political campaigns are, as a rule, men who, if not paid outright for their services, expect to get appointments if their side wins. Year after year you see the same men hanging around the polls, and hoping, through their connection with the organization, to be "taken care of." Gradually the government has been wrested from the hands of the people, and more and more—and as a consequence —the people have lost interest in it and influence with it.

Now the proposition is to restore to the people that supremacy which is rightfully theirs, and which they must have if this is ever again to be a government of the people. As this is even yet pre-eminently an agricultural country, the farmers are the people. With the millions of men directly interested in furthering their own interests, which are those of the people, and bound together in an or-

ganization, the usurpation of the politicians and corporations would be broken, and the real rulers
would govern. Considered in this light the American Society of Equity—the Third Power—is an instrument for the restoration of true democratic government in the United States, regardless of name
of party. No administration would dare to disre-
gard such an influence, or would think of tying itself up to the politicians and those who now use
them. Under such a system nothing would or could
be done without the freely expressed will of the
people. If they governed themselves badly, they
would still govern themselves, and would be responsible for all mistakes and crimes. With this
power and influence the people would regain their
old interest in public affairs, and the government
would no longer be forced to rely on the professional politician "for continuous activity in giving
effect to its decrees." In a word, it is proposed to
broaden the base of government and to put the
power and responsibility in and on the people. A
favor is something enjoyed by one at the expense
of others. Favors enjoyed by all are not favors,
but rights. If we can secure the granting of justice
to all and the withdrawal of privileges enjoyed only
by the few, we shall destroy the "pull" and the
whole system based on it. So this is a movement
for democratic government—government for all and
by all, in which all shall participate. With this secured most of the evils from which we are now suffering would disappear. The pull would not work
when there is nothing to be gained by it. The

people would not be interested in stealing from themselves. If there was nothing for corruption to win there would be no corruption. In brief, the remedy is to be sought in a simple adherence to what is the true American system, from which we have so widely departed, and in a loyal adherence to the old American ideals.

One other point is made by President Hadley that bears directly on this discussion. He calls attention to the fact that business and politics are now both regarded as games, and he says:

"A wider discretionary power for good or ill is placed in the hands of those by whome the public affairs of a city or state are conducted. These affairs will not be safe while politics is regarded as a game. * * * Under an imperialistic policy our government can not remain what it is. It must grow either worse or better. It can not remain a game in which the struggle for success is as far as possible disassociated from the moral sense of the participants. It will involve either a direct breach of trust or a direct acceptance of trust."

How widely this "game" theory of politics is held we all know, or, if we do not, we can easily learn by a few minutes' talk with a ward worker. Perhaps we ourselves have held to the theory. However this may be, the theory is wholly pernicious. For what is a "game" except something at which some one must win and some other one lose? It is the risk of losing, the hazard, that gives the game all its charm. There would be no betting on horse races if it were positively certain that every one would win; also no gambling on grain if every one were bound to lose.

The Farmer Will Not Forget the Question of
Price. See Page 105.

If success were sure for all, our gambling laws would enforce themselves—for there would be no gambling. What, therefore, are we to think of a political system administered by, or in the name of, a free people, which is avowedly based on the theory that some of the people must win at the expense of others of the people? Yet that is the present situation. It should be ended. An honest government is one under which every citizen, even the humblest, would win—that is, it is not a game. It is a business, and a business conducted for the benefit of all. And that is the sort of government that is advocated by the American Society of Equity. Politicians do not struggle, and plot, and bribe in order that they may secure justice and equity; what they seek is privilege. They play the game, and they play it for rich stakes. So it is proposed to uproot this game theory, for, as President Hadley truthfully says, our "affairs will not be safe while politics is regarded as a game." If we make it impossible, as we intend to do, for one man to win at the expense of another, we shall end the game business and destroy the interest in politics now shown by men who ought to be banished from politics. With the people in power, and with the government, which is now a great gambling affairs, turned into an honorable business enterprise, corruption, bribery and extravagance will disappear, and elections, instead of being fierce and degrading struggles for spoil, will be, as they ought to be, sober consultations regarding questions of principle and policy in which all will have legitimate interest.

CHAPTER XXI

While some may think him quite enchanting,
Heed not the politician's senseless ranting;
　　Down with his throne!
In your sturdy ranks are statesmen true
Who'd see that you received what's justly due.
Bring them forward, as you surely should do—
　　Have rulers of your own!

COMPELS A STRONG GOVERNMENT.

Much is said about the dangers of a strong government. But surely no one will deny that the government ought, at least, to be stronger than any citizen or combination of citizens. The power of all must be stronger than the power of less than all. Otherwise we shall have the rule of the many by the few, which is abhorrent to American ideas. So we shall have a government strong enough to prevent one man from injuring another. And it will make no difference how rich and powerful the would-be injurer is. In no other way than this can justice and equity be secured. The government must first itself be just, and then it must, standing above and outside of all classes and cliques, impose absolute justice upon all. We all know that weak governments can not do this. A feeble ruler is always, and of necessity must be, an unjust and oppressive ruler. In order to maintain himself he is forced to seek the support of the rich and powerful or of certain classes

of the rich and powerful, and to win their support
he must favor them at the expense of the rest of
the community. A study of the history of the South
and Central American republics will show that this
is true. To be just, a government must be great
and strong, owing no favors to any one, and granting none to any one.

To this extent, then, we intend to have a strong
government in this country. Putting the case in the
other way, surely no one will say that it should be
less strong than even the most powerful citizen, or
combination of citizens. We want all the people—
and not some of the people—to rule all the people.
And this, and this only, is self-government. We
may then start with the certainty that the success
of the American Society of Equity and the triumph
of the Third Power will mark the end of class rule
and of the favoritism that has grown out of it. Thus
we shall have justice and the destruction of all motives that lead men in power to be guilty of injustice. Surely that will be a great gain. Of course it
would be foolish to attempt to say what such a government might do, for it could do whatever it
pleased to do. What it pleased to do would depend
wholly on the will of the people. It is conceivable
that the new system might develop along socialistic
lines, and that the central authority might interfere
more than it does now with what we call private
business. Yet there is no tendency to the confisca-
tion of property nor anything that will check enterprise, nor limit ambition or kill incentive to efforts.
But if two classes of citizens got into a controversy

causing inconvenience and loss to the whole community, it is very probable that all the people, acting through their government, would intervene to protect themselves and to end the quarral. If it were found that the butchers were charging prices for meat out of all proportion to the cost of the cattle that they bought—as they have been known to do—the government, in the interest of all, would almost certainly order the price to be reduced. The coal strike of 1902-3 could have been ended before the evil effects of it were felt outside of the neighborhood where it started; and who will claim that immeasurable suffering, inconvenience and financial loss all over the country should be endured just because a few miners and operators disagree? If a government is not for this purpose, pray, what is it for? In the controversy, which it has been suggested might arise between the farmers and the consumers as to the price of farm products, the government would impose its just will on both parties to the quarrel and see that a fair and reasonable price was established. In a word, it would instantly ally itself with all the people as against any class that was seeking to win for itself an unfair advantage at the expense of society. As it is now it allies itself with a given class against the whole body of the people. Thus that situation would be entirely reversed.

But it will be asked, could such a government be trusted? Certainly it could be if the people can be trusted to govern themselves, as we all pretend to believe. And when we say that we believe in the principle of self-government we do not mean that we think that the people are infallible, and so incapable of making mistakes. What we do mean is that the people are honest, intelligent, swayed by good purposes, and are much better fit to govern themselves than any man is to govern them. We mean further that they will be much more patient under their own mistakes than they could be under the mistakes of any one else. They would recognize that the hurt came from themselves, so as there would be no one to punish there would be no basis for discontent or revolution.

It would, to be sure, still be necessary to decide questions of policy by a majority vote, and the danger of a tyranny by majority would not be wholly removed; but it would be greatly lessened. For we should have in government something of that cooperation which it is designed to introduce in the business of production. The government would be more directly by the people and less by the delegated agents than is now the case. And the overwhelming preponderance of the farmers would strengthen and broaden the foundation of government and would give many more people an interest in it.

Thus the American Society of Equity, merely by calling attention very sharply to the grievances of the farmers, who constitute the largest class in the country, and without having anything directly to do with politics, may be expected to transform our government by restoring it to its first and highest estate.

What does it matter if mistakes are made? They are made now. The people are quite as wise as the politicians and ringsters who now bear rule. And surely the politicians ought to be willing to admit that people wise enough to put them in power are very wise indeed. To hear the defenders of the present system talk you would think that presidents and congresses were never corrupt, nor wicked, nor incompetent, nor foolish. They compare the new scheme with an ideal system, and because it does not measure up to it they condemn it, forgetting that neither does the old system measure up to the ideal. Yet it must ever be borne in mind that we do not advocate any new system—no patent device or trick. What is advocated is old enough, namely, a government which shall be controlled by the people and not by the agents and servants of the people—a strong government, that will protect its citizens and afford that protection quickly—an equitable government, that secures justice for all. This is the true American theory from which, however, we have widely departed.

One thing which it is desired to secure is new in human governments, and that is justice. If that can be gained all will have been gained. Is it beyond our reach? For ages men have longed for it and struggled for it, but it has always gleamed just ahead of them, and they have never been able to reach it. Is it now at hand? Not ideally or in its fullness, perhaps, for this is an imperfect world of imperfect men, and selfishness is hard to kill. But substantially it can be secured. It can be secured, but only in one way—by enlisting selfishness (self-interest) in the struggle for it. If we can make a large majority of men see that it pays to be just, that they can not have justice themselves unless they are prepared to concede it to others, they will be as zealous fighters against injustice as are the most unselfish and idealistic of people. Men have in the past tried to eliminate selfishness. Now the purpose is to use it on the side of righteousness. The appeal must be made to the intelligence and self-interest of men as well as to their conscience. It ought not to be difficult to make sensible men understand that they would win more by freely yielding to every other man his rights than they could ever hope to win in a fierce scramble for unfair advantages in which they are as likely to be hurt as they are to hurt their brother. The farmer's cause will not be promoted—the Third Power will not rise—on the ruin of other enterprises, but by building up alongside of them will strengthen every other legitimate business and good institution.

A great economic writer has given us an allegory showing the wastefulness of a foolish and unenlightened selfishness. He once saw a cage of monkeys being fed. A plate full of food was placed before each monkey, but each one of them, instead of eating from the plate before him, wildly grabbed for the portion of his neighbor. And in the scramble much of the food was lost. What is suggested here is that each man should eat off his own plate and leave his neighbor to consume his meal in peace. Thus all would get enough, and the decencies would be maintained. Society at the present time is very like the cage of monkeys. In both cases there is selfishness, but it is of the silly kind. Surely we can order things better. If we can not, we might as well confess that self-government is a failure, nay, that men are not fit to live together in organized society.

CHAPTER XXII.

THE PLAN IS PRACTICABLE.

Then come along! Come along! Make no delay;
Come from every dwelling, come from every way;
Let Equity be in your hearts, and on your banners gay,
Then right and justice will prevail and dwell with us
    always.

Such is the argument in favor of the proposed society. For further details as to methods of organization, and rules for government of the society, I refer to the appendix and to the constitution and by-laws, where the details are set forth explicitly. And these have to do directly with another exceedingly important question. Some farmers may say that such a combination would be very desirable, that it would accomplish all the things I have said it would accomplish, and that in every way it would be a good thing for the farmers and the people. But they may ask: Is the plan practicable? This is the great question which reformers always have to answer, and, of course, it is right that they should be required to answer it, for it is to the test of practicability that everything must be brought. A flying machine would be most useful—if it would work. But unless a device of this sort will work there is no sense in paying any atttention to it. Always there is this terrible test. Can the American Society of Equity stand it?

I have not, in what has been said, passed over this question. For it has been shown that organization is the law of industrial progress; that other industries are organized; that all the forces of our civilization are tending toward a closer unity among men; that the farmers have combined successfully already (witness the Grange, Alliance, Farmers' Mutual Association and others), and that every change for the better that has taken place in the farmer's condition—his greater intelligence, his growing sense of dependence on others in the same line, his closer association with others through the medium of frequent mails, telephones, trolley lines, the growth of cities and towns in the rural regions, and his greater use of machinery—all points the way to organization, and makes it necessary, easy and inevitable. The American Society of Equity is thus working along natural lines and in cooperation with natural forces. So the argument in favor of the possibilities of organizing by this plan is reasonably strong as it now stands. As to its practicability and durability, these depend on the benefits it gives. But a little closer and more detailed examination of it may serve to allay the doubts of the more timorous and conservative. Of course, the great objecttion is that the scheme is too large and involves too many men. Organization, it is said, is easy when only a few people are concerned, but it is exceedingly difficult when it becomes necessary to take in millions of people, living in widely separated sections of the country, but this objection is based, not on the impracticability of the plan, but on the difficulty without conceding its impossibility. It will undoubtedly be harder to organize the farmers in such a way as to secure united action from them than it is for two men in the same city to form a commercial partnership; but the one is no more impossible than the other.

Surely the farmers in a certain neighborhood can organize without much trouble, and they can agree to abide by certain rules. They have done so and are doing this every day. So of the farmers in another and adjoining sections. Thus far the case is plain enough. If, therefore, the farmers in any given county have organized in the American Society of Equity—and they have in many—does it not follow that they can organize in other counties until a state is organized. If one state can organize another can. In fact, all the states can. If the farmers producing one important crop can organize into the American Society of Equity and get all the benefits it promises, and they have, is there any reason why the growers of other crops can not do the same? If the farmers in the United States can organize (and they have more than once, but on very poor plans), the farmers in Canada can organize, where the needs are as urgent and the conditions are very similar. Now if the farmers in America can organize on this new plan of the American Society of Equity, and for the beautiful and meritorious objects for which it stands, does it not follow that the farmers of Europe can organize, particularly since they need organization even more? I do not admit the necessity of organizing the farmers of Europe to accomplish all the objects of the American Society of Equity in this country, but organization there will follow. It will be a spontaneous lifting up or following in the lead of the American farmers until they are on the same level.

There is not a step in the process which may not be easily taken. Indeed, the work has already been begun and is now going forward with great rapidity. It would not be too much to say that the organization has already been effected. The problem is not one of the creation, but of the extension of the organization. That the organization can be formed has already been demonstrated. But there is another question which may give trouble to some people, and that is, Will the organization work? Unless there is good reason to believe that it will not, we are almost justified in asserting, even in the absence of affirmative proof, that it will, since the presumption is so strongly in its favor. At any rate we may say that the only way to find out positively whether or not it will work, unless it can be absolutely demonstrated that it will not work, is to try it. The man who builds a flying machine does not hesitate to put it to the test. Many men were sure that no ship could ever cross the ocean under steam. Yet when the trial was made it was found that the doubter was mistaken. So it is here. There is, as I believe, a great new machine. That it can be built has already been proved. Now we want to know whether it will operate. The machine is being built for benefits. We will leave you to judge if the plan as explained does not provide for every needed timber, all the wheels, levers and cranks; is there a nut, screw, bolt, rivet or nail lacking? Don't it look that all that is needed is the co-operative help of one million American freemen to man it, when it will start and continue forever to supply the needs of entire agricultural needs of this greatest of countries? In order to be sure either that it will or will not work we must give it a trial.

We have seen what it would accomplish, assuming that it will work. Are not these objects worth taking some risk—especially when the risk is so slight to secure? If the machine breaks down the loss to each individual will be inappreciable; if it moves, his gain will be tremendous. You risk infinitely more on every crop you put out or every head of live stock you put in the stall, not knowing whether you will get your money back or not. If the machine works, it will insure you a liberal return for every dollar invested, or every hour employed in all future time. But why should it not work? It all depends on the farmers. If they come into the organization, are loyal to its rules, are true to one another, and cooperate faithfully and intelligently for the general good, there can be no possible doubt of the success of the plan. No, I will not expect this. All do not need to be loyal, considering the great number of farmers, and the fact that only a small portion of any crop needs to be controlled at any time. If we admit that the great majority of farmers are stubborn, in fact rebellions,

yet they can not affect the accurate working results
of this machine. There will still be enough loyal
ones left at any time to insure success. In this respect the great numbers of farmers which, in the
past, was considered the great element of weakness
in a farmers' organization will be its greatest
strength, when working on the plan of the American Society of Equity. Give us a number equal to
what were in some former farmers' organizations
and the definite results will work out almost without an effort on the part of the individual farmer.
Farmers should remember that they are not to be
ruled from the outside. When the voice of the
American Society of Equity is heard, it will be the
voice of the farmers themselves.

So what we are to learn is not whether the organization can succeed, but whether the American farmers honestly want it to succeed; therefore, to doubt
the practicability of the plan is to doubt the farmers themselves; after the organization has been effected the farmers can kill it if they wish to, but so
can a man rob his partner. Railroads combine successfully, and yet how often do we hear of secret
cutting of rates in direct violation of the agreement
between the roads. So I admit that some of the
farmers might play the traitor to the organization,
and yet I hold that the organization would win in
spite of their treachery. But there would be few
such men among the American farmers; having
once decided to give the American Society of

Equity a trial they would see to it that it had a fair
trial.

The only people incapable of working together
in organizations are savages, idiots and the insane.
Among these a perverse individualism prevails. Are
we to class the farmers in either of these categories?
Organization is the great weapon of civilized and
enlightened men, and so it is peculiarly the weapon
of the American farmer. In his "Notes on Virginia," Thomas Jefferson wrote:

"Those who labor in the earth are the chosen people of God, if He ever had a chosen people, whose
breasts He has made His peculiar deposit for substantial and genuine virtue. It is the focus in which
He keeps alive that sacred fire, which otherw'se
might escape from the earth. Corruption of morals,
in the mass of cultivators is a phenomenon of which
no age or nation has furnished an example."

And writing to John Jay, in 1785, Jefferson said:

"Cultivators of the earth are the most valuable
citizens. They are the most vigorous, the most independent, the most virtuous, and they are tied to
their country and wedded to its liberty by the most
lasting bonds."

What they were in Jefferson's day they are now.
Yet it is of such men that we are asked to believe
that they, like the insane and savage, are incapable
of organization. The farmers are as intelligent as
the mechanics, who combine without difficulty and
make their combinations effective. They are even
as intelligent as the so-called captains of industry,
who, through their organizations, control both the

business and the politics of the American people. What the mechanics and capitalissts do, the farmers can and will do. To say that they can not organize effectively is to put them in a class by themselves and to rank them infinitely below all other classes. And that is absurd.

But all this argument as to whether it will work is largely irrelevent because it is working in some crops now completely, notably the tobacco crop, and has exerted its beneficial influences on all other crops.

One objection remains to be considered: There are those who say that the scheme is too great— that it is beyond the power of men to achieve. This is but another way of stating an objection already considered. But what are men put in this world for, if not to achieve great things? The very greatness of this enterprise, instead of being an objection to it, ought to be one of its chief recommendations. Further, if it has been shown that it is practicable, what matters it how great it is? The greater the better, one would think; besides, system is the servant of the twentieth century business man, and great enterprises frequently work out more definitely than small ones.

It is a stupendous campaign in which the farmers are asked to enlist. But that very fact ought to stir their ambition and inflame their zeal. Instead of saying that the plan can not be put in operation, we ought to set ourselves to a consideration of those qualities that are necessary in those who would make it work. Ralph Waldo Emerson—an American prophet who was never staggered by the great or impossible—has said that "nothing great was ever achieved without enthusiasm." It is so. Therefore, our duty is, not to pick flaws in the proposed scheme; not to make up our minds beforehand that it can not win, but to kindle our enthusiasm to such a point as to make failure absolutely impossible. The cause is worthy; the weapon is at hand and effective; the only weakness, if there is weakness, is our own doubting spirit. The appeal is for men to fight in the cause and to wield the weapon. With them—and they will be had—the Machine of Cooperation will be built. The Third Power will be a real power; the grand American Society of Equity will be a triumphant success, and agriculture will be lifted to the plane where it rightfully belongs.

CHAPTER XXIII.

Away with special privilege,
  Away with greed and gain,
Away with cunning schemes of men
  That equal rights restrain.

When Toil goes forth amid the fields,
  Its fruits mankind to bless,
Let Toil say what those fruits are worth,
  Let Toil its own possess.

FOR ALL COUNTRIES.

The plan outlined ought to appeal to European farmers quite as much as to their American brethren. With the cheap land in America, and boundless quantities of it, and by the large use of machinery, the farmers of the United States have forced the price of European wheat, and farm products generally, to an extremely low price. So all the farmers, and not merely those in the United States, have suffered from low prices and inadequately rewarded labor. This American invasion has not been a good thing for any of the farmers. For they have been engaged in a competition that was hurtful to all. Of course the farmers of Europe can not possibly raise prices as long as they are subjected to the competition of American products at the present low prices. The thing to do is, manifestly, to combine to raise prices. Restrictive legislation will accomplish little. In resorting to this, there is, too,

the further danger of raising prices so high that
people can not or will not buy. The farmers can
check the present competition by combination more
easily, and more effectively, than governments can
kill it by law.

And the key to the situation is in the hands of the
Americans. If they will refuse to compete with
Europeans on the present basis, and will combine
with them to lift the price of farm products all over
the world, it is clear that, though competition will
not be destroyed, it will be put on such a basis as to
make it possible for all to profit. Every advance of
price here, provided it be firmly held, will raise the
price of the competing product abroad.

A combination among American farmers even
without help from abroad would have that effect.
It would establish a level below which the European
farmers would not need to go in competing with one
another. But with all the farmers in the combination the effect would be much more marked.

It seems strange that the European farmers
should look for salvation to their most dreaded
competitors, but it is from these latter that salvation must come. For they have found that in beat-
ing their European rivals they have also injured
themselves. Now they propose to take themselves
out of the unprofitable struggle for cheapness. And
until they do withdraw from that struggle there will
be no hope for any one. So this chance is offered
to the farmers of Canada, France, Austria-Hungary,
Russia, the Argentine, far-off India, and, in short,
the world where food for man and beast are grown,

If a Farmer Goes to Washington   *   *   *
Page 40.

in the confident expectation that they will eagerly embrace it. The arguments that prove that organization will be a good thing for the American farmers prove, also, that it will be a good thing for the farmers everywhere. For the same conditions that operate against the former operate against the latter, and there is the additional element of American competition.

Let it be distinctly understood that the organizatinn proposed is industrial rather than political. For nations differ in their forms of government and in their political institutions, and a political program that would work well in one country might not work at all in another. Production, however, is the same the world over. Everywhere it depends on the three factors, land, labor, and capital, and the problem is the same everywhere, namely, to secure a fair reward to all three. There is no reason why the Third Power should not operate as effectively and beneficently in Russia as in the United States, in India as in the Argentine. The farmers in all these countries are interested in checking speculation, in preventing the speculators from playing the products of one against the other, and in securing fair prices for what they raise. In a word, their interests are identical. Therefore, all can easily cooperate.

The farmers of other countries need the society even worse than those of the United States do. They have smaller farms and they work dearer land —and land that is more in need of constant renewing and fertilizing. They need to make even a higher interest on their investment than is necessary in this country, in order to be sure of a decent living. When they come in competition with American wheat, grown on large farms and on land that is yet cheap, they are at a serious disadvantage. There is not a farmer in Russia who does not know that it would be easier for him to compete with American wheat at a dollar than with American wheat at fifty, sixty or seventy cents. And if the German or English buyers were unable to get wheat from America at a lower price than that established by the Russian farmers, it would be an equal chance that they would take Russian wheat. Nor are the American farmers at all disturbed at the prospect of all farmers getting good prices for their products. They know that there is a demand for all the staple crops that is ever likely to be raised—that the market is big enough for all. The trouble is that the crop of one country is used to depress the price of the crops of other countries, and thus all have suffered while now we want all to get good prices.

It is this well-known fact that makes international cooperation desirable, and to make the benefits of the society world wide. Buyers of farm products operate on an international basis. Sellers should, if they would protect themselves against imposition, do the same thing.

Thus business, and not politics, is the object of the organization. The question is not whether a man is a Republican or a Democrat, a Liberal or a Conservative, a supporter or an opponent of the government, but simply and solely whether he wants to end the bad, uncertain and unprofitable system of the past. Elevate his business on a plane with the best of others, and make the best possible man out of himself.

It is from this point of view that rulers and people alike are asked to consider this plan. The combination is one of the world's producers for their own, and so far the world's good. It is proposed to antagonize nothing except unfair commercial and industrial conditions. And when it is known that those conditions operate to injure by far the largest class of people in the world, surely no one can object to having them removed.

So the organization will be, and indeed has been, extended to other countries than the United States. The Russian farmers are roused, and are moving in the same path which the American farmers are asked to tread. Societies similar to the American Society of Equity will soon be organized in the Czar's dominions and other countries. The interest is intense wherever the plan has been developed. No man to whom it has been explained has failed to be convinced. Its simplicity, and, at the same time, its wide scope, its effectiveness, its justice and its equity, have all served to commend it to reasonable men. Whether a man lives in Russia or India, the United States, or elsewhere, he wants at least a fair chance to make his living, care properly for his family and accumulate a competency. On this platform all can stand. It is the platform of the American Society of Equity. And this is the reason why it is so well adapted to act internationally. The invitation, therefore, is as broad as humanity. The call goes to all, and from all. For their own good a favorable response is earnestly desired. It comes from men who are firmly determined to control their own business in their own interest, and to quit paying unfair toll to the speculators and middlemen who have so long preyed on the productive industries of the world.

CHAPTER XXIV.

Let justice reign o'er our mighty band;
  Let our hearts with triumph fill;
Let all awake, ere 'tis too late,
  And every foe we'll still.
In Unity we'll conquer all—
  Oh, may the day be near
When with God and right we will reign as might,
  With conscience bright and clear!

Oh, why should we, to whom life depends,
  Be trampled in the dust?
While others gain, we writhe in pain,
  For want of right and just.
If one and all would for duty strive,
  Then sorrow soon would end;
We supreme would reign and our rights we'd gain—
  On no one we'd depend.

FREEDOM OF ALL THE PEOPLE.

As a final word, it seems to be necessary to urge the thought that success would not involve the enslavement or control of any one class, but the freedom of all the people. It has been said that the struggle to which the farmer is invited is one for emancipation. What is sought is as little government regulation as posssible, and the widest possible opportunity for each one to work out his own destiny. The removal of obstacles rather than the imposition of new restrictions is the end sought. Undoubtedly men who prey on others must be restrained, but even this restraint will be in the interest of general liberty. That man is not free who does not get a fair reward for his own toil undiminished by tax for the benefit of his fellow citizens. So the vice of our present system is, that it is not based on liberty. And the farmers are those from whom liberty is withheld. So it all comes to a question of freedom. In doing away with the present abuses we are attacking not simply commercial and industrial unfairness and oppression, but tyranny. It is insisted that all men shall have all that they are entitled to. Liberty, then, is the great aim of the American Society of Equity.

And there can be no real justice where there is not liberty. For justice is, by its very nature, something that is due to a man; a debt owing to him; something to which he is entitled. When it is given or conceded to him as a favor or privilege coming from a benevolent despot, it is not really justice at all. Justice is not a thing to be granted, but one to be demanded. So when the American people came to frame their new and free government under the constitution they declared that one of their purposes was to "establish justice." They knew that a government could not be free unless it was just, or just unless it was free. And they were right. Surely this is a good precedent—one to which every American citizen should bow in reverence. But the appeal is not to one people, but to all people. The greatest merit of the plan is that it does not antagonize any government. It seeks the cooperation of all governments, which, no matter what their form, are without exception based on the idea that the good and prosperity of the subject or the citizen must be their chief consideration.

If the rulers of the earth believe this, and they all profess to do so, they will find a valuable and useful ally in the American Society of Equity. All that is asked is that the men who feed the world should themselves be decently fed. Even in the most absolute monarchies it is of the first importance that the people should be happy, contented and prosperous. And that government is wise which exerts itself to the utmost to secure that result. When this can be achieved without cost or peril to the government, it would seem as though no objection could be raised, even by the most absolute ruler, to any plan that appeared likely to bring the result to pass. Kingdoms have been known to go to war for the sake of diverting the attention of the people away from ill conditions at home. There have, in the history of the race, been many wars prompted by this motive. But such relief is only temporary. For after the war is over we find that the same evils exist, and that the burden of taxation imposed by the war only makes them worse and increases the discontent of the people. So, at most, war undertaken for this purpose is a mere palliative. What is wanted is a permanent remedy.

And the true remedy is one which is not only consistent with peace, but one which demands peace. The late Lord Tennyson wrote of his vision of what the earth was one day to be:

"Robed in universal harvest, up to either pole she smiles,
Universal ocean softly washing all her warless isles."

That is the ideal.   Abundance for all, general
content, the greatest productiveness, justice, honest
pay for honest toil, and universal peace—these are
the things that the American Society of Equity
would have the world enjoy.   To keep the people
happy is better than going to war to make them forget their unhappiness.   It is in this direction that
we must look for federation, not of Europe against
America, not of one class against another, not of
the people against their government—but of all
people, of all the nations for the general good.   It is
through such industrial and commercial alliance
that political alliances must come.   The Russian,
the American, the Argentine, the Indian and all
other farmers ought to be friends, not enemies.
They will be friends when relieved from the spell of
the speculators and gamblers in farm products, the
market manipulators and false crop reporters.   And
when they are friends their governments will be
friends.

So this society is not American except as it
started in America and at present is domiciled in
America.   It is world-wide, and there is not a toiler
in the world who will not be benefited by it.   What
has been said to, and of, American farmers applies
to all farmers, and this organization is meant for all
farmers.   It all comes to the scriptural doctrine that
the laborer is worthy of his hire.   To withhold his
hire from him, or any part of it, is to weaken all
government and to impair the foundations on which
society must rest.   While to insure him his just reward is to strengthen the social order and to build

anew the foundations of the political structures of
the world.

Years before it came to pass, Arthur Young, traveling in France, predicted the great revolution that
took place in that country more than a hundred
years ago. He based his prophecy simply on the
fact that the people were being robbed by the
church and the nobility, and robbed to such an extent that they did not have enough left to live on.
We are wiser in our generation, in that we do not
push our spoilation to such an extreme point. But
we want, not simply to avoid revolution, but to
make all the people happy. The question is, not
how much we can safely take from them, but how
much we can give them. And when we are asked to
give them only what is already theirs, in equity,
with the assurance that by doing so we shall make
them happy, shall we hesitate?

Peace, happiness, truth, justice, order, the death
of anarchy, firmly established governments, the
reign of law, contentment and satisfaction, together
with real and widely diffused prosperity, and to
crown it all a real federation of the nations—surely
these are things worth striving for. St. Paul said:
"Who planteth a vineyard, and eateth not of the
fruit thereof? Or who feedeth a flock, and eateth
not of the milk of the flock?" And the Psalmist
wrote to his people in their capativity: "For thou
shalt eat the labors of thine hands; O well is thee
and happy shalt thou be." We seek the fulfillment
of these prophecies. There is not a human being in
the world and not a government in the world that

will not be better because of the triumph of the Third Power through the American Society of Equity.

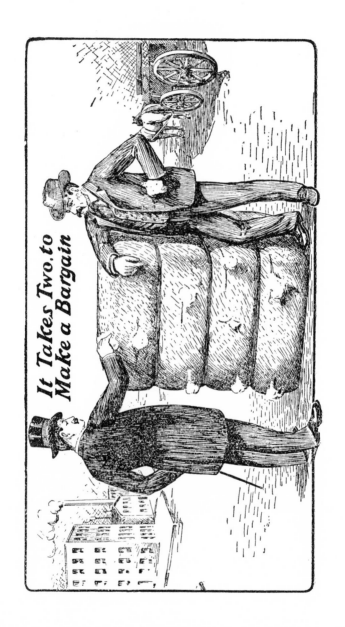

It Takes Two.to Make a Bargain

THE AMERICAN SOCIETY
OF EQUITY OF N. A.

The emblem of the American Society of Equity is symbolical of PRICE, being on an equality with PRODUCTION and CONSUMPTION.

APPENDIX.

THE BIRTH OF EQUITY.

Four years ago this very Christmas eve
    A mighty movement, glorious and grand,
Within this very city did achieve
Birth unto Righteousness and Equity:—
    A pure nativity, to bless our land;
To bless all lands beneath the sky's broad dome,
To make more safe the sacred rights of Home,
To bring to pass what Christ through His strong life had
       longed to see.

          Damned demons, Hell's infernal horde,
          At this event blasphemed the Lord,
             Who, with the aid of one great man
             Thus put in shape the glorious plan
          To bring all people in accord!

Like Christ, you walk midst scenes of dire distress,
    And by the Spirit you are led to be
Tempted by Satan in the wilderness,
    But let the Christ rise in you—and be free!
Be yours the Christlike sympathy and ruth;—
    Spurn Hell's hypocrisy, as He did then;—
    'Tis yours to save the starving souls of men
With the unleavened bread of sweet sincerity and truth.

          'Tis yours the fire of love to fan
          At which is forged the Master's plan—
             That hate, with which the world is rife,
             And land- and creed- and labor-strife
          End in the brotherhood of man!
                —Harry Albro' Woodworth.
Indianapolis, Ind., Dec. 24, 1906.

THE AMERICAN SOCIETY OF EQUITY.

What It Is—Its Chief Objects—Its Plans—What It Will Accomplish—How to Become a Member.

The American Society of Equity was incorporated and became a legal institution on the 24th day of December, 1902.

There was no design in selecting a date next preceding Christmas Day unless the design was on the part of an all-wise Providence Who directs the actions of men. There is, however, a distinct significance in the fact that the two greatest and best movements the world ever knew have their aniversary on consecutive days, December 24th and 25th. And there can be no doubt but that the birth of The American Society of Equity will in future years be celebrated in joy and thanksgiving, like unto the celebration of the day that commemorates the birth of Christianity. The latter will continue to be celebrated because it was the harbinger of "peace on earth, good will to men," the former because it marked the beginning of a new and glorious era of Equity, Right and Justice on Earth, and we may claim, will be a more potent factor in spreading Christianity than all things else, because it will remove the conditions that retard Christianity; and it will replace them with conditions favorable to its spread and the application of its doctrines.

THE NAME.

"Equity—Equality of rights; natural justice of rights; the giving or desiring to give to each man his due, according to reason and the law of God to man: fairness in determination of conflicting claims; impartiality."

"Equity is synonymous with or equal to justice, rectitude.

"Justice—The quality of being just, conformity to the principles of righteousness and rectitude in all things, strict performance of moral obligations, practical conformity to human or divine law; integrity in the dealings of men with each other; rectitude; equity; uprightness.

"Conformity to truth and realty in expressing opinions and in conduct; fair representation of facts respecting merit or demerit; honesty; fidelity; impartiality; as:

"The rendering to everyone his due or right; just treatment, requital of desert; merited reward or punishment; that which is due to one's conduct or mctives.

"Agreeableness to right, equity; justness; as the justness of a claim.

"Equity and justice are synonymous with law; right; rectitude; honesty; integrity; uprightness; fairness and impartiality.

"Justice and equity are the same; but human laws, though designed to secure justice, are of necessity imperfect, and hence what is strictly legal is at times far from being equitable or just.

"Justice, Rectitude—Rectitude, in its widest sense, is one of the most comprehensive words in our language, denoting absolute conformity to the rule of right in principle and practice."

The name, The American Society of Equity, will always indicate the purpose of this society. We can not offer any more comprehensive explanation than contained in the word "equity" itself. To give equity and receive equity, or to establish equity as a guiding standard in all relations of life and to compel fair dealing, or equity, in all business transactions, will always be the guiding principle of this society.

To accomplish this purpose, the society is devoting its effort to organizing the greatest class of our people—the farmers—and the one representing the greatest and most important industry—agriculture.

Once having accomplished the organization of the farmers, and this need not be to a complete extent, it is proposed to throw their numerical strength and the influence they can exert, by virtue of them possessing first of all the farm products that are absolutely necessary to the happiness, comforts and well-being of the country, against every form of iniquity existing in the country. There can be no doubt of the result when the millions of farmers make a demand for Equity. They will get it by virtue of their numbers and the importance of their business.

One of the first demands will be for equity in the price of farm crops. So important do we consider this that it is made the *first* or *chief* object of the society. With the old-time uncertainty of prices of crops, consequently the uncertainty attending agriculture, it would be useless to think of farmers combining for any good accomplishment. But with agriculture elevated to a level with the best of other business for certainty of profits, farmers will all join in the movement that has helped them, and will perpetuate it for the benefits and blessings it will continue to give them for all future time.

THE OBJECTS OF THE A. S. OF E.

Thus we come to the objects of the American Society of Equity. Read them carefully. All of them can be accomplished, and everything else that the people in Equity are entitled to and that may not be mentioned can be accomplished with farmers organized. Imagine what America will be when this society is established and all its objects are accomplished. Then consider that a movement as good as this, for everybody, can be established in a year if the people really want it and will do their part to get it. Each person's part is clearly shown in this book, and when you consider that you have often been deprived of your just rewards on what you sold; or taxed beyond an equitable rate on what you bought; many times exceeding all that is asked to cure the troubles for all time, will you refuse or even hesitate to embrace the apportunity now offered to secure your independence, in selling at least through this society?

Therefore, let it always be borne in mind that the first, great and immediate object of the A. S. of E. is:

To obtain profitable prices for all the products of the farms, orchards and gardens.

SOME OTHER OBJECTS ARE AS FOLLOWS:

To report crops in this and foreign countries so that farmers may operate intelligently in planting and marketing.

To lease or to have built and maintained, granaries, elevators, cold storage houses, etc., on the farms, at shipping points, and in the principal market cities, so that the utilities for storing crops and preparing for market may be under the control of the producers insted of owned or controlled by speculators and exploiters.

To end speculation and gambling in farm products.

To guard the consumers' interests and to protect them from overcharges, so the maximum consumption of farm products will result.

To open up new markets for American farm products in foreign countries and enlarge old ones.

To prevent the adulteration of food and marketing of food that is adulterated.

To secure new seeds, grain, vegetables, fruit, etc., from home and foreign countries and distribute them with the view of improving the present crops and giving greater diversity.

To secure legislation in the interest of farmers and the enforcement of good laws in the interest of all.

To establish institutions of learning, so that farmers, and their sons and daughters, may be educated in scientific and intensive farming, the best methods of marketing, and for the general advancement of agriculture.

To promote crop insurance against drought, flood, frost, and all the uncertainties of nature. Also fire and life insurance for farmers.

To make good roads.

To irrigate our lands.

To promote safe and equitable banking.

To cause child labor on the farms to cease as it largely has ceased in factories.

To keep the young people on the farm by removing the drudgery of farming and making farming attractive, reliable and profitable.

To produce conditions on the farm that will make woman's lot less irksome and more conducive to health and happiness.

To settle disputes without recourse to law.

To promote social intercourse to the extent of the fullest mutual benefit.

SCOPE OF THE A. S. OF E.

The American Society of Equity is a society for all Americans. In the word "American" as used here we include the citizens of the United States and Canada, although the people of the latter country prefer to call their part of the society the Canadian Society of Equity. It is also for all farm crops and its principles may be applied with benefit to all industries other than farming.

WHO ARE ELGIBLE TO MEMBERSHIP

While the American Society of Equity is primarily a farmers' society, yet it is not limifed to this class. But it says in its declaration, "for farmers and friends of farmers." Thus any person who wants farmers to come to the front and prosper, which means the prosperity of all the people; and who wants to see agriculture elevated, which will give greater stability to every business; and will help to establish this society and to accompiish its objects, is elgible to membership. As every fair-minded person will subscribe to the conditions, as stated, then this society is, in fact, *a Great American Society of Equity*, and for all good Americans.

THE ORGANIZED FORMS

The organized forms of the American Society of Equity are as follows:

THE LOCAL UNIONS; THE COUNTY UNIONS; THE DISTRICT UNIONS (NOT NEEDED FOR ALL CROPS); THE STATE UNIONS; THE SECTION UNIONS; THE DEPARTMENT UNIONS, AND THE NATIONAL UNION.

In the pamphlet "Crop Rich but Money Poor Farmer," sent free, is explained the functions of the various unions, except the Department union. This latter is organized for the particular crops or classes of crops that require different methods or different utilities for marketing. The purpose is to give the producers of the particular crops the opportunity to contribute toward marketing them independently of others who may not produce the same kinds. For example, grain farmers need elevators, but don't need cold storage houses; but producers of fruit need cold storage houses and don't need elevators. Hence we have the Fruit and Produce Department of the A. S. of E.; the Tobacco Growers' Department of the A. S. of E., and will have the Grain Growers' Dept., the Cotton Growers' Dept., the Live Stock Growers' Dept., etc., until every important crop or class of crops is equipped with its department union.

A BUSINESSLIKE SOCIETY.

A careful study of the organized forms of the A. S. of E. and its plan of directing the marketing of crops will disclose the fact that it is a business organization. (See "Crop Rich but Money Poor Farmer," a copy of which should accompany each Third Power book.) It is planned on a scale to correspond with the magnitude of the agricultural business of the country. Agriculture is by far the largest and most important business. It many times exceeds in volume and value any other industry. These facts apparently appalled other people and influenced them from attempting to organize farmers for the distribution of their crops. Or such attempts, when made, did not have the right plan and a sufficiently comprehensive system, and were failures.

MEASURES UP TO THE BEST SYSTEMS.

The reader should, however, understand that farmers are not going about solving their marketing problems in a slip-shod, slovenly way this time. An understanding of the plan will show that it measures up to the best systems employed by any of the great industrial, commercial or transportation companies. In comprehensiveness and effectiveness, when established, it will leave nothing to be desired. It meets all the requirements of the large and diversified businss for which it is intended.

Notwithstanding all this, the plan is perfectly simple, and in operation it will not be nearly so complicated or difficult to carry out as are the systems of tne great transportation companies. Moreover, when in operation the buyers will pay all the expense of operating it, which will be a new and novel thing for farmers who heretofore paid the expense of marketing other people's goods, in the prices they paid and did not pay a cent to market their own.

EQUITY A NEW IDEA.

Equity is a new idea in business, politics and society, we confess, but the masses, the common people, who outnumber the classes many times over, are demanding more and more of Equity in all the countries. Every reader knows this is true. They want it, and they are so numerous that they will have the power to get what they want, and what they are entitled to, when they have a good plan by which to make their power felt.

This is what the American Society of Equity gives them, and it is the only way through which the masses can make their power felt. Through this society they can kill all speculation, graft and exploitation, and substitute therefor Equity in all the relations of life. The *people* are the government, or ought to be. Under the American Society of Equity they will be, and when the society is developed in any country, the government of that country will be a government of Equity. Just imagine our Congress—our government—a Congress and government of Equity. It will be such soon, and then it will be *a government of the people, for the people and by the people*, as it was intended to be, and as it originally was.

NO WAR AGAINST ANYBODY.

In accomplishing its object the American Society of Equity will wage no war against any individual, business, institution, trust or government. Farmers will simply rise up and take what is theirs in Equity, and in doing this all other institutions will be leveled up or down; strengthened or destroyed; as in equity they deserve. The rise of the American Society of Equity will be like the operation of a law of nature—sure, certain, irresistible, but in fairness to all as each merits. *Dare any person go on record as opposing such a movement?* If he dare, he goes on record as opposing equity and confesses that his business is not based on equity.

HOW TO BECOME A MEMBER OF THE AMERICAN SOCIETY OF EQUITY—THE FEE.

The membership fee is $2.00, and it includes a year's subscription to **Up-to-Date Farming,** the official paper. The subscription price of the paper alone is $1.00.

If there is a local union in your neighborhood you should join it, paying the membership fee to the president or secretary. But if no local union, you should send the fee to your State union, if one; otherwise, to headquarters of The American Society of Equity, Indianapolis, Indiana.

THE DUES.

The dues to remain a member of the socieety are $1.20 a year, which also includes payment for the official paper. However, no dues are payable the same year the member joins.

MONEY; HOW EXPENDED.

The money received from fees and dues is used to educate farmers, organize them and establish the society. After it is established they can be less. But it takes money, and a lot of it, to educate a nation of farmers and revolutionize the business end of an industry like American agriculture.

It is hoped that every person who receives this book will become a member of the society at once. Thus he will help its development and it will help him even to a greater extent.

THE AMERICAN SOCIETY OF EQUITY AND ITS NEED IN OUR COUNTRY.

Address by J. A. Everitt, Founder and President of The American Society of Equity, at the Annual Meeting of the Society, E. St. Louis, Ill., Oct. 23-26, 1906.

Mr. Chairman, Ladies and Gentlemen:

I congratulate you on the auspicious opening of this convention. I am glad to greet you at this fourth annual meeting of the American Society of Equity and rejoice with you at the growth and accomplishments of our beloved Society, and in the contemplation of its future greatness and usefulness.

Our meeting in convention with a firm purpose to attain our avowed objects is one of the most sublime acts, when carefully considered, in the history of any country. Delegates are here representing every important farm crop. These delegates have come together for the main purpose of deciding what farm crops shall sell for during the next twelve months. Some people will say that it matters not what prices may be agreed upon at this convention— that the acts of this convention will have no effect on future prices. But they are mistaken. While the members of the American Society of Equity are not strong enough within themselves to compel the fair prices on all the crops throughout the season, nevertheless there are millions of farmers in the country who will look to the prices agreed upon as equitable by this convention and they will fix their minds on them and hold for them. Thus the minimum price idea and the doctrine of controlled marketing have taken hold all over the country and silently but surely the future prices of the crops are being molded. Looking back, we find that only two principal crops failed to sell up to the minimum prices since this society has been naming them. They were the crop of potatoes of 1904 and the crop of wheat of 1905. This being a fact, and in view of the further fact, that since the existence of the American Society of Equity there has been much more advance in each crop between the first months of marketing and the later ones than prevailed before, it follows that those farmers who held for the prices profited thereby. True, there have been some exceptions, but they are comparatively few.

But it is not vital whether the society is able now to influence the price for all of the crops or any of them. It is more important to know that farmers are at last on the right track to solve their problems, chief among which are marketing and price making. Each recurring annual meeting finds the society stronger and the new education more universal. The time is bound to come and will come soon when these conventions will be almost instantaneous in their effect on prices. That is, as soon as the price is agreed upon for any crop no more will be for sale at any other price, hence the price will prevail. I believe this will soon come to pass. Thus, when we contemplate the significance of this convention and future ones where the decision is made as to what the year's crops—representing the food and clothing supplies produced in America—are in equity worth, it is a thought that may well arrest the attention of every person in this country and millions in foreign lands who depend upon us for food and for the wherewithal to be clothed. It is a sublime thought. The realization is as certain as that people and domestic animals will continue to crave food and that humans will wish to be clothed.

Realizing thus the main object of our coming together we should pray for wisdom that all our acts may be governed by equity and that whatever is done may be done in the spirit of justice to all.

WHAT BENEFITS THE FARMER BENEFITS ALL.

Although this is primarily a meeting for farmers and for agriculture, yet everything that you do to benefit yourselves and your business, and all that you can with safety do, must operate to benefit every class, every useful industry, every meritorious institution and every person doing a legitimate business. For instance: if farmers are deprived of a fair share of the wealth they produce, all other industries will suffer in equal ratio. If, on the other hand, the farmers receive a fair reward, their gain will be reflected in the business done by merchants, bankers, professional men, laborers, etc., all down the line in country, towns and cities.

Before the time of the American Society of Equity it was generally considered that what one man, company or corporation gained in trade must be lost by another, and many enterprises were undertaken on this platform. But, with the farmers working on the plan of this society, it is different. The more the farmers gain the more they can and will give in trade to others. The higher agriculture rises in the scale that measures industries, the more it will exalt, strengthen and guarantee the integrity of all other useful industries and beneficial institutions.

Somebody said "the liberty of one man ceases where the liberty of another man begins." But not so with the A. S. of E. It will give to all men greated liberty, and for those who are not free industrially it will rend asunder the shackles that bind them, and leave them free forever.

WHAT THE WORLD OWES TO THE FARMER.

I verily believe farmers can not take unless they give in return. On the prosperity of farmers depends the continued prosperity of our country. Thus we can begin to realize their importance, at this time, and for all times.

They were the pioneers who subdued the savages, cleared the forests, drained the swamps and leveled the mountains. They have always kept, not only abreast of civilization in America, but ahead of it. The American farmers have always stood on the firing line of civilization; fought the battles, fed the people and fostered our industries and institutions.

As owners of the land they have given the mines of coal, iron and precious metals and wells of oil. Nearly all the natural wealth and much of the created wealth of the country have come from the farmers.

Hence we may say, "Hail to the farmers!" We greet them as the mainstay of the country and the people to whom are due all the rewards their position entitles them to. They have, by their patience and hard, honest toil, made the country great. But what has the country done for the farmers? Are farmers receiving their just rewards? Are they getting equity in dealings with others and from the government?

A WORD WITH A GRAND MEANING.

We speak of EQUITY. We have incorporated "Equity" into the name of our society. We have incorporated the principle, the attribute, itself. Who can correctly guage the meaning of this word or measure its depth and breadth as we want it to apply to mankind? Who can fully estimate the beauties and benefits to humanity, were equity to prevail in all the business relations of life, or who can measure the injustice and suffering if it is refused?

Equity means justice, impartiality, the giving or the desire to give to each man his due according to the law of God and man. Note that it means "Justice,"—a fair return, a fair reward, a fair exchange, a fair wage without partiality. We might say "a square deal," equal and exact justice to all and special privileges to none, or, equal opportunities to all.

Who will claim that equity, justice, impartiality and the granting to each his just dues are the rule in our land today? Or will contend that all have equal opportunities?

ARE ALL MEN FREE AND EQUAL?

Our country was founded on the proposition that "all

men are created free and equal." But are all free and
equal to-day?

Our government was saved and the union preserved on
the proposition that "all men are equal before the law."
But are all equal before the law? Do all classses receive
equal consideration from congress, legislatures and courts?

It is the habit of Americans to boast of freedom and independence. But who are free and independent in this
country to-day? Are farmers free and independent? I
might ask, is our government free and independent?

When I see laws made in the interests of the rich and
powerful and not in the interest of the masses; when I see
laws interpreted in favor of the powerful corporations and
against the masses; when I see the poor punished for trif-
ling misdemeanors and the rich go free after great of-
fenses against society, state, country and God, I cannot
but think ours is not a free and independent government,
hence how can all the people be free and independent?

That man is not free and independent who has not the
power to place the value on his own product, the result of
his own investment, skill and toil. The possession of this
right has been the contention all down the ages by every
people and class. Laborers contended for the power and
won; manufacturers contended for it and won; merchants
contended for it and won. Every class has now complete
or partial industrial freedom but the farmers. Yet the
farmers have worked harder and longer hours than any
others and have produced more desirable and valuable
goods than any of them. They are admittedly the backbone of the country and of all its industries. But, shame
to say, when it comes to putting a price on their own produce, thus setting the wages for their toil, that backbone
is so weak and farmers so wobbly, that they represent no
power at all, while the other people make the price, set
their wages and take the goods.

Does this not amount almost, or quite, to industrial
slavery? In times before the war the black slaves worked
all the time, and all they produced was taken by their
masters, who gave a living in return. I want to ask if
farmers have not done, and are not doing, practically the
same thing as these slaves did who could not help themselves, while the farmers can?

WHAT IS WRONG WITH AGRICULTURE?

I believe I do not overdraw this picture. I have in
mind the average farmer. He represents the great mass.
In a movement such as this, we must consider the average
man. We aim to produce conditions that will make the
average farmer prosperous—the one who lives on the aver-

age farm and produces average crops. The average farmer has not been as prosperous as he should be. There is something wrong with agriculture. Nearly everybody knows that something is wrong, but very few people know that there is a remedy and fewer know how to apply it. I want to tell what the remedy is and explain how to apply it.

THERE IS BALM IN GILEAD.

We see that business in other lines is not done as it was formerly, but farmers and their advisers have been slow to adopt the improvements in agriculture. Although they have seen the great industries organize and substitute co-operation for competition, to great advantage, they say "it can't be done for agriculture."

They have seen political parties organize and they have seeen them inaugurate the policy "To the victors belong the spoils," yet they say "farmers can't co-operate."

They have seen laborers organize against the opposition of employers, and they now see them stand shoulder to shoulder for fair wages, and yet they say farmers can not organize, although there is no person to oppose them.

They have seen many illustrations to prove that competition is the law of industrial death and co-operation the law of industrial life, yet they say "farmers can't organize," and "farmers can't co-operate," and "farmers won't stick."

We may well stand appalled at the spectacle of every other class and industry being organized while the farmers—our greatest class, numbering millions—are at the mercy of organizations, some of which have no mercy. Our most important industry is as yet unorganized and year after year is more exploited by the organized classes.

Such were the conditions when the American Society of Equity came and they still largely prevail, at this day. Many here to-day know that already the society has accomplished much to relieve these conditions. All who understand it and its principles believe that, through it, farmers will be fully emancipated from the industrial slavery of the past, and that their business will be exalted above any other in the country, where it belongs by all rights, human and divine.

MY ADDRESS.

My address to-day will consist of four parts. First, the foregoing introductory remarks; second, an explanation of the American Society of Equity; third, the need of an American Society of Equity; fourth, summing up of results. The second part—what the American Society of Equity is—might be omitted except that there are some members present who may not fully understand the organized forms of the society, and some non-members present who want to understand it, thus making it advisable to review it briefly. Naturally this address should include a review of the work so far accomplished together with recommendations for the future, but these must wait until a later hour. I think it is of the utmost importance that we should have a clear understanding of the society as it to-day stands, on advance ground, ready to take the final steps for its completion. Full comprehension should also be had of the need of this society in America's social, industrial and political affairs.

THE AMERICAN SOCIETY OF EQUITY.

What is the society? How is it constituted? What is its plan? What are its objects? How does it differ from former farmers' organizations? What right have its supporters to hope for greater results than were realized from former farmers' societies that had millions of members? These are questions that the uninformed naturally ask.

This is primarily a farmers' society, but it admits to membership friends of farmers. It is non-secret. It is a society for all farmers in America and for all their crops. It is not only the intention of this society to organize all farmers, but also to assist them in marketing all of their crops.

The objects of the society are numerous. I will not mention them here, but I will say that they cover everything to which the farmers are entitled in equity. The chief object is to secure profitable prices for all crops; and if this one object can not be accomplished, farmers need not try for any of the others.

The plan to accomplish the first object is to organize the farmers all over the country. Or, in order to secure profitable prices on some of the crops, to organize those portions of the country that are heavy producers of such crops. The farmers are organized into local unions, these into county unions, these into state unions (and sometimes into district unions) and the States into section unions. There will also be department unions. All the unions organize into the National union.

THE ORGANIZED FORMS AND THEIR FUNCTIONS.

A brief explanation of the organized forms and their functions will enable you to understand the plan. However, before entering into such explanation, I want you to understand that the machine of the American Society of Equity is planned on a scale to correspond with the magnitude of the agricultural business of the country. At the same time the plan reduces the work down to so simple a proposition that, in operation, it will not be nearly as large, complicated, or expensive as is a single large railroad system. Moreover, when in operation, the buyers will pay all the expense of running it. This will be the first opportunity farmers have ever had to pass the expense along to the next, although heretofore they have been paying all the expenses, including the expense of marketing the goods they have been buying. The agricultural business in this country is by far the greatest industry. It many times excels any other in volume and value of product and number of people engaged therein. These facts have apparently appalled other people and prevented them from attempting to organize farmers and give them a business system. Or such atttempts as were made were positively without a carefully prepared plan. I took all these things into consideration a few years ago when working out the American Society of Equity plan. I want you to understand that we are not going about solving farmers' problems in a slipshod, slovenly way. An examination and a perfect understanding of the plan will show that it measures up to the best systems employed by any of the great industrial, commercial or transportation companies. In comprehensiveness and effectiveness it leaves nothing to be desired. It meets all the requirements of a large and diversified business such as American agriculture. This I know by practical test in certain sections and on certain crops already organized and under control. It has been demonstrated that this plan will bring profitable prices for farm crops. All that is necessary is to use it. I realize that the success of a farmers' movement is not all in organization. The Grange and Alliance had millions of members, but did not accomplish all that the farmers needed, simply because they did not have the right plan, did not work for the correct objects and did not furnish a sufficient business system. They builded on the sand and soon went to destruction. They have demonstrated that an organization with a large membership and without a good plan and sound business system is powerless to bring about reforms.

A BUSINESSLIKE CONSTITUTION.

Let me put in your minds again a picture of the constitution of The American Society of Equity:

The Local Unions
The County Unions
The District Unions

The State Unions
The Section Unions
The Department Unions
And the National Union.

Does this not look like business? Looks very much like the machine of government for the United States itself, except that we have provided so that the directors can never control this machine as congress controls our country. The people will always be the sovereign power in the American Society of Equity.

IN OPERATION.

In business operation, for directing the marketing of crops, the local unions will receive daily reports from their members stating what each has ready to market, that is, only the part for shipping. All the local unions in a county will report to the county union, and all the county unions in a section will report to the section union. Thus each section will have a report each day of all the crops standing that they are being oppressed.
ready for market, or that will be ready in a few days, in the entire section. All the sections will report to the National Union and it will have a crop report every day, of the entire supply in the country for any day. The report of the demand will be gotten from the societies' representatives in the principal markets, reported to the section unions, and, in turn, the section unions will report to the National union. Thus, we will have a report of both the supply and demand each day. Each section union knows exactly where there is supply and where there is demand even to the railroads connecting, so that it will be an easy matter to so direct the supply that it will go out and meet the demand. I might enlarge on the beauties of this system if time permitted. But I want to say that it is the correct plan for farmers and will work, because it is working. This system of reporting will beat the government system ten thousand per cent. and will be almost instantaneous, while the government system is so slow that it is only of benefit to speculators.

IMPOSSIBLE? NO; SIMPLE!

You may say it will be impossible to get the report of demand, or it will be such a great undertaking as to be impracticable. But, like every other step in this plan, it is perfectly simple and reliable. You see, the supply of crops will be tied up out in the country or in farmers' warehouses. Then the representative, the man who represents the tied up, controlled, crops, will open an office in a central part of the city, install telephones and hang out his sign, and the buyers and handlers will be compelled to send their orders to him, or, well, if they are stubborn they will soon get mighty hungry.

THE EASE OF REPORTING NEWS OF SUPPLY.

The reporting will be done by telephone or telegraph, but may be done by mail or in person to the local unions. I do expect every farmer's home to have a telephone. It will be the greatest utility on the farm.

Just one more illustration to show how light the actual work of reporting supply will be. It will be easy enough for a local union to receive the daily report of each member who has anything to sell. If we say there are fifty local unions in a county, it will also be very easy for the county union to receive fifty telephone messages. Now let us assume that there are sixty counties in a state with eight states in a section. This means only 480 telephone or telegraph messages to get a complete report of all the crops ready for market in the whole eight states. Is there anything impossible about this? Could you imagine anything simpler or easier? Then, too, just think what is accomplished; and it all depends upon the farmers organizing into local unions!

Department unions are to give particular crops or classes of crops a large degree of independence in conducting their own business; and are also for the purpose of identifying producers of these crops, apart from others, so that they may hold separate conventions, provide special facilities for controlling and marketing, and contribute independently to such business, if necessary, through their respective department unions. Already there are organized the department of fruit and produce, and tobacco growers. Other crops will organize into department unions until each important crop or class of crops is perfectly organized. Remember, in all this machine and its operations, the American Society of Equity never becomes possesseed of any crops, but acts only in directing the marketing. This feature commends itself highly. Any intelligent person will quickly appreciate the superiority of this plan over the past ideas of marketing direct to the consumers, and of forming capital stock companies. The society, however, believes farmers must own or control all granaries, elevators, warehouses, cold storage houses, and other utilities for storing, controlling and marketing the crops.

Such is a very brief description of the American Society of Equity, its plan and system. Let us now consider:

THE NEEDS OF AN AMERICAN SOCIETY OF EQUITY.

Does this country need an American Society of Equity? Not only a Society of Equity to secure profitable prices for farm crops, but one that, in the full scope of the name, will accomplish many needed reforms?

The common people are aroused now as never before to the fact that the government is controlled by powerful industrial and commercial organizations, and they see that the tendency is to keep the masses in such a condition that they can be easily exploited and plundered.

To obtain profitable prices is a grand object. Farmers are entitled to them. We can appeal to their selfish interest to accomplish this object. Once having accomplised it, we can depend on the farms to continue the society for the profit it will give them every year. In this way we answer the claim that farmers "won't organize" or that they "won't stick together."

But when farmers are organized they can do more than get profitable prices. I am going to tell you some of the things they can do, through the American Society of Equity. After you understand you will say that this society appeals to all farmers, no matter where located, what crops they grow, or what their condition of prosperity. Also, to all other people who are tired of graft and exploitation and who want equity to prevail. Thus, while it is a farmers' Society of Equity on account of the great number of farmers, the importance of their industry and the great power that they can exert in an organized condition, it will be a national society, or truly an American Society of Equity, and can be used to secure equity for all Americans, in society, business and government. We need such a' society, such an organization, in this country now.

Instead of ours being, at the present time, a government of the people, by the people, for the people; it is a government by the rich and powerful to exploit and coerce 999-1000 of the people. In other words it takes 999 of the common average people, to work for and support one of the masters, sometimes called captains of industry, in the style he demands, and all the machinery of the government is working to perpetuate this condition. The law of the land has not beeen equity and justice. Freedom, liberty, independence and equal opportunities are not enjoyed by all. But the law of the land has been, and is, greed, graft, plunder and exploitation.

EQUITY A SCARCE COMMODITY NOW.

Equity is not in business; it is not in society; and we dare say it is not in all homes and churches. It is not in politics, in congress, in education, or in professions. It is not in the great struggles of capital and labor; in commerce or trade; in manufactures or science; in art or literature. Under present conditions, human nature is so warped as to be opposed to giving equity, and those who desire it can not compel it.

The present conditions erect a great barrier against equity and offer a premium on dishonesty. The conditions must be changed. New conditions must be produced guaranteeing to each man, woman and child, equal opportunities, promising to each justice, a fair return, a fair reward, a fair wage measured by effort and merit.

Give us conditions that guarantee these and the incentive to robbery will disappear, the necessity to graft will not be present and the ability to plunder and gratify greed will not exist.

These conditions will obtain when equity prevails, and equity will prevail when the American Society of Equity is thoroughly established.

ORGANIZED POWER THE ONLY POWER THAT IS FELT.

Individualism in society, in politics or in business is a condition of the past. The only people who count now are organized people. The only power that is felt is organized power. The farmers organized will represent such a numerical and industrial power as the world never knew before. Give us the farmers organized with the ability to speak through one head, and to throw their combined power on one spot, or to the accomplishment of a good object, and we will accomplish every desired reform, whether industrial, social, or governmental, in a short time. All that is necessary is for farmers to get together once more, but this time on a good plan so they may exert their power.

THE FARMERS' AWAKENING.

The power exists now, this very hour, but it is useless. It exists in the millions of honest, hard working people out on the farms. We may say the people who represent this power have been sleeping. But an awakening is coming. The former infant has grown to the stature of a giant, as it slumbered. Already we can hear the deep, powerful voice as the rumbling of Niagara demanding more of equity. Leaders have arisen who are teaching the truth, and, fed on truth, instead of deceptions, strength is coming to the limbs and body of the giant. Soon, with the inspiration of a new education, it will rise in its might and crush out inequity and iniquity whenever found, and establish equity and righteousness in their places.

THE PRESENT CRISIS.

We are now living in a time when something has to be done—at a crisis which has been looked forward to by able thinkers who predicted a great and bloody revolution. There will be a revolution; and it will not be the less forceful, the less decisive, because it is a bloodless one. Those who now control the markets may, in their fancied security, sneer at such an organization as this. But if so, then they forget history; they forget other instances of the power of the people when they finally reach a clear understanding that they are being oppressed.

"Backward look across the ages and the beacon-moments see,
That like peaks of some sunk continent jut through Oblivion's sea;
Not an ear in court or market for the low forboding cry
Of those Crisis, God's stern winnowers, from whose feet Earthly chaff must fly;
Never shows the chance momentous till the judgment hath passed by."

The present crisis will be bloodless because the blood has already been spilt. It was the blood of our fathers, freely offered in that other crisis which gave us the United States —a land which should and must be fully free. Through their grand patriotism this generation has the power to enforce their just demands without the awful instrument of War. And so this movement is a peculiarly American one, and will carry out the spirit of our country's constitution as nothing has done before.

THE AGE OF INDEPENDENT THOUGHT.

A wave of reform is sweeping over the country. Independence in thought is becoming prevalent. Take our own people, the farmers. They are reading and thinking to-day more than they ever did before. This portends progress. As rapidly as they learn the truth, they will no longer be deceived and misled by their old false teachers and leaders, who were, in reality, their drivers and masters. This wave of reform is evidenced by the writings and speeches of our president, Mr. Roosevelt, several governors of States, Lawson, Steffens, Sinclair, Miss Tarbell, and others. Hundreds of newspapers and magazines are also spreading the wave. Combined they have poured a great Niagara of effort against the old conditions, and have caused the waves to rise mountain-high, but very little good has been accomplished.

We may compare the great effort to the Niagara river rushing onward and down to the sea. The effect is spectacular but nothing more. Or to a huge boiler under which fierce fires have been built, generating enormous quantities of steam which is allowed to blow off into the air where it is lost, because there is no engine attached to use it. I tell you, these agitators may continue on that plan for fifty years, and the last condition of the country will be worse than the first. You may wait for a dozen presidents, fifty reform governors, as many congresses, and a thousand newspapers, and as many brilliant writers and the reforms will not be accomplished without a machine of the people through which to work.

THE DUTY OF THE PEOPLE.

The courts are ineffective, legislatures are impotent, and congress and the senate is the machine of the present great and powerful combinations, and will remain so until a greater power than these arises. Congress makes laws and there its functions end. When a representative of congress was asked why a certain law was not enforced the reply was "It is the duty of congress to make laws but it is for the courts to enforce them and for the people to see that they are enforced."

For the people to see that they are enforced. But the people are not organized, and I have said unorganized people are powerleess.

We see that enforcement of laws depend on the people; that unorganized people are powerless. Therefore, does it not follow that the people must organize in order to see that the laws are enforced, as well as to secure any reforms that they need? There must be a different machine than congress to safeguard the peoples' interests.

"New occasions tech new duties; Time makes ancient good uncouth;
They must upward still, and onward, who would keep abreast of Truth;
Lo, before us gleam her camp-fires; we ourselves must Pilgrims be,
Launch our Mayflower, and steer boldly through the desperate winter sea,
Nor attempt the Future's portal with the Past's blood-rusted key."

THREE NOTABLE LAWS—ARE THEY JUST LAWS?

The last congress was declared to be the greatest and best the country ever had because it made three notable laws, viz: The railroad law; the denatured alcohol law; and the packing house law. These laws were supposed to be in the interests of the masses, but in reality the railroad law was wanted by the railroads, engineered by the railroads and the railroads will benefit enormously by it. The alcohol law was wanted by the Standard Oil Company, and although they appeared to oppose it, their opposition was only to direct the legislation in lines that best suited them. This law, I predict, will be the basis for one of the greatest trusts that the country ever had—a subsidary trust to the Standard Oil Company. The packers could hardly have asked for a better law in the interests of their business and the government pays the expense of inspecting and becomes the guarantor of their goods. Let us consider these laws for a minute.

THE RAILROADS' POWERLESSNESS AND THE RAILROADS' POWER.

The railroads were powerless against the demands of the Standard Oil Company, the combined packers and other powerful combinations for special rates, because if one would refuse, another road would grant the concession. Thus, without desire on the part of the railroads, the rates were ground down until they were not making the profit they wanted on the immense tonnage carried for the big shippers. To preserve them from these shippers and protect themselves from competition amongst each other they had congress make the railroad law. It is conceded that the railroads' earnings will be enormously increased both from freight and passenger service because of this law. Why, then, should the railroads oppose it? They may oppose any feature that does not exactly suit them, and we read that the Interstate Commerce Commission is liberal in the interpretation of the law. But why does a law need "interpretation?" Why do the words not mean just what they say, or why are words not used in laws that mean just what is intended? But recent laws were not made that way, and that is why so many lawyers, in preference to farmers, are sent to congress, to make laws that may be interpreted to meet their clients' cases. I have said that the railroad law is beneficial in increasing the earnings of the roads, and, I believe, will protect some small shippers from discrimination in favor of the large ones, but the very things that would benefit the masses of the people are not included. For instance, we hear little complaint about the rates charged, as compared with the complaint about uncertainty of arrival of shipments. If a farmer ships a carload of hogs or grain to market he does not know when it will arrive. Or, if I buy a carload of paper I can not make definite calculations on the time of its arrival. The merchant knows he can not make definite calculations on arrival of his goods, and must order far in advance. And so it goes on all freight all over the country. The railroads delay nearly all the goods they carry for an unreasonable time. There is absolutely no dependence on their service and they make no restitution to the shipper or receiver for damages he may have incurred. Notwithstanding the high-handed methods of the railroads in handling freight they impose a penalty on the public as soon as it holds one of their empty cars more than 48 hours. Thus they make a law and enforce it against the public, while the public has no law or power to enforce penalties against them, while the loss to a merchant on a carload of goods may be many times as great as the loss of an empty car is to the railroad. The public needs an amendment to the railroad law requiring the roads to move freight a certain minimum number of miles in each 12 hours, and if they don't, then let there be a penalty. Then the receiver and shipper can calculate exactly when the goods will be received, because the road will move them promptly rather than pay damages. It can be done, and will be done, when the masses have power. Also the matter of freight rates can be made so simple, and at the same time equitable to the railroads and the public, that a schoolboy can figure just what the charge will be between any two points. Also, if he knows the number of miles, he can calculate when freight will arrive or be delivered at destination.

ARE THE LAWS IN THE PEOPLES' INTEREST?

The packing house law calls for an expenditure of $3,-000,000 to place the government guarantee on packing house products, thus giving them freerer and surer entrance into home and foreign markets, causing larger consumption at higher prices. The packers could hardly have asked for a better law in the interests of their business, and the government pays the expense of such a law as this, with the money of the people! True, legislators owned by the meat trust tried to lessen this expense by holding out for an appropriation of only one million dollars—being an advance of only $250,000 over the cost of an inspection which allowed the people to be poisoned by wholesale. It stands at three millions at present, which is after all, cheap enough, it would seem, with one hundred added establishments all over the country to be looked after, and with the original one hundred and fifty to be thoroughly inspected, instead of in the farcical manner which formerly prevailed. Probably the public is even worse off now, because its eyes are being closed by the lullaby which says we are safe—which was always a dangerous song. And how can the public be safe, if it was poisoned before, for the very lowest estimate of the cost of adequate inspection is six million dollars a year? And how can the beef trust fail to be pleased with the law, which practically leaves it just where it was before, with this difference, which under the circumstances, is startling—the government puts its endorsement on all beef trust products, passed by what any one should see is still an inadequate inspection.

But can the government inspection, as at present carried on, ever be satisfactory? The government is establishing a system that can not be carried out. If it is necessary for the government to label and guarantee packing house products, it is as necessary for it to put inspectors in every wholesale grocery house, in every drug house, in every cannery, in every creamery, in every seed house and in nearly every business house and factory in the country. This would set about one-tenth of our people as inspectors over the others, an impracticable scheme to say the least.

DENATURED ALCOHOL—STANDARD OIL'S PRETENSE.

But it is in the denatured alcohol law that we find the hand of an expert manipulator. The Standard Oil Company pretended to oppose this law, which I believe, was planned and promoted by that trust; and I also believe it will be the principal beneficiary.

This is one of the many instances where the creed of that organization has seemed to be that of Hosea Biglow's "Pious Editor.":

> "In short, I firmly do believe
> In Humbug generally,
> For it's a thing that I perceive
> To have a solid vally;
> This heth my faithful shepherd been,
> In pastures sweet heth led me,
> And this'll keep the people green
> To feed as they hev fed me."

That is, until the people who should own these pastures learn to oppose Humbug with Equity.

In criminal cases the lawyer usually looks for a motive. Let us see if there was a motive for the Standard Oil Company to want the tax removed from alcohol.

The consumption of gasoline has increased enormously during the last few years. It is a bi-product and its production is limited by the consumption of kerosene. If gasoline was produced in sufficient quantities to keep up with the enormously increasing demand it would result in an overproduction of kerosene, a condition which the Standard Oil Company did not want. Therefore, the problem was: How can the demand for power, fuel and lighting oil be met and at the same time not injure our business and even, perhaps, benefit us? I imagine the Standard Oil Company reasoned along these lines when first the problem of being able to meet the increasing demand for gasoline, or a substitute for it, presented itself to them.

They hit upon the denatured alcohol. They know there is enough vegetable matter going to waste in this country to produce alcohol that could largely, if not entirely, displace coal, wood, oil and gasoline now used for heating, lighting and power. But they must be careful or they will destroy their established graft on the people. They go to congress, and get this law through with such safeguards (to their interests) thrown around the production, handling and sale, that it can not possibly sell low enough to be a competitor of kerosene or gasoline. It is even noised around that, with their characteristic acumen and firm and unyielding methods of applying pressure, they have obtained control of the distilleries of vegetable and wood alcohol.

I am giving considerable time to this subject, but I consider it is important to show how the public is duped and also to show the necessity for an American Society of Equity to safeguard its interests. According to the regulations made, individual farmers, or groups, will not be allowed to have distilleries, where they can make at small cost their own light, fuel and power, but the alcohol must be manufactured in large central places—"on the distillery premises, where alcohol is produced, in special bonded warehouses." That lets out the farmers, who especially desired and demanded an equitable denatured alcohol bill; and that lets in the Standard Oil Company, with the distilleries they have lately secured. In short this at once places the industry in the hands of the same class of people who have always exploited "the masses." The adulterants prescribed are ten gallons of wood alcohol and one-half gallon of gasoline to one hundred gallons of alcohol. The wood alcohol is now worth about $1.00 a gallon, which puts ten cents on each gallon of the denatured product. On account of the greater demand fo rwood alcohol, we may expect the price of wood alcohol to advance very much, thus benefiting the manufacturers, whether the Standard Oil Company or others. The price, it has been stated, will not be less than thirty-five cents a gallon. Thus, instead of forcing the price of gasoline down, which by the way has doubled in a few years, this alcohol law will, I predict, raise the price of gasoline still higher. This looks reasonable when gasoline and denatured alcohol are direct competitors and the latter is not intrinsically worth the difference in price. I intend to leave this matter for you to think about, but before leaving it I want to say that the farmers have again been betrayed in the interests of the parasites that have always been fastened on their backs. It is possible to find a cheap denaturer and one that can not be placed under the monopoly control. Also, distilleries should be allowed in all communities to utilize the waste products. Anything short of these will absolutely deprive the millions of our farmer producers and other millions of consumers, of the great blessings God intended they should realize when he made nearly everything that grows out of the earth to yield a product, when wisely used, so esential to the comforts and welfare of humanity.

THE LUSTS OF TRUSTS.

So we have allowed our heritages to be squandered or monopolized by a few individuals, and the masses held to to pay tribute for what should be almost as free as the air we breathe. As we view these things and as we contemplate the destruction of our forests and the present high prices of lumber, the acquiring of all the coal and oil lands by powerful syndicates and the enormous prices for coal, iron and steel we will soon be compelled to pay, we naturally wonder whether somebody will not soon get a grant from congress to organize an air and sunshine trust.

THE A. S. OF E. A MIGHTY ENGINE.

I realized fully, the conditions four years ago when I devised the plan of the American Society of Equity and intended it, when established, to strengthen congress, legislatures, presidents, and all who sincerely want to help the common people in their demand for equity. It was my purpose to build a mighty machine of the farmers and their friends. This machine will take the energy of the hundreds of writers, and instead of allowing it to waste, like the waters of Niagara, we will confine it in carefully prepared channels and direct it against all inequity and all inequality. The power will be irresistible.

Or, through this engine of acomplishment, we will direct the great volume of steam generated in the enormous boiler referred to, so that the steam will turn its wheels, and the machine will work and run on for ever, giving blessings to all mankind.

The American Society of Equity is the first machine of this kind ever proposed. Do you agree with me that such a machine or organization is necessary? Will you not admit, in the light of past experiences, that it is useless to wait on congress, legislatures, the organized classes who have been exploiting you, or even on Providence for your salvation? Does it not now appear to you that the surest and quickest way to accomplish reforms for the people is through the people themselves—the people organized?

ITS COMING POWER OF REAL GOOD TO THE MASSES

If our government was intended to be, and has been, in times past, a government of the people, by the people and for the people, how can we rescue it from greedy exploiters and deliver it again to the people? You can only do this by organizing the people and making them a power. I do not mean to organize them into this or that party, neither need the American Society of Equity have any political significance, but the reforms can be acomplished through an industrial and social organization. Such an organization will not depend upon the fortunes of politics but no matter what political party is in power, its demands for equity will be heard and granted. Give me the American Society of Equity established and I will accomplish more of real good for the masses than Roosevelt, Bryan or Hearst can accomplish in twenty years.

If these things are true, and I appeal to any fair-minded, intelligent American citizen to decide whether they are not true, then we can begin to realize the needs of an American Society of Equity and the power of such an organization along lines such as I have outlined, a society that gives to farmers all they need in business and, at the same time, by virtue of its great overpowering strength, numerically and industrially, can quickly accomplish all the reforms that the people of all classes are asking for. These reforms will not come about in any other way or through any other medium. The individual may as well understand that he or she has no choice. It is either to accept salvation through the American Society of Equity or forgo salvation altogether. Organizers of the society should thoroughly understand the position this society will occupy and what it is capable of accomplishing. Then they will not appeal to any man or woman in vain. Whether the individual desires more profit in business, better social conditions, more certainty industrially, or purer politics, this society will give them all. Its members can even now

"Down the future see the golden beam incline
To the side of perfect justice, mastered by their faith
    divine."

"THERE'S A GOOD TIME COMING, A GOOD TIME COMING."

The completion of the American Society of Equity means the solution of all the following vexatious problems.

They will then be solved in equity to the people and the institutions:

Steady, uniform and profitable prices for farm products will prevail.

The end of speculation in farm products will be at hand.

Markets at home and abroad will be enlarged.

Elevators, warehouses, cold storage houses, etc., will belong to or be controlled by the producers.

Unnecessary toll gates between producers and consumers will be removed, guaranteeing lower prices to consumers and steady values.

Adulteration of food will end. This alone will wonderfully increase farmers' markets.

Farmers will reap the benefits from new discoveries in their field, from improved machinery and from the utilization of waste products, instead of having them appropriated by others.

Then farmers will control production as well as marketing.

Child labor on the farm will cease as it has in factories.

Boys will stay on the farms.

Farms will increase in value.

Higher intelligence will pervade rural communities.

Protection will be given farmers from the products of cheap labor in foreign countries and our island possessions.

Good roads can quickly be built all over the country.

Parcels post, post currency and postal savings banks can quickly be secured if they are wanted.

Honest insurance and safe banking will be among the things desired and obtainable.

The trusts will be regulated.

Business men will find most of the present-day uncertainties removed, and business failures will be almost unknown.

In acomplishing all these things no war will be waged against any trust, institution or government. The only demand will be for equity. Is there any class or corporation that will go on record as opposed to receiving and giving equity?

THE TOBACCO GROWERS TAME THE TOBACCO TRUST.

Tobacco growers organized on the plan of the American Society of Equity. They compelled the tobacco trust (one of the most powerful and, as has been claimed, most soulless in the world) to be decent and give equity. The trust is still in existence and the farmers are glad to do business with it on their (the farmers') own terms. Thus, instead of trying to "bust the trusts" the American Society of Equity will tame them and make use of their fine machinery to serve the people in fairness and equity, as they should.

Then the government will become good and strong and able to cope with all its problems, because compelled to do so by the people, through their own organization. Then the people will be sovereigns and the government will be returned to them. Hasten the completion of the American Society of Equity, and its blessings will pervade the country for every people and for every industry.

Does it not appear that every person, every institution and every newspaper should help to establish the American Society of Equity, so that all the benefits which it only can give, may be quickly realized?

"LET US, THEN, BE UP AND DOING."

Remember, our troubles will never end and the benefits will never be realized unless we each do our part. Results will not come through promulgation of a plan. We must build the machine, following the plan as a guide. We will not be saved by what we want done but by what we do. Prayer and trusting in Providence will never build the American Society of Equity. While we watch and pray we must also work and wait, work for the completion of our society and wait with all patience, upheld by the certainty that this good movement, once started, will never down, but will go on to full fruition. Great movements are not accomplished in a day. But more has, I believe, been accomplished in four years by the American Society of Equity, than was ever before accomplished in the same time, in any movement for the emancipation of the masses from bad conditions as deeply rooted as are those that encompass us at this time. I don't want to get away from the fact that much depends on the farmers. Others can help and will help. But farmers must look ahead to the fact that this movement is to dignify their business by making it certain and profitable. They must lift it out of the miasmatic atmosphere that has surounded it. They are now called upon to take their position on higher and more exalted ground, from which they can constantly see the promised land. Build your machine, then use it, and it will send the pure and healthy blood of co-operation through all the veins and arteries of your industrial body.

ORGANIZE!

Organize a local union in each school district, a county union in each county, a State union in each State, a section union in each several States, a department union for each important crop or class of crops. Thus, your machine will soon be built and your good ship "Equity" will soon reach the harbor forever safe from the shifting winds and changing currents that have tossed and imperilled it in the past.

CO-OPERATION IS THE LAW OF GOD.

The law of God and the universe is co-operation; the law of government is co-operation; the law of the production of the fruits of the fields is co-operation; the law of the perpetuation of the human race is co-operation; the true law of business is co-operation. "God helps those who help themselves" and "The stars sang together." All speak of co-operation. If the sun and moon and stars and earth would not co-operate, but would each go it alone, or in competition, dire results would follow. Or if the sunshine and rain would not co-operate with the seed and the farmer to produce the fine grain and fruit, how vain would be our labors!

We see competition only in the case of farmers and weeds. The latter compete with the crops and give a great deal of trouble. The former compete with each other and have carried on a guerilla warfare resulting in immeasurable disappointments and inconceivable misery. Surely God ordained the law of co-operation while the law of competition was hell-born.

God is love, equity, co-operation. He is always ready to help us and co-operate with us if we will help ourselves. He has promised many places, in His Word, and, He never enters into competition with us. On the contrary, the devil established competition, and through this instrument he breeds hatred, envy, jealousies, suspicions and physical and industrial murders. The devil of competition I warn you against.

I believe I have made my case against the old, bad, competitive system, as it is still used by farmers, and in favor of the Godlike system of co-operation. A few more words and I will rest the case with you, ladies and gentlemen, as the jury.

ORGANIZE!!

I want to say to farmers, you must organize. By the unalterable rule of right and the eternal fitness of things you must change your system. You now have, for the first time, the right plan and are directed for the right objects. Give this society the same membership that you gave the Grange or Alliance and the work will be done now and forever. Give the members one-tenth of the benefits this society is capable of giving and they will never abandon it. Before many years, yes, I believe, before many months, equity, which is next to righteousness, will be established.

Some claim that this movement is socialistic. Suppose it is, it is attainable socialism, and desirable socialism. A socialism that gives every man his just dues according to all the laws of God and rights of man. A socialism that does not confiscate property, limit ambition, destroy incentive, or deprive any man of his reward, measured by merit.

It has also been defined as analogous to Christianity. It is even this because it contends for equity, gives equity, believes in justice and teaches the golden rule.

TRULY AN AMERICAN SOCIETY OF EQUITY.

As I have said it is not for one class of people but for all the people. It is not strictly a farmers' society of equity but truly an American Society of Equity and, with equal truth, it may be a society of equity for every country on the earth. For all lands; for all governments; for all classes, without distinction as to creed, religion or color, as far as the sun travels, wherever its principles are accepted and its plan adopted it will bless mankind.

THE GOLDEN AGE.

This is going to be the grandest age of the world. There are greater and better movements in progress now for the reform of the world and the uplifting of humanity than ever before. The people have aroused themselves; and soon, with the matchless plan of the American Society of Equity, all graft, speculation, gambling, exploitation and plundering will end. People in the hearing of my voice will be glad they lived in this age rather than in any other, because it will be the age of equity. I believe these predictions will come true.

THE DAWN OF EQUITY.

The dawn of Equity has now appeared, the sun of equity is rising and its bright beams will drive away the dark clouds of ignorance, selfishness, and suspicion. Understanding is coming to the minds of the misguided; soon, very soon, the rays of equity's sun will break in its full glory and flood the earth.

America will lead in this movement as she has led in others for the betterment of humanity. Through the American Society of Equity and, by the new power, all social, industrial and political bondsmen will be made free.

I may say in the words of Whittier as we contemplate the transformation that is sure to come:

> "The air of heaven blows o'er me;
> A glory shines before me,
> Of what mankind shall be—
> Pure, generous, brave and free."

I thank you.

_____

THE AMERICAN SOCIETY OF EQUITY ANALOGOUS TO CHRISTIANITY.

C. P. GERBER.

In the early days of the Roman Empire was produced the simple, yet sublime system of Christianity. It had the comprehensiveness and directness requisite to give it authority as a universal religion. In few, but plain, convincing words it laid down the principles of human rights and of Divine law. It defined the nature and defined the sanctions of virtue in the clearest terms; it tore away every covering from vice and denounced, without fear, the favorite ambitions and follies of men. It was humble, unostentatious, very simple in all its forms, carefully refrained from all interference with established governments and presented many new and consoling truths with great force. It would have seemed that it had only to speak to gain a hearing and take a leading place at once in the work of the future. The few unprejudiced among the great, multitudes of the poor and oppressed and many whose minds recoiled from the vices, crimes and skepticisms of the age, heard and embraced it with joy. It rebuked with the utmost severity the ambitions, the injustice and the love of luxury that were prevalent in that age, and that were most distinctly Roman. It was persecuted with the greatest vigor for hundreds of years, but persecution called public atttention to it,—won it sympathy, and it spread continually beneath the surface of society.

The brutal features of Roman character were gradually softened under its benign influence. Its teachings awakened a disgust at the atrocious crimes so prevalent in that age, and established a new standard of judgment in the community.   Christianity created a purer moral atmosphere in Rome, even while being persecuted with the utmost barbarity.   It was the doctrines of peace proclaimed among nations who knew no occupation so glorious as war, whose institutions all rested on conquest.   It proclaimed the rights of men and the equality of all persons and classes before the Divine law.   It scorned alike gorgerous cremonies of worship; the subtleties of an imperfect philosophy; and pride of place and power.   It is not possible to imagine a greater contrast to all the customs and thought, prevalent in those times.   The most sensual of all the races, it exhorted to spirituality; to the most cruel it preached meakness and forbearence; it recognized as equals the great and the small, the ignorant and the wise, the bond and the free.

For all these causes Christianity was slow in penetrating society and moulding the work of institutions, but it spread so extensively that a clear-sighted emperor found it politic to profess it in order to gain the support of so large and vigorous an element, against his rivals in power.   It had maintained its growth by its real superiority, and has always remained the most powerful and productive agency among the influences that aided the progress of mankind. It was actively aggressive, and had made of the barbarians, who overthrew Rome, converts to the faith before the invasion, and thus broke the force and diminished the disastrous effect of the fall of the empire.   Christianity, through those trying times, showed a youthful vigor by which it eased the fall of the old civilization, and abounded in valuable services to the civilization yet to be.   But the high patronage and active part of Constantine in the affairs of the church had the effect to corrupt its simplicity of manners; such as the adhesion of the Greek philosophers, who infused into its doctrine their crude theories and adulterated its teachings.   As a consequence, much that was foreign to its essential character long continued associated with its promulgation and institutions.   Christianity is destined to return, in time, to is orgnal form and purity, and in the employment of its primitive powers will crown the work of civilization.

Now note the analogy:

The A. S. of E. is simplicity personified, and is practical in its application.   It is the grandest, sublimest idea for the betterment of the economic conditions of mankind ever conceived by mortal mind—it is the application of the essence of true Christianity to mundane affairs.   It has the comprehensiveness, and the directness, requisite to bring about peace and harmony between all the varied industries of a free government. By a few plain, axiomatic truths it teaches the principles of human rights as measured by the standard of Divine law; it recommends that all business affairs be conducted on lines of equity, therefore has no need of secrecy or secret obligations; proclaiming its doctrines and teachings to all, it is ever willing to stand in the glare of the searchlight of eternal truth. It is very simple in its forms, therefore, it can be readily understood by all who would see the beauty of the plan and profit thereby. It carefully refrains from all interference with the rights of others, but presents its own claims with dignity and force. The plan being so plain and practical, it would seem that every fair-minded man, who would have equity prevail, would embrace it and thereby serve his own interest and the interest of his fellowman. But, as in the case of Christianity, a great many are blinded by prejudice and are led by the false dogmas of former (now dead) organizations, and are still deterred by the delusive phantoms of the dead past; while others, led by selfish avarice, care nothing for the interests of mankind at large or their class, as illustrated by the attitude of many of the so named "farm journals," and see no merit in any move or plan, unless it brings sheckles to their pockets.

But the opposition and unjust criticisms by those who would decry the A. S. of E. brings many able, broad guaged and liberal-minded recruits to its standard. While it is hindered, and handicapped in some localities, its plan is penetrating and permeating every fiber, woof and warp of our economic structure, and the merit of its plan is the most potent influence in bringing about the reign of civic righteousness, of which the signs of the times indicate a fulfillment.

Never in the history of organizations has there been a plan so misjudged as that of the A. S. of E. Even many of its members have but a slight conception of the grandeur and lofty purposes of its plan. It is being measured by the mercenary standard by which other organizations are actuated and controlled. Like early Christianity, the A. S. of E. is built on a higher plane. It has a field of its own —a field where the noxious weeds of antagonism do not grow, neither can the burrs of bitterness and strife mature therein. A field lying on the lofty plane of equity where grows the choicest of fruits, among which are good will, peace, contentment and happiness to all mankind.

While the underlying principles are as old as the dealings of Deity with man, yet the application of those principles to every industry covers ground never traversed by any human institution. It stands before the world demanding that all business transactions should accord with the spirit of Equity and that all dealings of man with man should be based on equity. Its plan is adaquate to meet every contingency that might arise in human affairs. Christianity created a purer moral atmosphere in Rome and proclaimed the doctrine of peace among a nation whose highest aspiration was war and whose institutions rested on conquest. The A. S. of E. teaches that all transactions be measured by the standard of equity, at a time when we, as a nation, are standing on the crumbling banks of that treacherous stream—remorseless greed—whose waters have swept to destruction more nations and made serfs of more men and women than any other of the treacherous streams that ever surged over the blasted hopes and fond aspirations of once socially equal and happy homes and a free and independent nation. It teaches peace, good will, harmony and good fellowship between all industries, and equal and exact justice to all men, at a time when insatiate greed would create warring factions in the ranks of the masses of the various industries, thereby estranging and weakening tne forces whose concentrated powers are so essential to bring about the reforms on which the welfare of the masses and the perpetuity of a free government depend.

It is scarcely possible to imagine a greater contrast. The basic principles of the A. S. of E. and all exclusive organizations are as different as day is from night, and as far apart as the antipodes. The A. S. of E. demands that every one shall have all that justice and equity entitles him to—no more, no less—and is willing to give as much, and that no one should have any special privilege, regardless of station or occupation. Thereby it takes a broad-gauged, liberal-minded view of the entire field of humanity's plane. From the very nature of humanity, all exclusive organizations are, in a measure at least, actuated by selfish ideas which will naturally lead to narrow-minded views, and will, in turn, bring about controlling methods foreign to a Christian spirit, and to the disadvantage of those on the outside. It has been an axiom in business, that what one party or company gained, another must lose. Not so with this society. It lifts all up who are below the level of equal opportunity and who are not realizing a fair reward for well directed effort put forth. At the some time it will level down those, who, through special privileges are getting more than their share as compensation for equally well directed effort. At the same time it can not have any tendency to destroy incentive or limit ambition.

It is not surprising in this age of greed and grasping methods that many, even of the well informed, should be led into error's ways by pernicious, delusive dogmas, and that many able thinkers should stand aloof from all organizations. On the one hand they have seen organization after organization spring up, mush-room like, but when brought under the searchlight of justice and equity, they melted away like dew before the morning's sun. While, on the other hand, when the grand soul-inspiring, elevating plan of the A. S. of E., with its comprehensiveness and its direct methods is presented they can sacrcely believe that a plan so complete, so perfect in all its details, could be carried to completion.

As in the case of early Christianity, the leaven is at work. Much, very much of the awakening of the civic conscience, the independent thinking by the masses at this time, is due to the teachings of the plan of the A. S. of E. No matter how much it may be decried, misrepresented and mis-comprehended, it will stand forth in its pristine vigor as burnished gold that has been tried by fire. It scorns the subtleties of imperfect plans and methods, and maintans its growth by its real superiority, and will ever remain the most powerful influence for the emancipation of the toiling millions of all classes and in all parts of the earth, from industrial serfdom, and be the great leveler, socially and industrially.

MY CONVERSION.

Address by Hon. R. H. Elliston, Williamstown, Ky., before the Annual Meeting of the American Society of Equity, East St. Louis, Oct. 23-26, 1906.

Mr. President, Ladies and Gentlemen:

I have the honor to appear before this national convention as a delegate from my County and State Unions, not as a practical farmer, but as a merchant, living in an agricultural section and drawing my commercial sustenance from an agricultural community, and therefore being as deeply and fully interested in the betterment of the farmers' condition as the farmer could possibly be himself.

It is the only farmers' organization to which I ever belonged, and the only one I was ever invited to join. I acidentally heard of this society only a few weeks ago. I was passing our court house and I heard the voice of a speaker within, whose ringing tones and earnest manner attracted my attention, and I went in to see and heard a man, who, I soon learned, was the Hon. H. B. Sherman, national organizer of this society, expounding a new gospel of justice and equity, specifically applying to the farming and agricultural class, and generally to all mankind. He was doing it in a manner captivating and convincing, and elucidation of the plan and to fairness and justice of its teaching.

He likened his own conversion to the doctrine he was teaching to the sudden conversion of Saul of Tarsus, through the teaching of a book he had read, denominated "The Third Power." I said to myself, "I must have that book. Any book that could convince a man like Sherman, and fire his soul with the enthusiasm, and his brain with the clear conception of the sublime doctrine he was enunciating, was worth making a great effort to procure." I procured the book and raed it carefully. I have been more or less a book buyer all my life, and, while this book only cost 25 cents, I have not one single volume in my library that I regard as the equal in value of this one. I will not repeat in the presence of the distinguished author of this book and to his face the exalted opinion I have of it, butI will say what I said to my County Union after reading it, "That if our people could be educated to carry into execution its beautiful, equitable and sublime doctrine, so as to reap the benefit of its full fruitition, as I believe they can and will be, this little book will became unto our nation a second declaration of independence, more valuable for relieving us from wrong and oppression than even the first one." Why should not I and all honorable and honest merchants, who are nothing more or less than the necessary and legitimate distributors of agricultural, industrial and commercial commodities, stand for this? Why should not all men having a community of interest with the farmer and a common welfare with his own, take up this most righteous cause and help him to push it on to success and the attainment of a position to which he has always been entitled, but never permitted to enjoy, and thus equally help and benefit ourselves?

If there is one class of people, it seems to me, that should be entitled to more reverence and more respect, than any or all other classes, it is the farming class. Practically placed in position of all the land God created in this world of ours, and who in His Almighty wisdom and His unfathomable chemistry endowed it with capacity to bring forth products of food and clothing, He commissioned those farmers, divinely commissioned them to take unto their hands His agencies, and, by the toil of their hands and the sweat of their brows, feed and clothe the world. No man can ever convince me, nor will any right thinking man be convinced, that it was it was a part of this great plan and a condition of this great commission that the man carrying this great burden and responsibility should be defrauded out of his just proportion of the value of his own product.

His commission is not only to feed and clothe the body and minister to the physical wants of mankind, but the still further duty is put upon him of maintaining the social, moral and intellectual advancement of mankind.

I heard a learned scientist who had delved deeply into the questions of sociology and who gave his conclusions not only as his opinions, but as the opinions of all men, experts in the same lines of investigation, make this kind of statement:

"Take a great city like Cleveland, or Cincinnati, or St. Louis, and let its own population reproduce, or procreate itself, free from country influence or intervention; feed and clothe these people as the farmers must do or they would starve, but have no other intercourse with them; don't go into business with them, don't intermarry with them, or have any other relation with them except to feed and clothe them, and in three generations, or about sixty or seventy years, they will become a race of degenerates, socially, morally, physically, intellectually, and, of course, financially; a rotten, ruined and revolting excrescence of humanity." An awful picture, is it not?

So, gentlemen, the farmer not only feeds and clothes the world, but his rich, warm blood coursing through a healthy body, his brawny muscle, made hard and strong under the skies and in the sunlight of heaven, his brain clear and comprehending, free from unhealthy environments, must vitalize and revitalize all the functions and endowments of the human race and hold it in the line of advancement and progression. And yet they are doing all this gigantic work for humanity without organization or co-operation among themselves, and without the power to protect themselves in trade with these very people who are so dependent on them.

I welcome this grand movement that is destined to bring to the farmers what is their own, but which has so long been withheld.

THE FARMER AND HIS POWERFUL FRIENDS NOW RATED AS ANTAGONISTS.

From Up-to-Date Farming.

Not less than two billion dollars are invested in plants for the manufacture of cotton goods, besides the great sums invested in the manufacture of by-products of cotton, such as cotton seed, oil, etc. Add to these sums the amounts invested in flouring mills and other machines for converting the grains (cereals) into thousands of different usable articles. Then the sums invested in the woolen mills and other great factories for the conversion of raw farm products into articles for use, as well as the, we presume, equally great investments in the manufacture of the machinery used in all these great enterprises.

These references open up a line of investments stupendous in the sum of money involved, in the number of people employed, and in the amount and importance of the work done. Every part and particle of these great investments depends for success, for existence, upon the work of the farmer and the products of the farm. Were these withheld by a failure of the soil to produce, or the refusal of the farmer to furnish them for a single year, each of these enterprises must cease to operate and go into bankruptcy, and a continuation of such failure or refusal would make all this valuable machinery worth no more than old iron at the junk shop.

And now must come in another long line of sufferers—those engaged in transportation, in providing fuel, in building cars, and in making the machinery that builds them. Also those engaged in the distribution of the finished products—wholesalers, jobbers, merchants.

What, then, should be the relation existing between the farmers and all this vast line of investments? That of the closest friendship certainly—the friendship of absolute dependence and mutual interest.

But an element coming between the two has for its own selfish interest inculcated a feeling of antagonism that is harmful to both interests. This midway element, by the most hellish means, has so long sought to rob the producer by forcing the price to him down, and then to rob the manufacturer by forcing the price to him up, that a feeling has been engendered in the breast of the manufacturer that to succeed he must get the producers' goods at the lowest possible price, and he feels that he must oppose every effort of the former to increase the reward for his labor.

In this the manufacturer is mistaken. His best interest lies in reasonable and STEADY prices—prices that enable him to make his own prices with safety, and to gauge his output with certainty. Thus is the farmer's movement to control the prices of his products as much in the interest of the consumer of those products as it is in his own, and should cement the friendship between them that would never have been broken but for the Godless greed that came between them. The producer of the raw material and the manufacturer that converts it into things of use are logical friends, and their friendship must be restored, and it will be by the controlled marketing proposed by the farmers, and the steady prices that must result therefrom.

SHALL FARMERS FORM A UNION.

From Up-to-Date Farming.

The most frequent criticism we have of the attempt to organize the farmers for the object of making their own prices comes from people who are opposed to unions and trusts. They have seen and probably suffered from the iniquities of some unions and of some trusts until they have come to the conclusion that they are all bad, or that they are bad in principle.

> "A good principle, not rightly understood,
> May prove as hurtful as a bad."—Milton.

Or a good principle abused in its application may prove bad, and it is often so.

We have a letter from a subscriber who orders his paper stopped, because he is not in favor of a farmers' trust, but is in favor of ridding the country of all trusts. Also, Mr. Leroy Templeton, of Indianapolis, a large farmer and stock raiser, recently spoke before the Farmers' Congress of Indiana. We never heard a man tell of more troubles in the same length of time, than affected his business, and he attributed them all to the trusts and unions. He said, in part: "I am opposed to a farmers' union. It is undemocratic, unfair and wholly selfish for the farmers to form a union to set the price on their crops."

He further said: "I hate unions of all kinds, and it is not right for farmers to join a union."

From the Farm Journal we quote as follows: "We are in receipt of the following from an Indiana subscriber, 'Hit the trusts and monopolies a little harder; but let there be no farmers' trust.'" Replying, the Farm Journal says, in part:

"The trusts have been hit so hard lately that we feel like dropping the subject for a while. The largest proportion of them seem to have the stuffing nearly all knocked out of them. As for a farmers' trust, we see little sign of that rising above the horizon. It would be harder to manage by far than most other kinds of trusts, and, as has been proven, is so far an impossible task."

Referring to Mr. Templeton's claim that it is "undemocratic, unfair and wholly selfish for farmers to set the price on their products." Since somebody puts the price on these crops, why not the farmers? Does he think the farmers would not be as fair as the speculators, gamblers, middlemen, or food trusts? Since the farmer produces them and knows what they cost in investment, labor, loss of fertility, wear and tear of material, etc.; since he knows his needs in the way of living, what he should have for his family, for taxes and for profit; why should he not be the person above all others to price the produce of his own creation? If the farmer has no moral right to price his products, who has? How can this right be morally claimed by a food trust, the speculators or middlemen? Will Mr. Templeton or any person answer?

The American Society of Equity is purely and simply a farmers' co-operative society. It is not a trust in any way, shape, form or intent. It proposes to organize the farmers into a union where they can all get reliable information about crops, values, markets, etc. It will, through its board of directors, decide what is a fair and equitable price for each crop that is produced, basing the price on production and consumption. The price will also have a direct bearing on the COST of production. The society differs with the gentlemen who deny that the farmers have no moral right to price their goods. It most emphatically demands that right for the farmers above any other person, company, class or trust.

The Farm Journal's statement that to form a farmers' trust has been proven to be impossible may be true, but if it refers to their right and ability to price their own products, it is mistaken, or at least the proof has not been submitted to us. We think there is proof quite to the contrary in the behavior of the markets every week.

Is it not a fact that when the farmers market hogs liberally, the price goes down, then when the receipts are small, the price goes up? It is the same with all other farm crops. The farmers do this. But as long as there is not a head to the whole business, and until all farmers have the same advice about the same crop, at the same time, uncertainty will prevail. With a known price, farmers will quit marketing the moment the buyer won't take any more at that price. Do you begin to realize the simplicity of the plan and the absolute strength of the farmers' position? Every day we see proofs of how this plan would work out as accurately as the addition or multiplication tables when enough farmers are organized.

But to go back to a farmers' union: Let me ask those who oppose unions, or "hate unions," as Mr. Templeton said. Do you hate the union of the thirteen colonies that fought against oppression and through co-operation won freedom and independence? Do you hate the union of the States when they fought to preserve the union of the North and the South, and thus guaranteed the greatest and most glorious country the sun ever shone upon? Do you hate the union of the counties in any one of our States which co-operate to make up our great commonwealths? Do you hate the union of heaven and earth which co-operate to make the great universe produce the fine crops of grain, fruit and vegetables and the beautiful flowers? Do you hate the union of man and woman joined together by God to co-operate, so the race may not perish from the earth?

Do you really hate the union of capital that co-operates to develop the wonderful resources of our great country, or of laborers who co-operated, and who have truly dignified all labor except that on the farm? Do you not realize that our universe, our nation, our States, our cities, our business, our very being, are all dependent on union and people who howl against unions in toto, have shouted without due consideration. The trouble is not that we have unions, but that we have not enough of them. It would be simply preposterous to think of this country without them. They are the natural result of our wonderful development. It is the natural evolution from the savage state to one of the highest development—the passing from a state of guerilla warfare, political and industrial, to a federation of mutual interests, whether national or individual. More unions is what the country needs. When everything, everybody and every industry in the country is organized, unionized and of our industrial, political and social existence. Then, when everybody and everything is organized, each will be as strong as the other. There will be no weak to be dominated by the strong. Then will the THIRD POWER arise; equity will prevail thoughout our land and America will be the model to shape the destiny of all other nations.

Farmers, don't listen to the false teachers. Others have organized. It was natural they should, and they will not disband their organizations. In fact, it is not wise that they should. It is your duty to organize. It is the mission of Up-to-Date Farming and the American Society of Equity to organize you, and unionize you, until you are as strong as the other classes, and so you can price your products as they do theirs. The union of the farmers will be the greatest union—greater than all others combined—a union that will temper all other unions and deprive them of their power to extort and injure.

Until the government lets the farmers fix the tax they shall pay; until the banker opens his vault and says to the borrower, "Help yourself and fix the rate of interest you will pay;" or the merchant opens his doors and says, "Take my goods and pay your price;" or the manufacturer says to the farmer, "Use the machine and set your own price;" or the laborer renders his service at the price fixed by the employer and complains not; or the client and patient set the price for the lawyer's and doctor's service; until then we shall champion the farmer in his legal, moral, yes, Divine right to fix the price of his products—the result of his toil—the wage for his labor. "The laborer is worthy of his hire."

EQUITY APPEALS TO ALL CLASSES

John P. Stelle, in Up-to-Date Farming.

We are aware that in our advocacy of equity the rights of all must be not only respected, but they must be carefully guarded. In securing an equitable price for wheat, for instance, if that price be an advance on the prevailing one, the price of the bread of the consumer who is not a wheat grower, is likely to be increased also. Likewise, if we secure better prices for corn and hay, beef and pork, frut and vegetables, the consumers of these articles who are not producers of them, are likely to have to pay more dearly for them. And if we increase the price of tobacco in the in-

terest of the grower, the smoker and chewer must ultimate-
ly pay the increase.

In these facts superficial thinkers see an irrespressible
conflict, and conclude that it is imposible to accomplish
the first great purpose of the A. S. of E., the securing of
equitable and profitable prices to the producers for all
farm prodcts. But in these same apparently conflicting interests we see the strength of our position, and the certainty of the accomplishment of our purpose.

Take the wheat grower and the cotton grower. The latter is a consumer of flour and not (as a rule) a producer of
wheat, but he is one of the wheat grower's best customers.
The wheat grower can not impair the cotton grower's ability to consume without injuring himself. Hence his interest lies in making the cotton grower able to consume the
greatest possible amount of flour. How can he do that and
at the same time hold his grain to a profitable price? Evidently by aiding the cotton grower to bring his product to
a corresponding—an equitable—price.

But the wheat farmer is an abundant user of cotton
goods. When the price of cotton goes up the price of cotton
goods follows, and the wheat grower must pay more for his
cotton fabrics, thus making his consumption of cotton
goods more expensive, perhaps limiting his use of them,
and thus cutting down the demand for such goods, and re-
acting upon the cotton grower himself. How can the latter
avoid this impairment of his market? By standing in with
the wheat grower in the latter's demand for better prices
for his grain.

Here comes in a mutual interest and equity, which the
unthinking world has failed to see. The cotton grower is
not concerned about a higher price for flour if he can have
a correspondingly higher price for cotton; and the wheat
grower is not concerned about a higher price for prints and
other cotton fabrics if he can have an equitable price for
wheat. Self interest, therefore, the strongest power to influence human action, binds the two together, and impels
them to join each other in a mutual demand for equitable
prices for the products of each—a demand so powerful
when combined that the world can not turn a deaf ear to it.

"But is not this a mere swapping of dollars so far as the
wheat and cotton growers are concerned?" Perhaps so as
to the amount of their own consumption of each other's
products; but the prosperity of each depends upon the value
of his surplus, and, while the price of that which is consumed by each is increased the price of each one's surplus
is likewise increased, and its aggregate value is made greater. These farmers do not depend so much upon each other

for their gains as upon those who produce neither wheat nor cotton, and the profits derived from these make up the sum of their prosperity.

This brings to view another class who consume both wheat and cotton products, but produce neither—the great body of wage laborers. Can the demands for equitable prices be reconciled with the best interests of this great class so deservedly of the kind consideration of society, and can they be marshalled under the same banner, and held together by the same ties of self-interest? Certainly.

Nearly all classes of wage earners are already united in compact unions that give them greater or less power to enforce their demands for remunerative pay. The greater the ability of the wage earners to eat abundantly of healthful food direct from the farms, and to gratify their desires and tastes for an abundance of comfortable and even fashionable clothing, the better patrons are they of the producers of the material of which these things are made. This brings into lively exercise the self-interest of the wheat grower and the stock raiser, the cotton planter and the wool producer, the poultryman and the fruit raiser. Would not the labor unions feel that they have powerful allies in the enforcement of their demands could they so rate these great productive interests? Thus organized that is exactly what they would be, allies of the wage earners; self-interest would make them so.

But the matter of greatest interest to the wage earners, and that which opens up to them the best opportunities for savings, without resistance to or controversy with their employers, and without any disturbance of the industrial progress of society, or loss of time on their own part, is a reduction of the cost of living so that they could eat more and wear more, and yet save more, on the same wage.

Nearly all the supplies of the wage earners are in the merciless grasp of monopoly. The price paid the producer does not measure the price charged the consumer at the point of final distribution. Between the consumer and producer the princely profits of monopoly are annually growing into millions. Here is where the sweat of the farmer toiler and the sweat of the wage laborer mingle and flow in a sea of unearned wealth for the benefit of neither, but to oppress both. The producer and consumer, brought thus together in equity, stops this fatal drain of life energy, and, dividing the cruel stream where it now pours its constantly augmenting tide into monopoly's coffers, sends one branch of it to increase to an equitable price the reward of the producer, while the other goes to diminish to an equitable charge the price taken from the wage earner

consumer, thus knitting these great industrial classes together in the ties of self-interest and benefits, stronger than
those of secret pledge or mystic ceremony.

We are not unmindful of the interests of the smaller
producers, of the growers of the minor crops, whose rights
are just as sacred, and who are just as much entitled to,
and must have, equity, and whose every interest may be
even more easily reconciled to and worked out by this common plan, but we have purposely made use of the three
great classes of production and consumption, and we have
brought out the apparently most irreconcilable phases of
their relations to each other, to show, as we think we have
done conclusively, that their interests are in harmony, and
that beneath the Aegis of the American Society of Equity
their true relation will be found, and a new era ushered
in for industrial humanity.

CAPITALIZED CORPORATIONS NO RE-
LIEF TO FARMERS.

From Up-to-Date Farming, June 15, 1904.

Uu-to-Date Farming stands in glad support of whatever
may serve well the best interests of agriculture, and of labor in general; but the mere claims of an institution, and
the interestingly detailed results which, it is argued, must
follow it, are not sufficient to warrant its support. Let
everything come under the keen scrutiny of investigation,
and what can not stand the severest test of reason, may
well be left alone.

A farm paper now lies before us which heralds the formation of what claims to be a giant corporation of farmers,
with a capital stock of half a million, with the privilege
of increasing it to five millions. This corporation is
headed by prominent people, and it proposes to knock out
the farm machinery trust in the first round. Should it do
so, who would probably be the gainer? The new combination would have to crowd out the old one before it could
get the field, to do which it must become stronger than its
antagonist, and, therefore, just as much of a monopoly. It
would be crowded with salaried officers managers and
foremen, and perhaps be managed just as extravagantly and
with just as little regard for the inner life and interests of
agriculture. Human selfishness is much the same the

world over, and only awaits the opportunity to manifest itself. But this is only a suppositional view of the probable, we may say, the natural result of the corporation should it be successful.

Another view of the enterprise is a far more important one. A capitalized corporation is nothing without money. Capital stock is not money; it is something issued by the corporation presumably to represent an investment—is given out in exchange for money. This particular corporation invites farmers to take its stock at $25 a share. The situation at present is this: The farmers have the money; the corporation has the stock. If the plans of the promoters be carried out, and they succeed in getting the stock taken by the farmers, the situation will be this: The corporation will have the money and the farmers will have the stock!

This is not saying the corporators are dishonest, or that they are inordinately selfish in their designs. They are men of business prominence. But this change of money and stock must take place before a wheel of the corporation can move; then the future of the money and stock must depend on the success or failure of the enterprise. Certain it is, the money will never be swapped back for the stock, for it must be expended or absorbed beoore either success or failure can be reached.

We also have on our desk a circular outlining the formation of a corporation of tobacco growers and providing for a capital of $5,000,000. It, too, has the names of prominent men at its head, not one of whom, however, so far as we know, is a tobacco grower. The money is to come from the same source as that of the former one, from the farmers. In this case the tobacco growers are to put up the money, and the same change in possession, the same change in relation to money and stock, must take place as outlined in the case first recited.

Again we protest that we do not accuse these people of dishonesty, but their plan, if carried out, simply creates a rival to the tobacco trust, and involves the two in a fight to the finish. The new concern must take the money paid in by the tobacco growers as a fund with which to fight their antagonist on his own chosen ground. It is safe to conclude that the money would be thus absorbed, and the tobacco growers would be left where they began, minus some good money, plus a large amount of discouragement, and in the hands of a trust grown all the more arrogant because of its victory. "The man behind the gun" may be all right, we would not intimate that he is not; but it is the man in front of the gun, out in the field whence the moiney is to come, that is in danger. "We help farmers to to help themselves," declare the promoters, but those same farmers are asked to "tote" the fuel—to furnish the money to buy their own tobacco, and to pay somebody a big price to show them how. They don't have to buy their own tobacco; it is theirs already. Why not simply hold it until some one else is ready to buy it at an equitable price?

This is the plan we advocate, and it takes not a cent of capital stock. Besides, if the tobacco growers were able to put up five million dollars, they would not need anybody to "help the farmers to help themselves"—they could help themselves without help even from "the man behind the gun."

A letter just received from a very intelligent gentleman, writing from Kentucky, gives an account of the formation of a similar corporation among the growers of Burley tobacco in that State. It was capitalized, it seems, at $10,-000,000. The tobacco growers were to furnish one-fourth of this, or $2,500,000, and then capitalists were to furnish the remaining three-fourths, and the corporation was to buy up all the Burley tobacco at 9 cents a pound, and after having been finally sold, net profits (profits after all expenses and salaries had been paid) were to be distributed as a dividend among the stockholders. Buying was to begin December 1. Nearly $2,000,000 were subscribed by the farmers, but fortunately none wah paid in—it was not to be paid until the whole scheme was completed, which proves that its promoters were sincere and honest.

The farmers held their tobacco until the time came for the company to commence buying; but the entire amount required to be taken had not been subscribed, and the big loan could not be secured. The time was put off three or four weeks, the farmers still holding their tobacco. Christmas came. Still the loan had not been secured, and still the farmers kept their tobacco off the market, still awaiting the success of their own effort. Along in January things began to happen. The market had run dry. The factories had no material to work upon, and could get none. The growers did not have to wait any longer; the country was full of buyers, and the growers named their price—better prices than they had received for years Why?

Not because they had formed a corporation, for the corporation had done nothing. Not because they had subscribed for capital stock, for they had not paid in a cent. It was because they had held their tobacco off the market until the market had to have it. and then they made their price, or could have done so had they been organized to that end. Their corporation absolutely failed, but they scored a notable success on this plan of controlled marketing, without knowing it.* And thus it goes. Great capital stock corporations never yet have brought relief to the farmers as a class. They must fight well drilled armies that are already in the field; that have their batteries planted and masked; their gunners trained and masters of their parts, and victory in this way can only come to the farmers at the end of a struggle which shall annihilate these intrenched veterans. It never comes.

The West is being thickly sown with these mush-room corporations, and there are indications that a crop is being prepared for the South. Much effort may be thus wasted, and perhaps some good money lost, but no permanent good will ever be accomplished.

Now, we are entirely willing for the American Society of Equity to be measured by the same standard with which we have gauged these stock corporations, and the same arguments may be used where they will apply. We are incorporated to make us amenable to, and to give us the protection of the law; we ask no subscription to capital stock, because we need none; we have to fight no corporation, because we are arrayed against none; we are rivaling no business concern, because we are not in business in the sense that they are; we are not asking farmers to furnish money to buy tobacco or any other farm product, because they already own it all. We simply teach them how to hold what we have until the market calls for it at an equitable price—a price which compares justly with the prices of what we have to buy, and carries with it a reasonable profit. We court investigation, invite comparison, and challenge a denial of the efficiency of the plan of the A. S. of E.

NATIONAL CROP CONVENTIONS.

HOW PRICES MAY BE INTELLIGENTLY MADE AND POSITIVELY
MAINTAINED.

From Up-to-Date Farming, 1904.

The closing year has been prolific of important lessons. rrice-making and marketing have been studied by the rural

---

*Later, in 1906, the Burley tobacco district accepted the A. S. of E. plan and in a few months organized and accomplished all they attempted to do through the capital stock corporations.

population as they never were before, and it has been proven that the producers of farm products can control the market and make and maintain prices. The remaining lesson to learn is the best way to do it. The American Society of Equity is not a stickler for methods. It set out to prove that the farmer need not trail along after all other classes, that he need not look from his toil-worn fields to see everybody else putting prices upon the work of his hands while he alone must toil on, aimlessly, almost hopelessly, and accept for his products whatever the buyer chose to offer. We have accomplished that purpose. We have proven that the farmer, though a toiler, is abreast of other toilers, that he possesses every right that belong to others, and that from the very nature of his products, food and raiment for the race, his is the vocation which makes all other vocations possible, and without which none of the others could be. We have demonstrated that, by a simple act of ordinary business, he can secure these rights which he has so long waived in the interest of others, and for himself make and secure profitable prices upon whatever he produces that may be needed by his fellows or their domestic dependents. It only remains, as we have said, to determine the best way to do this.

The methods adopted for other great purposes, and the successes achieved, point to a national convention—a convention of wheat growers, of corn raisers, of cotton planters, of tobacco raisers, of fruit growers, of live stock men—of every great agricultural interest. Assembled thus, we may pattern after the political conventions, and act through committees. Not only supply, demand, market and price may be considered, but other questions affecting the industry may be discussed, making the convention an annual summing up of the lessons and experiences of the years, and of suggested advancements for the year to come.

Who can calculate the benefits that would result from such conventions, and who would be better qualified to make suitable prices upon the various products than such a convention of the producers of them, acting primarily through a committee of the most intelligent, most conservative, and most judicious of them all? Such action ratified by the convention, would go to the country with a force, and be received with a confidence that no other action could claim, unless it were the action of the government itself, and it is questionable whether even than would carry with it so great a weight of confidence.

But would such action be accepted by the masses of the various lines of production? We may reason from analogy and say emphatically YES. And this is a good year in which to say so, because the proof is so near at hand.

The national conventions of the political parties meet every four years. They adopt platforms that have never been considered for a moment by the masses, and in most instances, name condidates that have not previously been spoken of. In only a few cases are the candidates a reasonable certainty. Yet the wires scarcely cool from the flash which tells the news when the respective party masses accept the result as their own act—the platforms as being the embodiment of their most sacred principles and profoundest convictions, and the candidates as being the ones of all others whom they most delight to honor.

Can it be said that people so intelligent as those of America are less devoted to their personal interests than they are to their political parties, which, laud them as you may, are but ephemeral aggregations gathered around some fancied purposes, and whose principal, if not only, beneficiaries are the few that may obtain office? We do not believe it. Give the American people a chance to rally around the standard of their own prosperity—the foundation of their homes, the welfare of the families, the success of their calling—and they will do it with an enthusiasm and unanimity that will put every doubter to the blush and every enemy to flight.

What of a penalty? No penalty will be needed but the penalty of privileges abused, opportunities neglected, and willful loss. What incentive? The incentive of benefits, of just reward for toil, of an honorable place among men, of a home established and a family provided for—the incentive of honest and honorable prosperity. The voter that ignores his party action is a "bolter," the laborer that refuses to recognize the union is a "scab," the farmer that would not accept the work of a convention of his kind would be—the future must coin the word. The lessons and successes of the past point to a full accomplishment of these great purposes in the near future.

HOW TO CALCULATE THE FARM VALUE OF CROPS.

ON THE PLAN OF THE AMERICAN SOCIETY OF EQUITY.

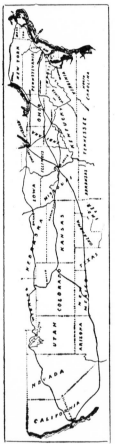

The American Society of Equity is being built for every farm, garden and orchard crop. It is for the grain grower, the stock feeder, the dairyman, the poultryman, the tobacco grower, the fruit grower, the cotton grower, etc. As soon as it is in operation it will benefit the largest operator, no difference where situated, or in what line engaged, and also the smallest operator—owner of a few rods of ground—by securing stability and equity of price, which means stability of prosperity.

The central head or National Union of the society will print in the official paper a price that any crop is equitably (to producer and consumer) worth. This will be done as soon after the crop in this country is secured as it is possible to decide the yield from reports from members and local unions. The price will be known as the MINIMUM price, and will be based on some leading market. For instance, grain and stock prices will be based on Chicago, cotton on New York, beans on Detroit, etc. (The Pacific Coast and territory tributary, can have their own bases and the plan will work the same for them.) Markets elsewhere and the farm price can be calculated from these bases, being enough less to equal transportation and the cost of handling. Of course, there will be many places where the local markets will take all the products, and the price under these conditions is usually higher than where a surplus is produced. The home market should be cultivated to the greatest extent possible.

Refer to the map and let us see what the farmer in Central and Western Kansas ought to have for his wheat on the basis of $1.00 per bushel at Chicago. The rate of freight to Kansas City is 16 cents per cwt.; from Kansas City to Chicago is 14 cents; total, 30 cents per cwt., or 18 cents a bushel. Deduct this from $1.00 and we have 82 cents. If the farmer in Central and Western Kansas receives less than 82 cents on the basis of $1.00 for No. 2 red at Chicago the difference is what the middle men charge for handling it.

There is another thing farmers should notice. The railroads charge 16 cents to carry wheat 200 miles west of Kansas City, but only 14 cents for the 500 miles from Kansas City to Chicago, or as 8 to 3. This looks like an injustice that should be wiped out. Also, the through export rate from Kansas City to Great Britain and other foreign ports ranges from 29 cents to 33 cents, only twice as much as is charged to carry grain less than across one State. There is no equity in such an adjustment and it is clear such enequalities can only exist because farmers have not put themselves in a position to resist them. They can quickly change these things when organized.

Referring again to the map, the rate of freight from Chicago to New York is 20 cents; therefore, wheat that is worth 82 cents in Kansas, $1.00 in Chicago, is worth $1.12 in New York, plus a fair price for handling it. This should be the case if equity prevails, as the populous east must get its supply from the grain fields of the west.

Eastern farm consumers of western grain and meat need not be concerned if the western farmers get good prices. This is not a movement for a good price on one product or a few, but on every product. The vegetables, fruit, dairy products, poultry, eggs, etc., of eastern farmers will advance proportionately.

The entire agricultural business needs reorganization in its distributing end. Gross discrimination must end. Equity must prevail and these things all depend upon the farmers. Elevators and shipping associations in the Mississippi Valley won't cure the trouble, but may aggravate it. Nothing less than a national organization when a million or more farmers will speak through an authorative head will be effective. Under such conditions the farmers will rule— they will be irresistible.

HOW THE SOUTH HAS BLINDLY
SUFFERED.

From Up-to-Date Farming.

More than fifty years ago the British Board of Trade concluded that the lower they could force down the price of cotton, the more the American planter would be compelled to raise to make a living; that the increased production would furnish increased supplies for their mills; and that it would afford additional leverage to be used in making the prices still lower. This policy was agreed upon, and has been adopted by all the Cotton Exchanges of the world, and it has been steadily and relentlessly pursued ever since, with various results, of course, as season conditions have favored or thwarted their purpose, but always in the loss of the planters, not in absolutely lower prices, perhaps, but in prices below what conditions warranted.

This selfish and cruel, and, we may say mistaken, policy, has cost the cotton growers immense sums of money, or, rather, has prevented them from realizing vast sums they have honestly earned, and to which they were justly entitled. So great a difference has this made in the business of cotton growing that many good, industrious and economical people who ought now to be in independent circumstances, or, at least, well to do, find themselves and their families with a scant living, in many cases short of the common comforts of life.

Until very recently the results of this miserable policy have been accepted by the cotton planters as a decree of fate, as the best they could expect, and something entirely beyond their control. But a different teaching has lately found its way into the South, and there has been a wonderful awakening, a revolution in sentiment, and an absolutely different system of marketing. The farmer has learned his power, and he now knows that, as the first owner of the things he produces, he is the logical price-maker, and that no one can get them from him without his consent. He will no longer suffer the wrongs to which he has so long patiently submitted. Instead of the cotton crop of the present year going blindly on to the market as heretofore, it is going into storage rooms, there to remain until the demand calls for it at prices that mean reasonable profits to the grower, but, in no sense, excessive to the mill. Indeed, as we have argued so many times, and, we think, conclusively, the mills may get their supplies cheap-

er than under former methods, for the prices will be
steady, free from corners and manipulation, and they will
come direct from first hands instead of from the hellish
pits of speculation. Two simple words have brought about
this great change in sentiment and marketing—organization and co-operation, and it is not at all out of place to
say that Up-to-Date Farming set that wave of thought in
motion, and the American Society of Equity crystalized it
into action.

TO WHOM BE THE CREDIT?

**THE RESULTS ARE MORE IMPORTANT THAN THE
POWER THAT ACHIEVED THEM.**

From Up-to-Date Farming.

"Credit for dollar wheat is not given unanimously to the
national administration; one farm paper claims that it did
it. Isn't there danger of an over-production of such modesty?"

We find the above paragraph in a prominent farm publication, one whicn is ably conducted, and one, too, which
is usually not afraid to lead out in reform lines. It takes
no act of the imagination to determine that Up-to-Date
Farming is the paper referred to by our contemporary. We
do not know that we ever made the claim alleged, but it
has been made for us and we have not hesitated to speak
of the part we have played in the matter. We concede such
a claim seems extravagant, and to the mere onlooker as
preposterous, but in these days all classes seem willing to
give even the devil his due. A brief review of the situation can not be harmful.

It is very evident that some influence is at work among
the people that never was before; that something is affecting the markets as they were never affected before. In the
face of the conceded large corn crop, commercial reports of
the highest authority tell us that traders who have been
in the habit for years of making large sales abroad to be
shipped later, in advance of the purchase of the grain,
relying upon their ability to purchase the grain at their
price at time of shipment, are having to buy back their
sales because they cannot purchase the corn to ship, not

because there is a lack of corn, but because the farmers refuse to sell at the price. Such a state of affairs was never known before.

It is also conceded that there is a large cotton crop, the latest government report putting the yield at more than twelve million bales; and yet the manipulators find it impossible to force the price down materially and hold it there. From a single report recently issued by a prominent member of the New York Cotton Exchange, A. Norden & Co., we make the following extracts:

"South Carolina. Farmers holding extensively.

"Georgia. Atlanta—The farmers are holding their cotton to a greater degree than we ever remember. Macon— This market is completely blocked, everything being held for ten cents.

"Alabama. Montgomery—Planters are either holding their cotton at home or bringing it to the market centers and storing it—probably selling about one-third or one-half. Troy—Marketing has been free up to about the first of the month. Since then after cotton commenced to decline below ten cents, there has been a general holding back, and receipts all through this section have been light. Thomasville—One-third of the amount ginned is being held by farmers.

"Texas. Houston—In all my experience of twenty-six years in spot cotton I have never seen such an indisposition to sell spot cotton."

And so on. Our private advices are still more general and more emphatic than the above. The same is true of corn, of wheat, of oats, of beans, of tobacco—of nearly all the leading market crops. It was seen and felt in the wheat market of 1903. In 1904 it appears, as we have said, in all the prominent crops, to an extent that puzzles veteran traders, men who have been on 'Change all their business lives.

Is any one willing to say that this disposition to hold crops off the market until a satisfactory price is reached, is accidental, that it took hold upon the farmers without and reason for it, that it invaded the wheat and corn fields of the North, the cotton plantations of the South, the tobacco fields of Kentucky, Virginia, North Carolina and Tennessee, the bean fields of Michigan and New York, all purely by accident at the same time, and simultaneously demanding the same price for the same crops?

This state of things, this condition of the market, was never known before. It cannot be accidental—mere chance. There must be a cause for it. Similar cropconditions have prevailed before. Wheat light, corn abundant; cotton and potatoes large; tobacco, beans and hay moderate to large. These conditions are not anomalous. But that farmers are holding them for a specific price made by themselves, and getting it—this is the feature that is new, and that is puzzling the veteran traders. As we have said, there must be a cause for it, something at work that has not previously been exercised, some connection and understanding among the producing forces that has not before existed— some power behind it all that was never before exerted? Find this and you will find what led up to dollar wheat and has so effected other prices and demoralized the market manipulators. It is not a question of modesty; it is a question of fact, of history now—a question of importance to producers of all time and countries, because it shows what can be done, and demonstrates their power to secure prices that shall reward them for their toil.

In December, 1902, the American Society of Equity was organized based on equity in all the business relations of life. Its first great object was declared to be "to obtain profitable prices for all products of the farm, garden and orchard." Up-to-Date Farming, which had previously advocated this new and strange doctrine, was made the official paper, and began a systematic campaign to build up the organization and secure the first object. It taught unequivocally that the way to do it was by controlled marketing, to unitedly fix a price and to hold the products until the price was paid—advocated the precise action that it is now acknowledged has been taken, to the discomfiture of old-time market prophets and confident price manipulators.

It is not necessary to say, in the face of such recent history, that this paper was compelled to fight the first battle single-handed and alone. Not another paper in all the country advocated it. On the contrary, many of them openly opposed it, others ridiculed it. The editor of one, more prominent than most of the others, confessed in a letter over his own signature, that, though he did not care to fight Mr. Everitt in the open, he would be glad to give him a thrust under the fifth rib. We speak thus not boastingly, but simply for the truth of history, and for the encouragement of those farmers whose superior intelligence and firmness have proven the truth and won the victory— a victory greater in its results and benefits than any won on the field of battle.

But to the proofs. In May, 1903, wheat was selling below 70 cents a bushel. The editor of this paper, who is also president of the American Society of Equity, believed the price too low as compared with the cost of production and the general level of values. He hatily gathered all available statistics, both of production and consumption, which convinced him that for the crop of 1903, $1.00 per bushel would be no more than an equitable price, thaht every bushel that sold below that price failed to bring the producer what was justly his. May 25, 1903, he issued his famous Dollar-Wheat Bulletin, setting forth those facts and urging farmers to hold their wheat for that price. Members of the Society at once accepted the bulletin in good faith, and acted upon the advice. Many of the farmers who had read this paper did the same. But the agricultural press uniformly ridiculed the idea and discouraged such action, many of them unscrupulously atacking the personality of the advocates of the doctrine. The trade manipulators and gamblers in wheat prices of course fought it by every means their accumulated wealth and recklessness of truuɪ enabled them to bring to bear.

But Up-to-Date Farming unflinchingly stood in the breach, and defended the right of the farmers to price their products, and urged the holding of the crops as the only means of accomplishing it. Shipments began to slacken, the "visible" was reduced, shorts commenced to cover, the price began to climb, and the dollar was reached months before the crop of 1904 was ready for the harvest.

The history of the crop of 1904 is a repetition of that of 1903. Long before the crop began to mature, the country was flooded with reports of tremendous yields, and the speculators began to bid low prices for future delivery of the grain. Many sales and purchases were made below 80 cents. This paper and the society it represents bided its time. We had means of information the sepculators knew not of, and were advised of the gigantic plans that were laid for a great rake off at the farmers' expense. July 20th, was issued the bulletin of the society declaring the equitable price in Chicago far the 1904 crop to be $1.20 per bushel, and announceu a total yield far below any estimate that up to that time had been made. Since then the estimate of the society has been vindicated by the very highest authority, and the price of wheat, in spite of all efforts and influence to pull it down, has stood well up toward and at the $1.20 mark, and in the great milling centers it has gone beyond it.

We may well submit the cause to the decision of an intelligent unbiased public. But, as we say in the heading to this article, the results are more important than the power that achieved them—important to a hard-working, poorly paid, but deserving class of people, who have long felt the injustice done them, but did not know their power to secure redress. Important to other producers, the growers of other crops, who have likewise borne the burdens of an ungrateful world, but who now see clearly the way of relief.

And the greatest victory of all is in the fact that we no longer stand alone. The doctrine of controlled marketing has taken deep seat not only in the minds of the producing people, but it is being taken up by powerful molders of public opinion, and its potency is conceded by its most interested opponents. Let us reiterate our appeal to the growers of all crops—stand by your products and secure your price and just profits by controlled marketing, by holding your crops until the demand comes, and you will get your price.

THE UNION LABEL.

One of the strongest weapons of organized labor is the union label. The organized workers have forced its use on almost every article produced by them to distinguish it from what they call "scab" produced articles, so that their friends may not be deceived into patronizing those unfriendly to organization.

Farmers have organized heretofore but it has been in a desultory way, and no attempt has ever been made to use a label. Indeed, they have acted as though they felt themselves underlings, subject in their productions to the whims and speculations and peculations of others, with no right on their part to claim distinction for what they grew, or to exercise any control over its quality or price.

But things are becoming different. Lessons are being learned and acted upon that were looked upon as almost treasonable two years ago. It is a fact that the farmers are coming to the front, and they are asserting their rights in a voice that is being heard from Maine to California, and from the wheat lands of the Northwest to the Carolinas.

Why not designate the product of union farmers by a label? The A. S. of E. provides one. It is seen at the head of this article, and we are sure that even its design must be admired. The monogram of the society occupies the central position, around which appear the words. "The American Society of Equity." The band of fellowship encloses this in a protected field, bearing above the "National Union" and below "American Farmers," the "of" in the monogram completing the legend, "National Union of American Farmers." Then on arms stretched out as to take in the world appears the words "Union Label."

As the success of the A. S. of E. will solve the farm labor problem and make a demand for millions of laborers at the market price of wages, it is very sure that products thus marked, whether wheat, oats, hay, cotton, corn, fruit, butter, eggs, or whatsoever, will attract the attention of union laborers in the cities, who are the leading consumers of our products, and receive their decided preference, creating a special demand for the products of union farmers. But this fact must also be borne in mind: This label must stand as a guarantee of honest goods. The package designated by it must be as it is represented to be, for the whole society stands, tentatively, at least, as its guardian. There is no question but the use of this label, with this proper and necessary restriction, would add very materially to the demand in the market, and to the price.

BOARDS OF TRADE ARE THE DEVIL'S WORK SHOPS.

Henry B. Geer in Up-to-Date Farming.

Labor—all labor—has the God-given right to protect itself. Whether it is labor of the factory, the mine, the counting room, the printing office, or labor on the farm, the same inalienable right exists. The factor in creating, in remodeling, in making wholesome for the human body, in making beautiful for the eye or pleasant to the taste, is the fundamental factor, and the mere fact of its primary position in the order of life should make it first in line of protection, and the division of returns from successful results. This is the natural viewpoint of all well-meaning, honest and equitable men. But there is an element in the commercial life of the world—a barnacle rather, that has engrafted itself on the produce of the earth—a sapsucking, unholy, godless thing, that is holding up and gorging itself on labor's portion. This thing is the soulless, non-producing, conscienceles speculator or gambler in farm products. It is ill-gotten gains turned loose to the detriment of the producer. It is the wealth of the inequitable thing manipulated to throttle equity. Boards of trade as now run are the devil's work shop engaged in forging profits for the non-producing class from the results of honest labor. It is the greatest blight in the body economic—a danger that threatens the very life of the farming industries of America. It is a bold, fearless, devilish power that often defies the laws of the municipality and the State. It has no base in justice and honor, and exists simply because of the indifference and former neglect of the one power that can dethrone it—the grand, majestic, sweeping strength of co-operative production—of organized farm interests and farm labor. Its injustice has grown because justice has been blinded; its inequity has been tolerated because there were none who raised a cry for equity; because the individual farmer was impotent in his feeble strength.

This is the conditon that has obtained under inaction, the natural result of indifference and neglect on the part of the producers. It is fattening of the unworthy, while the deserving ones, those who have all along been putting forth their strength, laboring honestly and continually on the farm, have grown lean in purse and crib. It is illustrative of the old proverb of "saving at the spigott and wasting at the bunghole." The farmer has labored diligently and honestly, and in doing so, he was conscious of his strength in manual labor, the work shop of his brain became dusty and cobwebbed, in so far as the proper guarding and distribution of the fruits of his labor are concerned. He has all along been short-sighted in the matter of marketing his produce. He has plowed, sowed and reaped; and then dumped the fruits of his labor into the lap of the conscienceless speculator, who has not hesitated to manipulate the market to his own selfish ends, after allowing the farmer an inequitable portion. And thus has come about the hold up of labor's portion. In this way has inequity all along prevailed, until now, after a realization of the unfavorable conditions, an awakening on the part of the producers that is becoming general—co-operation and organization—is beginning to obtain, where it should have been in existence years and years ago. A demand is now being made by the farmers for a release of labor's portion, and an equitable distribution of the rewards of honest industry and thrift.

This is the purpose of the American Society of Equity. It has for its chief object the betterment of the producing class; the advancement of the farmer's interests in every legitimate manner; and this without making war on any honest interprise in any other field.

No purpose, however, can be accomplished without the hearty co-operation and support of these most vitally interested, a fact that makes it incumbent on the farmers to adopt active measures to strengthen themselves, to organize and co-operate in the marketing and distribution of the products of their farms.

The question, the agitation and the demand for equitable prices is now a vital issue—one on which the farmers everywhere can, and must, unite to their mutual benefit. The issue is sharply defined, and the fight is now on. Labor's portion in the returns for the produce of American soil is now at stake. A long pull and a strong pull is now being made to rescue the farmers' crops from the grip of the gamblers, and it needs only united effort to succeed. Let labor hold back her portion for once; let the men who grow the crops store them at home as largely as possible, thus letting the market manipulators waste away for the want of subsistence, and the victory will be won. No one has either the moral or the legal right to put a price on the produce of the farm, but those who grow it, and for this principle every American farmer should hold out till the last ditch.

The producers can win. They are sure to win in the long run, for they have equity on their side, and they have the crops on the farm where they were grown. The thing to do is to make the storage at home as great as possible, and the offerings as meagre as financial conditions will permit; and then it will only be a question of a short time until the dealers will come to the producers and gladly pay the price the latter shall have put on the product of their labor. And then it will come to pass, that labor's portion will be delivered to the hands that wrought it, and not be held up by intermediate parties who have no legal claim to it, morally or commercially.

HOW MUCH MUST BE CONTROLLED.

There is one feature of controlled marketing that has not been much studied. Many think it impossible for farmers to make a price, however equitable, on their products and sustain it, because those products, at least of the main crops, are in such tremendous quantities.

But the selling price always depends upon the part that sells, and when we come to the statistics the selling or shipping part is surprisingly small when compared with the total crop. And when we speak of the shipping part we do not mean that only which is sent abroad, but that which leaves the county where it was produced. In other words, that which is consumed by other than those who produced it. Our figures below are based on those of the Secretary of Agriculture, and are, therefore, authentic.

For instance the wheat crop of 1906 was 750,000,000 bushels. The shipping part of this crop, that which left the county where produced, was 435,000,000 bushels. The corn crop was 2,900,000,000 bushels. The shipping part was 725,000,000 bushels. The oat crop was 964,000,000 bushels. The shipping part was only 218,000,000 bushels. The potato crop was 300,000,000 bushels. The shipping part was 150,000,000 bushels.

Now, suppose these crops had been short one-half of the shipping part. Does any one doubt there would have been a panic on the market and prices would have soared above the minimum set by the farmers? If one-half of this shipping surplus could be controlled by the farmers would not the effect be the same? There isn't a question but that the price would be maintained.

Therefore, it only remains for the farmers to control 217,000,000 bushels of wheat, 362,000,000 bushels of corn, 109,000,000 bushels of oats, and 75,000,000 bushels of potatoes to absolutely control the prices of these crops.

Another feature is equally surprising and that is the acreage. It is only necessary to control 14,000,000 acres of wheat, 11,960,000 acres of corn, 3,500,000 acres of oats, and 937,000 acres of potatoes.

Go into a still farther analysis and consider the farms. Basing the acreage on a reasonable average, to control the wheat crop it is only necessary to control 280,000 farms; for corn, 209,000 farms; for oats, 70,000 farms, and for potatoes, 93,750 farms.

It can be done. And it will be done. The reign of the crop gambler is ended.

PROOF OF THE FALLACY OF COMMON FARM TEACHING.

Its Logical Result is Poverty for Farmers.

(John P. Stelle in Up-to-Date Farming, Jan. 1, 1907.)

Up-to-Date Farming has contended that the constant strain of the schools and the press, and the Department of Agriculture also, to push farmers to raise more and bigger crops without a word as to marketing or obtaining steady and remunerative prices, was a one-sided education, and not the best for the farmers, whatever it might be for the rest of the world. The schools and the press have frowned at us, while the Department of Agriculture has bestowed upon us a kind of pitying smile.

We now have before us the Secretary's report for the crops of 1906. In Mr. Wilson's usual way, he has no trouble to show that the farmer is the richest man in the United States, and that the crop of 1906 was the greatest one the country ever produced—eight per cent. greater than that of 1905; ten per cent. greater than that of 1904; fifteen per cent. greater than that of 1903, and forty-four per cent. greater, almost double that of 1899.

But when we come to a definite analysis, we find our contention sustained in a most remarkable manner. And the Secretary admits it; at least, his own words and figures concede it.

"While the value of the cereals," says the Secretary, "drops about $40,000,000 below the total of 1905, and about $12,000,000 below the total of 1904, the number of bushels for 1906, which was 4,688,000,000, was 120,000,000 bushels above the yield of 1905, 570,000,000 above the yield of 1904, and 835,000,000 bushels above the yield of 1903."

There we have it in very plain English words and Roman figures. In 1906 the farmers produced 120,000,000 bushels more of the cereals, adding thereto the additional labor required to plant, cultivate, harvest, market and otherwise handle 120,000,000 bushels more of the cereal crops, and after all was done "its value," says the Secretary, "is less" than the previous crop of 120,000,000 bushels less of grain.

In other words, the wages of the cereal producers of the United States was reduced $40,000,000 below what they were paid the year before for less work, and they were not notified of the reduction until after the labor had been performed!

Deal thus with the wage labor of the country and every furnace would go out in the factories, every wheel would stop in the mills, every locomotive would stand dead on the track, and every mine would become as dark and silent as the long night which dwelt there before it was discovered. Are the millions of agriculturists less powerful than the wage laborers? or are they more humble, more timid, more subservient? The above are the facts as Secretary Wilson officially proclaims them. What are the farmers going to do about it?

It is no mitigation to say that gains were made in other crops more than sufficient to overcome these losses. These gains still sustain our contention that it is wrong to continually urge increased production unaccompanied by means of sustaining prices. The gains were made on crops that made normal or reduced yields. The crops that were normal or partially failed, saved the farmers from loss in 1906.

"On the side of gains over 1905," says Secretary Wilson, "two short crops are conspicious; hay leads with a gain of perhaps $80,000,000 in value, and the oats crop is second, with a gain of possibly $14,000,000."

Mr. Wilson says on page 10 of his special report to the press, that the hay crop "is short by perhaps 8,000,-000 tons;" yet on page 9 that "hay leads with a gain of perhaps $80,000,000 in value."

In other words, the 8,000,000 tons of hay the farmers did not raise, netted them exactly $10 per ton! And the 120,000,000 bushels cereals they did raise in 1906 more than they raised in 1905, cost them a net loss of $40,-000,000! They would have been $40,000,000 richer if they had not raised that 120,000,000 bushels of grain!

Now, don't sneer at Up-to-Date Farming; consult Secretary Wilson, and read this article through to the end.

In the use of a word Secretary Wilson is at fault, the word value. He says "the value of all cereals dropped about $40,000,000." The value of a bushel of wheat produced in 1906 was precisely the same as that of a bushel of wheat produced in 1905, if the quality was the same, and there is no intimation that the quality of the 1906 crop was inferior to that of 1905. A 1906 bushel makes exactly as much flour and feed, containing the same nutritive elements as a 1905 bushel. It is the price that dropped and not the value.

Who was benefited by this $40,000,000 loss sustained by the farmers? Not the consumers of cereals certainly, for the nickel loaf is a nickel loaf still and the restaurant or hotel dinner costs precisely the same. The local prices of flour vary slightly, but scarcely enough to be perceptible.

Who, then, gained by the drop in price? Evidently the powers somewhere between the producers and the consumers. Who made the lower price that caused the farmers a loss of $40,000,000? The law of supply and demand? Bosh! Who administered the law? The same powers somewhere between the producers and consumers. And there you have the whole thing in a nut-shell. These mysterious "powers" got the farmers' $40,000,000, and they pull the strings that make the school, the press and the Agricultural Depertment hop like jumping jacks to the tune of constantly increased production, without a note for marketing or price.

It is not enough to say that farmers gained on an average. You can't average these gains and losses in justice to farmers. Farmers produce different crops, and no one yet has said that the gaining farmer must divide his gains with his losing neighbor. That is too absurd for even an agricultural expert.

Well, what should the farmers do? They should make the prices on their products, and control the marketing of them. There was a very small percentage of these cereal crops of 1905 on hand when the crops of 1906 were ready for the market. As we have said, every bushel of 1906 was of value equal to every bushel of 1905, and it cost no doubt as much to produce it. And the world needed every grain of it, but it did not need it as it came in a golden deluge from the thrashing machine. Keep it off the market until the extra bushels will bring extra dollars, instead of taking dollars from you out of the legitimate proceeds of the whole crop.

In brief, our position is this: Raise big crops, but so market them as to get their legitimate value, an equitable price. Under the Equity system of marketing a big crops is a blessing; under the gambling system of devilish greed, a big crop is often a curse, a source of loss, as proven once more by Secretary Wilson's report of 1906.

GOVERNMENT AID TO AGRICULTURAL SCHOOLS.

What the Schools Should Do.

(John P. Stelle in Up-to-Date Farming, Feb. 22, 1907.)

The United States government has been, and is, very liberal in its support of agricultural schools. Several institutions, known as government grant schools, now receive $25,000 a year each from the national treasury, and an effort is being made at Washington to increase this allowance $5,000 a year until the annual contribution shall be $50,000.

This shows that our government, and in the main those who administer it, are not unfriendly to agriculture. Why they are not need not be discussed, except that we may say if the farmers were more positive and discriminating in their use of the ballot the ruling powers would be more friendly still.

It is quite proper, though, for us to consider this government aid. An analysis of it shows that the design of it all is to increase production. In this the schools with all their progress, all their investigation and research, all their experimentation and study, have signally failed. The average yield per acre has been but very slightly increased. Notable triumphs have been won by "intensive farming" at the stations, but when the crops of the country are bulked and averaged, the average production has varied only as the seasons have varied.

And, indeed, it may be better for farming that it has been so. The success of farming depends upon three elements—cost of production, quantity produced and price received; and the profits (hence the success) are entirely in the price. The efforts of the schools have been directed altogether to cheapness of production and increase in yield. In both, as said before, they have failed. Education and invention have given improved methods and diminished manual labor, but cost of machinery (wear and tear) and higher wages bring the cost of production up to, perhaps above, what it was in the days of our fathers, or even of our grandfathers.

Now, don't understand this as an argument against the schools, nor a belittling of what they have done. We appreciate the schools and their work and we would not do without either, but it is the part of wisdom to look at the truth, to see the schools as they are, and make them better.

It is said in high circles that price depends upon the relation of supply and demand. If that is so, increasing the supply without increasing the demand must diminish the price; and as the farmers' profits are in the price, the efforts of the schools to increase the production, had they succeeded, must have diminished the profits of farming by reducing the price. This is conclusively proven by Secretary Wilson in his report for 1906, in which he shows that three very large crops brought the farmers $120,000,000 less than the same crops much less in quantity and no better in quality, brought the year before.

As we said before, the three elements of success in farming are cheapness of production, quantity produced and price received.

Now, what we want the schools to do is to continue their efforts for a cheaper production and for increase of yield, and we are entirely willing that the government shall aid them in it, but we want them to take up the still more important element of price. If, as they claim, they can have nothing to do with price because it is governed by the law of supply and demand, then their every effort to increase the supply is an effort to lower the price and injure the farmer for the benefit of those who do not farm. We defy any one to dispute this proposition so long as it is based upon the contention that price is governed by the law of supply and demand. And every cent given the schools in pretense of aid to farming while these conditions prevail is a fraud in that the success of its alleged purpose would injure farming for the benefit of other callings.

The schools must teach marketing as well as production. For their encouragement, we may say they are mistaken in their entire theory of the law of supply and demand. It is not the quantity produced that governs the price, but the quantity marketed. It is throwing the stuff on glutted markets that destroys the profits of farming, and that made posible Secretary Wilson's famous figures of last year. Teach the farmers that, whatever they produce, they must not glut markets, and teach them how not to do that, how to name a reasonable price and to keep their stuff or get it; and then the more the schools teach the two things they now teach, the better it will be for farming and the world. But the effect will be different from what is now aimed at by the schools themselves. the cheapening of production will bring fewer hours of labor, and the increased yield will lead to the cultivation of fewer acres, and yet the world will be fully supplied all the same, or the theory of the schools, with their increased production and the intensive farming of the experiment stations are at fault.

With controlled marketing, farmers will very soon learn the quantities required for consumption, and they will not cultivate two acres when one will suffice. The first idea, cheaper production, will enable the farmer to make his price lower and yet have a profit. The second, cultivating fewer acres, will give him rest and recreation, and opportunities for improvement and outings with his family, and it will make room for homes for the thousands that every year need homes of their own.

Do you say farmers cannot be taught to control their marketing? Are not the schools teaching more difficult things? Is there anything American schools, especially those sustained by the United States government, cannot teach? To say they can't is to belittle the schools; to say they dare not is to handicap them; to say it is not within their province is to take them out of the list of agricultural beneficiaries.

PRODUCTION WITHOUT REGARD TO DEMAND.

Farmers Constantly Urged to Produce More.

The key-note of all who atempt to educate farmers, outside the lines of Equity, is to grow more. grow more; strain every effort to grow more! Farm institutes are held for this purpose, farm product trains are run for this purpose, the agricultural press devote every energy to this end, and great expositions are held to encourage it. The logical effects of such increased production upon price and values is not considered. They are clearly shown in the following article, which appeared in Up-to-Date Farming March 22, 1907:

Chicago announces a great corn exposition for October 5 to 19, 1907. This is well. We like to see interest in all of our great industries; and it is pleasant to note that prominent people, great and successful business men, merchants, bankers, manufacturers, railroad men, stockyards managers, theatrical people, leaders in commercial associations, department store men, college professors, men high in newspaper circles, etc., take such a lively interest in what has always been regarded as the humble vocation of corn growing. All these classes figure in the promotion and management of this proposed corn show, and in addition thereto we note the name of ONE CORN GROWER, Mr. E. S. Fursman of El Paso, Ill. We do not wish to be presumptive, but in the absence of anybody else to do it, we desire, in the name of the humble corn producers of America, to thank these distinguished people for their generous (they propose to expend $150,000 on the exposition) and unselfish (not being corn growers they can have no personal interest in the matter) action, and welcome them to the list of promoters of a great but humble industry, that for many years until recently has had to "plod its weary way," "unhonored and unsung."

But what is the object of this great show? We learn from the announcement of it: "It is the desire of the management to demonstrate that it is possible for the average corn grower to produce GREATER YIELDS." "It is easily possible to INCREASE THE YIELD FROM TWO TO TEN BUSHELS PER ACRE." We look in vain for any other object except that there is one intimation that the quality may be improved.

Now if the corn growers are failing in what the world has a right to expect of them, and are not producing corn enough to supply the world's needs, then it is well enough to jog them up a little just as the driver uses a lash when his team goes too slow, and to show them how they "can easily produce from two to ten bushels more per acre." But if they are supplying the world at reasonable prices, where is the kick?

In 1901 the corn growers of the United States produced 1,522,520,000 bushels; in 1902, 2,523,648,000 bushels; in 1903, 2,244,177,000 bushels; in 1904, 2,467,481,000 bushels. (See Government "Crop Reporter" for February, 1907), and in 1906, 2,900,000,000.

The acreage to corn in the United States for the same years was: In 1901, 91,349,928; in 1902, 94,043,613; in 1904, 92,23ᴸ,581; in 1905, 94,011,369. (See Year Book of the Department of Agriculture for 1905, page 657.) We have not an official statement of the acreage of 1906.

Now all of these gentlemen, so far as we are advised, hold that the price of all commodities is determined by what they call the law of supply and demand. The average prices paid for corn for the years named were as follows: 1901, 60.5 cents; 1902, 40.3 cents; 1903, 42.5 cents; 1904, 44.1 cents; 1905, 28.8 cents. (Year Book 1905, page 661.) We have not the average price for 1906. The demand was fully supplied during those years at the above prices. Had it not been fully supplied there would have been increased competition in buying which would have increased the price. The announcement of this corn show to increase production has not a word to say about increased demand.

Now, in case of complete success of the purpose of the exposition, which the management declares to be easy, the corn situation would stand thus: The yield per acre in 1901 was 16.7 bushels and the price per bushel was 60.5 cents. Add the ten bushels per acre proposed by this exposition management, and the yield would have been 26.7 bushels per acre. Then by the rule of simple proportion, if 16.7 bushels per acre supplies the demand at 60.5 cents per bushel, a yield of 26.7 bushels per acre would supply the same demand at 37.8 cents per bushel. The yield per acre in 1902 was 26.8 bushels, and the average price was 40.3 cents per bushel. Add ten bushels per acre, and, by the same rule, the average price would have been 29.3 cents per bushel. The average yield per acre in 1903 was 25.5 bushels, and the average price was 42.5 cents. Add ten bushels to the yield per acre, and by the rule of proportion the price would have been 30.5 cents per bushel. The yield per acre in 1904 was 26.8 bushels, and the average price for that year was 44.1 cents per bushel. Add ten bushels per acre as proposed, and, by proportion as before, the average price would have been 32.1 cents per bushel. The average yield per acre in 1905 was 28.8 bushels, and the average price was 28.8 cents per bushel. Add the exposition management's ten bushels per acre, and, by simple proportion, the average price would have been 21.4 cents per bushel.

Take another view of it. In 1901 the farmer had 16.7 bushels per acre, which, at the average price, 60.5 cents per bushel, was worth $10.10. With the gain of ten bushels per acre, he would have had 26.7 bushels to sell at the proportional price under the law of supply and demand, of 37.8 cents per bushel, and it would have been worth

to him $10.09, one cent less than his normal 16.7 bushels.
In 1902 he had 26.8 bushels to sell at 43.3 cents per bushel,
worth $10.80. Under the same conditions with the in-
crease, he would have had 36.8 bushels to sell at 29.3 cents
per bushel, which would have been worth to him $10.78,
two cents less than his 26.8 bushels brought him. In 1903
he had 25.5 bushels to sell at 42.5 cents per bushel, which
was worth to him $10.83. Under the increase proposed,
the demand remaining the same, he would have had 35.5
bushels to sell at 30.5 cents per bushel, worth $10.82, one
cent less than he got for his 25.5 bushels. In 1904 he had
26.8 bushels to sell at 44.1 cents per bushel, worth $11.81.
With an addition of ten bushels he would have had 36.8
bushels to sell at 32.1 cents per bushel, worth $11.74, four
cents less than he got for his 26.8 bushels. In 1905 he
had 28.8 bushels to sell at 28.8 cents per bushel, which
was worth to him $8.29. With an addition of ten bushels
per acre he would have had 38.8 bushels to sell at the
proportionate price of 21.4 cents per bushel, which would
have been worth to him $8.30. Here he gets one cent for
his increased ten bushels. In all the other cases he lost
his entire ten bushels and something besides. In other
words, the buyers would have gotten the crops with the
ten bushels per acre added for less money than they got
the crops as they were actually produced.

Here we may have a reason why these people who are
not corn growers are so anxious to increase corn production, with no proposition to increase demand or to maintain price.

These concerns are all heralded as of great interest
and benefit to the farmer, but unless they are coupled
with a corresponding increase in demand and the main-
tenance of the price they are a financial injury to the
farmer should they accomplish their purpose.

THE TREE OF AMERICAN INDUSTRIES.

C. Hayes Taylor in Up-to?Date Farming.

The farmer bears upon his back the burdens of the
world, and it is upon his arm that our national welfare
leans for support. The soil of our farms, watered by the
sweat from farmers' brows, has nurished the Tree of
American Industries until by its phenomenal growth, the
wide spreading branches have overshadowed the world. And

while the farmer toils and sweats below to cultivate the tree, vampires and parasites have nested in the branches, feeding on the choicest of its fruits, and dropping down only enough to allay the pangs of hunger to the workers beneath. These buzzards, hawks, crows and vultures are "the men up there who are doing the work." Our government has tried to clip their wings, but that has not diminished their voracious appetites. Something else must be done. Success on the farm can never be assured until these birds are routed. The way is open before us. If we would assert ourselves and take our rightful place in the business world we must make us a ladder every round of it built of an honest demand for equity, and we must add round after round to this ladder until it is as tall as the tree itself. Then we will climb step by step until we reach the top, and when we get up there—woe be unto those parasites!

The American Society of Equity will furnish us a foundation. Every one of its objects will make a round to the ladder that will bear us nearer to the top of the tree. It will go far towards making a connecting link between wealth and its creators. It will secure to us all opportunities to make our farms a grand success that present conditions make impossible.

Now, brother farmers, reason this matter out with cold facts. When you come to the inevitable conclusion that farmers must organize, warm up these facts in the fires of self-interest until they glow a white heat, and set yourself about the task of burning their brands into the brain of every farmer you meet. Here are the facts:

The buyers have organized and they won. The coal interests organized and won. The railroads organized and won. The manufacturers organized and won. The steel men organized to steal more, and they won. The meat men, the produce men, the lumber men, in fact most all the men have organized and won. Won what? Success. Everyone of these men, all of these combinations, are dependent on some other people, and yet they won. Who are they dependent on? On the farmer—on you. Without you they can not exist. You are the first cause; they are the last effect. Suppose *you* organize and control your own industry. Then you become the rulers of the world.

Do you say, "I don't believe farmers can organize?" That unfounded belief, my dear sir, is the only stumbling block in the way of our complete success. I say unfounded belief, and I speak from conviction. What reason can you give for that belief that is not contradicted by truth, necessity and experience? The spirit of the times demands that we place our faith in ourselves. No one will refute the statement that if farmers would co-operate, they *could* place agriculture on a basis that could not be undermined, and would make farming a successful, certain and delightful business instead of a life of drudgery. Then, if that be true, the man who hangs back for fear that farmers will not pull together, is the *only* enemy to our organization that can cause its failure.

Consider the matter carefully, rationally. Every farmer wants success. He is willing to work for it. He is a man of sound sense and honest purpose, and I have faith enough in his intelligence and justice to believe that he can and will make use of all fair means to further his own interests. He will work for better crops and he will establish equitable prices as soon as he sees his way.

Our work, then, is one of education. Let us make our organization a common topic of conversation, the same as we do our crops and field work, until we fully understand its benefits. Let us take fresh courage in our strength. This nation and its government was founded under circumstances far less promising than was the American Society of Equity. Show as much interest in your society as you do in your political party. Give it the same loyal support and allegiance as you have to that, and you will have secured to yourselves and your posterity the blessings of a home in a land where men live and labor under the banner of "Equity for all."

THE AMERICAN SOCIETY OF EQUITY A FRIEND OF ALL.

Unlike Any Other Farmers' Society.

When farmers, smarting under wrongs they could not entirely understand, realized that they must organize so as to meet organization with organization, they very naturally looked no further than to the business men they knew for the source of their trouble. The idea did not occur to them that the prices of their own products might be too low and unfairly and improperly made. They had been taught all their lives, as they yet are taught by many whose reason for such teaching is incomprehensible, that the prices of farm products are made at the fountain head of trade in accordance with some mysterious law, and, therefore, they must be right—at least that they were irrevocable. Hence if there was a lack of equity, an unfairness in prices, the farmers at that time concluded it must be in the prices they were required to pay.

Their efforts were, therefore, directed to a reduction of retailers' prices. Where merchants were stubborn or could see no place for a reduction of prices, the organized farmers formed companies and established stores of their own in opposition to the local trade. Some of these stores made creditable success, but most of them were miserable failures.

This theory and action on the part of the farmers inevitably created antagonism between organized farmers and business men. So bitter became this antagonism that business interests still hold to it, and whenever farm organization is suggested to local merchants, or even to the wholesale trade, it is at once concluded that an enemy to them is being built up, and they vigorously oppose it.

But this is not true of the American Society of Equity. This organization is unlike any other farm organization in that it is built on an entirely different foundation, erected upon a different theory, and aims to an entirely different accomplishment—*Equity in all the business relations of life.*

This society holds that the price of farm products are the ones that are arbitrarily and unfairly made, that while supply and demand each have a limit and their relationship varies, the adjustment of the proportion between the two constitute the law of supply and demand, but that in making the prices in the ordinary speculative way, as published in the market reports, these principles are wholly ignored and prices are made that will best serve the purpose and profits of speculators, who buy cheap to sell high.

Taking this view of the business situation, it is eminently the province of the Society of Equity to wrest farm products from the hurtful hands of speculation and gambling and give them greater permanency in price and more equitable adjustment. This price may be higher and it may be lower than sometimes made by the speculative forces, but it wi.l always be remunerative to the producers because the profits revert to them instead of flowing into the coffers of those "who toil not, neither do they spin," and yet be no more costly to consumers. This can be done, the society claims, and has proven it, not by withholding needed supplies, but by keeping the market supplied only as actual demand calls for it, stringing it along through out the season instead of pouring whole crops upon the market at times of maturity to become the playthings of the bulls and bears of speculation, and the means of extorting unfair prices from consumers.

This theory of farm organization and accomplishment places, or should place, the Society of Equity in the most friendly relations with the legitimate business interests of the country, and they with it. Indeed the society has fully proven its friendliness by opening its doors to business men, inviting them to membership, welcoming them to its councils, and working hand in hand with them in building up home interests. The Society of Equity has no secrets from the world; its propositions are plain business ones. Its success makes farmers better off financially, increases their ambitions, refines their tastes, multiplies their wants, gives them the ability to satisfy them and this makes them more liberal purchasers.

The merchant, therefore, or professional man, or anyone who is unfriendly to the society is too narrow in his views and selfish in his actions, and he is blocking the path to his own best interests. In many localities the business and professional men understand this and have become members of the society and are helping to lead it on to maturity and to success. In others they give it every assistance by counsel and good words.

In such localities it takes eminently the proper form—that of pure mutuality of interests, leading to "equity in all the business relations of life." And so may it be in every locality.

CAN PLANTING AND PRODUCTION BE CONTROLLED.

Under the old conditions, no. Under the new conditions yes. In the past, attempts have been made to regulate of limit the acreage of particular crops planted. But the result was that many farmers quietly put out a larger acreage and often increased the acreage and yield. Under the new system when farmers are organized into unions all over the land, if the order goes out to reduce the acreage 10 per cent., or 25 per cent., and the farmers agree to do so, the agreement will be carried out. What farmer, who broke an obligation that was entered into for the good of all, would face his brother farmers in meetings? The farmers when organized on the plan of the A. S. of E. can regulate their planting if it becomes necessary, outside of it they never v ill.

A WONDERFUL CAMPAIGN.

The Following Five Articles Bear on the Tobacco Growers' Success in Organizing into the American Society of Equity—Any Crop Can Do as Well.

CLOSED IN A BLAZE OF ENTHUSIASM.

From Up-to-Date Farming, Jan. 15th, 1907.

Seldom has any campaign among people, for any purpose, closed in such a blaze of glory as did the Kentucky tobacco growers' campaign for controlled marketing at Winchester, January 2, 1906.

The meeting was for a general roundup of the work among the Burley growers. "Nothing," says National Organizer Sherman, "in our history can run in the same class with the campaign just closed, for vigor, untiring work and determination, nor in its far-reaching results."

"The people have been wild," continues Mr. Sherman, "since 9 p. m. last night, when we made the official declaration that we had won the victory and I read the figures showing that we absolutely controlled the tobacco crop of 1906. They hugged each other and beat each other over the heads with their hats, and in every conceivable way acted like mad."

In the banquet that followed, Mr. Everitt was spoken of as the Moses who had pointed out the way, and Mr. Sherman was hailed as the Aaron who had held up his hands, and led on to the promised land. Cheers of the wildest nature greeted every sentence, and Mr. Sherman, who was present was made the hero of the hour and the librator of the people, a greater general in peace than was his illustrious kinsman in war, declaring him an adopted son of Kentucky.

"The spirit in which the campaign closed," writes Mr. Sherman, "was the most demonstrative I ever witnessed."

The executive board held an enthusiastic business session, elected officers, selected an executive committee to be practically in continuous session. Plans were arranged for carrying out details, and they will now completely cover the territory with local unions, and be ready to go ahead next season, and complete the A. S. of E. structure without the need of so much as the "sound of a hammer."

The warehouses of Louisville and Cincinnati had their agents at the meeting and were anxious to finance the pool. The banks of Central Kentucky were there also to see that the business did not get away from them. The "can't-be-dids" all disappear when Equity's banner gets to the top of the pole, and money is just as eager to help the farmers when they get in a position to help themselves, as it is to help tae corporations and trusts.

The tobacco growers have won the first victory, and have thus set an example for the producers of all other crops. If wheat, corn, cotton, etc., cannot do the same, who is to blame?

THE BURLY TOBACCO GROWERS' SUCCESS.

From Up-to-Date Farming Jan. 22, 1907.

All previous records in organizing the farmers were undoubtedly surpassed by the recent achievement of the American Society of Equity in the Burley tobacco districts of Kentucky and Ohio. This district is composed of nearly forty large counties, and previous to January 1, 1906, had no organization. In fact, active work in organizing did not comence until about September, four months ago. Then it began in earnest. National Organizer H. B. Sherman passed through the district in September, and, by his stirring eloquence, thoroughly aroused several counties. During the summer, H. E. Swain, of Smithfield, M. C. Rankin, of Bethlehem, Dr. G. W. McMillen, of Falmouth, and a few throughout the district, and organizing locals wherever possible. The officials at headquarters secured a large list of names in each county, and sent floods of literature into the district. A number of organizers were appointed, and a meeting of delegates from the several counties met at New Castle, in Henry County, on the first and second of October and organized a district association. Delegates were appointed to attend the annual meeting of the tobacco growers department of the A. S. of E., and some steps were taken to plan and execute a systematic campaign. These steps were carried still further at the annual meeting, and a "Whirlwind Campaign," led by National Organizer Sherman, was put into operation. A big meeting was held in Winchester on November 1st, and the plans were perfected. From that time on, the work has gone forward with all the excitement of a horse race, or a presidental election. The distirct had determined to secure control of 50 per cent. of all tobacco in the district by January 1st, and though it was a stupendous task, they succeeded in

tying up more than 54 per cent.—a marvelous accomplishment. Such ability and such determination behind the
sound principles of the A. S. of E. can bring success in
anything.

Let it be remembered that the first tobacco ever pooled
anywhere was pooled in 1905, when less than 20 per cent.
of the 1904 crop of tobacco in the Green River district was
all that was pooled. Since that time the amount pooled has
been growing rapidly, but nothing like the growth in the
Burley district. Success has crowned the efforts of the
organization in the Green River district, and a still greater
success awaits the Burley growers if they remain steadfast
and hold firmly to the faith (and to the tobacco). The
effect on prices has been marked. The highest prices paid
in years are now being offered. Surely the plan of controlled marketing has been fully vindicated, and those who
oppose it have no longer a shred of argument to support
them in their untenable position.

The Burley growers will continue to take pledges for
1906 tobacco, until January 12th, and it is probable that
more than 60 per cent. of the crop will be tied up and sold
through the society. Let them adopt the same plan of selling now in operation in the other organized tobacco districts of Kentucky, and in Virginia and Tennessee, and
the growers will from this time forward make prices profitable to themselves.

THE FARMERS SHOUTING VICTORY.

Mr. J. A. Everitt:

Your letter of congratulation is at hand, and I am glad
to express to you our deepest appreciation and sincere
gratitude for the A. S. of E., Up-toDate Farming and the
great Third Power, together with your unstinted aid in
perfecting this organization. Without this literature, we
could never have won our great victory in the "Burley
Patch," notwithstanding we were never short of anything
that could combine to bring the farmer forces together.
Farmers and their families and their friends are rallying
around bonfires, shooting anvils and big guns all over the
district. New Years will be a second Day of Independence
to our people, and the beginning of a new era in the prosperity of our country.

We have surprised everybody and ourselves, too, in
this organization, as no one anticipated such results in so
short a time. And while I have headed the campaign, directed her battles and sacrificed much time and money to
win the victory, I am deeply indebted to National Organizer

H. B. Sherman, State Organizer Robertson, C. M. Hanna, and especially to the gallant boys of old Pendleton, who never faltered nor flickered either in war or peace, but were always ready for an onslaught, and were never satisfied out of battle. I have for them the greatest admiration —Conrad, Crecelius, Galloway, Marquette, Loomis, Bartin and others.

You will always have our kindest rememberance for making it possible for our farmers to unite.—G. W. McMillen, Falmouth, Ky.

A WAY TO WIN COMPLETE SUCCESS.

"Where there's a will, there's a way." We all know it and we are making good use of our knowledge here in the tobacco districts. It is our will that practically all of the tobacco grown in 1907 shall be sold through our organization. We desire to give our plan a perfect test—one in which all the farmers are on one side and the buyers only on the other. Up to this time we have had but a portion of the farmers on our side—the others are working with the buyers. We want no dividing line between farmers.

We are going to make a determined effort to induce every farmer to pool with us for one time at least. With eight out of every ten already with us, we are going to those other two, and say to them: "We want you to help us make a complete trial of our plan. For this one year we ask you to join with us, put your tobacco with ours, and act with us, so we can see what we can do, if we have all the tobacco and the buyers can get none except through us. We have helped you much, harmed you none, and we deisre only to help you more. We only ask you to make this one trial, and we depend on the results to keep you with us. It is worth trying."

Fellow members, organizers and secretaries: Can we do this? We can if we pursue proper methods, work with energy and determination and that bull-dog grit that knows no refeat, and you will never succeed at anything if you don't work. We shall not fail unless we fail to try. Few men will refuse, after the abundance of proof they have had that we can succeed, to give us as good a show as possible for a single trial. Now is the time to complete this new and novel campaign. Appoint your committees now. Be careful in making your appointments. Secure men who have ability and influence. Appoint the best diplomats you have—the men to whom the non-members will listen respectfully. Circulate pledges, secure members and organize local, and county unions wherever there is an opening.

Go to them with the pledge. Treat them fairly and court-
eously, and strive earnestly to induce them to help us make
this year the full proof of the possibilities in controlled
marketing. Waste no time, but let us utilize every moment
in working out our own salvation.—C. Hayes Taylor, Sec.
of A. S. of E., Department of Tobacco Growers.

THE TOBACCO SITUATION.

C. Hayes Taylor, in January 22, Up-to-Date Farming:

Four of the principal tobacco growing districts are now
well on the road to success. They have become permanent organizations, and fixtures in the business world. The
tobacco trade has been compelled to recognize them and
to deal with them. These are the Burley, Green River,
Stemming and "Black Patch" districts. The growers therein are satisfied that they prosper with an organization
where they failed to prosper without it. There is no indi-
cation of their going back to the old chaotic conditions.

Virginia has accomplished much though not in proportion to the districts above mentioned. Special attention
will be given to the Virginia district this year. Virginia
dark tobacco ,worth more always than the western types,
is now selling for less than the tobacco in the west under
organized control. This is not as it should be. Virginia
tobacco is worth more, and should sell for more than western tobacco. A portion of the Virginia corp is controlled
by the organization, and that tobacco is being sold at prices
commensurate with its value. Yet it is not selling as
readily as it should, or would, if the growers in that state
would control the marketing better.

From all appearances there is still a surplus of tobacco in stock. The final report of the crop statistical department in Washington shows an increased production for
1906 over the crop of 1905. A well posted tobacconist in
Louisville, Ky., states that the production in the Green
River district for 1906 is undoubtedly larger than the production of 1905. Now, when will the growers learn that
more tobacco does not always mean more money. There
is more money in a crop of the right proportion than there
is in either larger or smaller crops. Why should a farmer
raise an extra thousand pounds if he gets no more than he
could get for his crop without the extra thousand? Our
principles teach us that the world will use so much tobacco,
and no more. It will have that much, no matter what the
price so long as it is within reason. It would use no more
even at the lowest prices ever paid. When we produce more
than that amount, the buyers buy it, and store it away.

They could afford to buy it and throw the surplus away, for without controlled marketing they could buy 10,000 pounds for less money than they would have to pay for 6,000 pounds if only six thousand pounds had been produced. Therefore, they can afford to buy the extra 4,000 pounds, even if they destroyed it, and I have known manufacturers to give away hundreds of thousands of pounds in advertising. They could afford to do it, for it cost them nothing. The fact that buyers take the large crops does not prove that one year's production will be consumed in one year. Suppose, for instance, the annual consumption is 650,000,000 pounds and the annual production is 750,000,-000 lbs. The buyers will buy what they need, and then will say they don't care for the balance. The next year they have 100,000,000 pounds surplus, and they put prices where they please. 750,000,000 pounds are offered them, when they only require 550,000,000, having a million surplus. They can, without controlled marketing by the farmers, buy the two crops of 1,500,000,000 pounds for say, six cents a pound, or for $90,000,000. But now suppose the growers are organized, and control the acreage. They know only 650,000,000 pounds are required, and they produce only 650,000,000 pounds. They demand ten cents per pound, and as the consumers demand that much tobacco, they will sell it all that that price. Hence, they sell two crops of 650,-000,000 pounds each for $140,000,000. With 200,000,000 less pounds of tobacco they obtain $40,000,000 more in cash. Now, Mr. Farmer, do you not see how the buyers can afford to buy all your tobacco at a low price, even though they do not need it? Are you pursuing a good business policy by giving them the surplus and pay them to take it off your hands? Think seriously over this matter, and always remember that more tobacco may mean less profit. Also that organized farmers can control planting as well as they can control the crop after raised.

The proper, sensible method for the farmers is this: Raise only what you believe to be your proportion of a crop that is suited to the market. If you find you cannot sell it all, you have absolute proof that you have a surplus. Then cut down acreage to meet it. The buyers will not take what they do not need unless by doing so they can get what they do not need for less money, and they are wiling to hold the surplus until there is a short crop year. This was the way the evening up was done in the past. The pproducer will hold the surplus and then quit producing another. It is clear to a thinking man that no matter what price he gets for a surplus, he looses money, for he could get more for his crop without the surplus. Buyers can sell but so much tobacco each year. It brings them so much money. They are willing to pay a certain sum for enough tobacco to supply that demand. They will not pay more for twice as much tobacco. I have repeated and reiterated this principle, because I want to thoroughly convince you that there must always be some money lost in the production of a surplus. It always brings distaster to any class of business men, and it will reduce our profits proportionately to the size of the surplus. Grow less tobacco, make it better in quality, control the marketing and you can make all the money it is possible to make from the production of tobacco. Think about these things. And then act.

FINANCIAL BENEFITS.

The American Society of Equity appeals to farmers from many vantage points as we have already shown. But in no sense does it appeal stronger than from a financial point of view. The time is past when farmers will be content with hard work and a mere living as returns from the farm. This kind of independence has lost its attractions, also the fear of a return to low prices and all the resultant evils, including mortgages, is so strong that farmers will embrace any plan that will insure against it. The A. S. of E. plan does insure against these things and does guarantee financial benefits. There are no stronger inducements than profits. Therefore, we appeal to you to join this movement on account of the financial benefits that are sure to come. While it is not intended to make all farmers rich, yet it is intended to give all farmers opportunities EQUAL to those enjoyed by any other class of citizens; investments, skill and effort put forth being considered. If you know of no other reason why you should join the A. S. of E., join because you will make more money by belonging. It matters not how much you farm or how little, nor what you raise. The A. S. of E. is for every section of the country; for every crop, and for every individual engaged in any kind of agricultural pursuits, and will benefit all and bless all mankind.

YOU ARE INTERESTED IN THE AMERICAN SOCIETY OF EQUITY.

BECAUSE it is the only society for farmers that has a practical plan, and inducements strong enough to hold members. The inducements are financial profits.

BECAUSE farmers must co-operate to raise their business to a level with others. They never can do it individually, and no other class will do it for them.

BECAUSE you are now working for other people at wages set by them. (You get your wages through the price of your crops.) The A . S. of E. will allow you to make your own prices and wages.

BECAUSE this is the only plan that will enable you to set your own price and get it.

BECAUSE you are absolutely not required to do anything that is not agreeable, profitable and to your interest to do.

BECAUSE it is not necessary to go to any meetings or lodge if you have not the time or inclination.

BECAUSE you can be a member and co-operate with other members, no matter where you live, if reached by the U. S. mail.

BECAUSE it is not a secret society.

BECAUSE it antagonizes no people, class or legitimate business; and every person, no difference what his or her business or condition, will be benefited.

BECAUSE it never fails to benefit every member from a few dollars to hundreds of dollars every year.

BECAUSE it has made hundreds of millions of dollars for farmers already in increased and maintained prices, and in advice to farmers when to market.

BECAUSE it is non-political, and because it has the strongest safe-guards to keep it out of politics.

BECAUSE there is no capital stock to buy and no intricate machinery.

BECAUSE every member gets advice from headquarters, and all get the same advice at the same time.

BECAUSE this one society is for all farmers, and society for all crops.

BECAUSE its crop estimates are the most reliable, and it has never made a mistake in its recommendation of of prices.

BECAUSE it will insure you a profitable price on every crop whether large or small.

BECAUSE through its workings you will increase your crops and enlarge your markets, as well as increase your price and profits.

BECAUSE it will insure a steady flow of crops to market over the whole year, instead of a flood at one time and a dearth at another.

BECAUSE it will kill speculation in farm products.

BECAUSE it will double the value of your farm and decrease the drudgery of farming.

BECAUSE it will solve all the difficult farm problems that have bothered farmers for years, and which are getting more serious every year.

BECAUSE it will be the greatest and strongest society or union on earth, and you will be proud to belong to it.

BECAUSE every member will receive the most helpful farm paper printed, and the only one in the world that teaches how to get profitable prices for farm crops.

BECAUSE every person that joins brings the time neare when perfect results will be realized. NUMBERS make strength. A large number of farmers in the A. S. of E. and the reading one paper that gives them truth about crops, markets and prices, will be irresistible.

BECAUSE It has already done agriculture more good through education than all other farmers' societies combined.

BECAUSE it has taught farmers CONTROLLED MARKETING, which has made for them hundreds of millions of dollars.

FARMERS, WHAT ARE YOU GOING TO DO ABOUT IT?

M. Wes Tubbs.

Dare you dare to lie inactive when a dozen men to-day
Make a dozen million dollars on your crops whene'er they
    say?
Dare you let them price your produce, price the things
    which you must buy?
Make you pay them double tribute; whate'er you sell, what-
    e'er you buy?
Dare you rest in dumb submission, let a wrong so flagrant
    cry?

Are you sleeping? Are you crazy? Do you work for pleas-
    ure now?
Are you on your seaside outing? Is your wife in Europe
    now?
Are your children off to college while the servants hoe and
    plow?
Nay, your life is naught but drudg'ry, naught but work
    from morn' till night,
While your wife and children, also, need must enter in the
    fight.

Yes, you feed the world in plenty; keep ten million wheels
    in motion;
Run the steam cars and the steamboats on the land and
    on the ocean;
Fill the shop and mill and factory; locate marts of trade
    and business;
Build up cities, states and countries; form the backbone of
    the nation;
Pay its bills in noble fashion; even own the earth it's built
    on.

But alas, where is your portion? Who has got it? Can you
    find it
In the billion-dollar steel trust, or the oil trust, or the
    meat trust,
Or the multi-headed food trust? In the dividends of rail-
    roads,
Telegraphs or telephones? Yes, in all of these you find it,
Find your wealth 'mid pomp and glory, 'mid the gorgeous,
    rich and splendid.

It is theirs. They have got it. You produced it. How
    about it?
Are you willing to continue being robbed of your just
    profit?
Will you bolt and say the farmers will not hold for better
    prices;
Will not join in a farmers' union; are too jealous of each
    other;
Rather let a stranger fleece them than to help their near-
    est brother?
If you bolt, go hide your "physog," narrow-minded, jealous
    weak,

Shut yourself in some dark closet, let the newsboys' union
    speak;
Even they in councils profit, so do bootblacks through
    their unions;
But the farmers are too foolish; are too jealous, weak and
    fitful,
Get you all such flagrant nonsense, farmers shall in union
    counsel!

We shall form a mighty union, large in numbers, strong in
    power,
Which will solve in perfect justice all the problems of the
    hour.
We shall price our own farm produce, price it at a profit,
    too,
And command the world to pay it. Hold until our price
    does come,
Then, you farmer, have your portion; then your new life
    has begun.

You no longer are a farmer, bound and shackled by a mar-
    ket
Made by brokers for their plunder, from your hard-earned,
    well-filled basket,
But a farmer, king in power, who commands a recompense
For his many weeks of labor, for his toil and his privation,
That he, too, may take an outing; take a well-earned, long
    vacation,
Spend a day off at the seaside; send his wife to Europe
    now;
Send his children off to college; let the servants hoe and
    plow.
Nay, the farmer is not sleeping; is not crazy working now,
But a man of means and muscle, well developed at the
    plow,
Who in mental calculations, rules the world and markets
    now.

SHALL FARMERS PAY SOMETHING TO MARKET THEIR CROPS.

Farmers are the only people in the country who produce
all they can, but don't spend a dollar to get a good market.
Manufacturers often spend more to market their products
than to produce them. Merchants appropriate a large percentage of their income to advertising to secure better and
larger markets for their goods. Laborers join their unions
and pay a considerable percentage of their wages into the
union to secure a good market for what they have to sell—
labor. And so it goes. Who, besides the farmer, having a
commodity to sell is not willing to go to some trouble and
spend some money to find a good market? Yet the farmers'
goods are in the greatest demand—they are absolutely essential. If farmers would adopt the same plan as others do,
they could put their prices just as high as they want to.

SIXTY-FIVE IMPORTANT QUESTIONS ANSWERED.

There is not a trouble affecting agriculture that co-oper-ation by farmers will not cure. There is a solution in co-operation for every problem in the agricultural book, and for nearly all the other problems of our social, political and busines life.

Q. Why should farmers organize?
A. So they may exert their combined forces to secure whatever they are entitled to. Unorganized they have been the prey of other people who have organized, and single-handed a farmer is no match for them. This might be il-lustrated by a bundle of sticks; take them one at a time and they can easily be broken, but taken collectively they resist the attempts to break them. A single farmer work-ing alone is the weakest person in the country, because there are more of the same kind of people in competition with him. However, organize the farmers so they can ex-ert their combined power and we will have the greatest union and the most powerful union on earth.

Q. Can farmers organize?
A. They did in the Grange, Alliance, Farmers' Mutual Benefit Association and other societies by the millions. Therefore, they can again, if there is a good reason for it. The reasons are more numerous and urgent now than ever before.

Q. Can farmers co-operate?
A. The farming industry is the same all over the coun-try, and practically all over the world. Farmers all have their investments for one purpose, and all labor to one common purpose, viz.: to produce the necessaries and com-forts of life. Laborers, on the contrary, are subject to many varied conditions, as found in the factories, stores, banks and mines, on the railroads, in cities or country, etc. They are also influenced by many interests of their em-ployers and frequently attempts are made to prevent them from organizing and co-operating. Yet they have organ-ized and do co-operate, and have secured great benefits from such co-operation. If laborers can co-operate for their mutual good under such conditions, who dare say that farmers cannot, when no fair person will oppose the farm-ers' organization on the plan proposed by the American Society of Equity? On the contrary every person doing a legitimate business will help the organization, because it will help him. Farmers are surely as intelligent as coal miners and factory employes, and surely they can see it is to their great interest to co-operate for every good thing. It has been said "Every class of people can co-operate ex-cept Indians, idiots and the insane." Do farmers belong to any of these classes? We will see if farmers must be classed with the above after giving them a trial on a good plan.

Q. Will farmers stick together?
A. Give them all, or half, or quarter, of the benefits that the A. S. of E. promises, and you cannot drive them

apart. Appeal to their self-interest—selfish interests, if you please—and they will stick to the thing that makes them money and elevates their calling.

Q. Does speculation injure farmers?
A. It certainly does. It is the greatest curse of the country. Usually farmers' crops are sold months before they are grown, when, if conditions justify higher prices the speculators won't let the price go up until their contracts are filled. The boards of trade are the devil's workshops, in which the earnings of farmers are forged for the benefit of a few individuals who become immensely wealthy.

Q. Is not cheap food a blessing to the world?
A. Cheap farm products and everything else dear is not an equitable condition. We care not how low the price of farm products is if all commodities were on the same basis. All we ask is a fair price—in exact relation to the prices of other goods. Cheap farm products will soon put farmers out of the list as liberal buyers.

Q. What are the speculative commodities?
A. Agricultural products, railroad shares and mining stocks.

Q. Why are these selected to speculate in?
A. Because of the uncertainties attending them.

Q. How can agricultural products be removed from the list?
A. By making prices certain. By fixing a price once a year, when the crop is produced, and getting that price. This is equitable. The farmer has as much right to do this as the manufacturer, the banker, the lawyer, the physician, the gas man, the ice man, the union laborer or any other person on earth. Besides. the farmer has a better chance to enforce his demands than any of the others. His goods are indispensable; the others may be done without.

Q. When is the time to organize the farmers?
A. Now is the time. There are more farmers in an independent condition now than for many years. This is the time to organize and keep prices up. Have you not noticed how the speculators price your crops down as soon as crop prospects are good? Don't you want good prices for good crops? Then the blessings will be equally distributed. Organize now and not when mortgages are plastered all over your homes.

Q. Will farmers' business grow worse?
A. Lines opposed to the farmers—and they constitute every other industry, profession and consumer in the country—are being drawn closer in organization and co-operation. As they all get their living from the farm, they will employ sharp practices that the stirring times have developed to beat down the farmers' prices to the very lowest level. True, there will be seasons of short crops, when prices will stay up, but in seasons of large crops there will absolutely be no sustaining power to prices of farm products except what the farmers furnish. Farmers are furnishing much of this power now, but we want a power that will be effective for the first bushel, pound or bale as well as for the last. I defy any person to show me the man or set of men in a trade, who will not try to protect himself. This grasping, greedy disposition is not the spirit of Chris-

tianity, but it is human nature. The weak are always opposed by the strong and the unorganized by the organized. There is absolutely no safety or good prospect in this country for an industry not organized, and unorganized classes are powerless.

Q. Are there not too many farmers to co-operate?

A. This is a popular fallacy that sound reasoning will dispel. The great number of farmers will be the great element of strength in farmers co-operating. For instance, all the farmers don't need to hold crops at any time, as the markets will take immense quantities of supplies every day. All that will be required will be enough farmers to control that part that goes on the market and creates a temporary over-supply or surplus. This over-supply makes the low price on all. Take, for example, the year 1901: all crops except wheat were short; everything—corn, oats, fruit, vegetables, meat, etc.—brought high prices. Why? Because there was no oversupply at any time and the buyers were eager to get all that was offered. Now let us see how about wheat. It was a large crop. The price ruled low. Why? Because growers of wheat fed the market faster than it needed it. Yet the entire crop was consumed, although it was the largest crop the country ever raised. No business can maintain prices or control prices that markets a year's supply in a few months. Co-operation is intended to produce the same condition that prevails when there is a short crop—i. e., keep the market hungry or willing to receive at the price set—the demand **seeking** the supply. This can be done by controlling the supply and keeping it back on the farm or in farmers' warehouses and letting it go out gradually over a year. With each crop there is one or two states that produce such a large part that they could control enough supply to compel the fair price on all, if the producers in those states were organized and co-operating on the plan of the A. S. of E.

Hence, we see that in the great number of farmers there must always be enough who will control the comparatively small part that has come on the markets in the past, and made the temporary surplus, and this plan will be reliable regardless of any weak or stubborn farmers.

We train ourselves to watch ourselves,
    Until we find at length
We've made our very weakness
    The pillars of our strength.

Q. Is the American Society of Equity a good name?

A. Yes, considering the power of the farmers when co-operating, it is necessary to have a motto that will influence their actions. For instance, the farmers organized, and in possession of all the food and clothing supplies, could practice inequity if they wanted to to a dangerous extent. If they were actuated by greed as are most of the great trusts, they could put the prices of the necessities of life so high as to work hardship to all other classes.

Therefore, the originator of the plan of the A. S. of E. selected this name as a promise by the farmers that they would give equity, and a notice to the world that they would expect **equity**. Equity means justice, right, honesty, impartiality. It will make the world better to the extent to which it is recognized and practiced. No man can hide behind it with a plea of ambiguity, as it is one of the most

uncompromising words in the English language, covering
not one shade of selfishness, unfairness or onesidedness. A
society founded on equity is founded on the solid rock of
fair dealing and righteousness. No better foundation word
could be found for the society and other people.

**Q. If farmers get profitable prices, will they not over-
produce?**
A.   Take into consideration the fact that in the last
fifty years practically all our great western and northwestern states were brought under cultivation, and immense
areas in the older states cleared, drained and made productive, yet all the products have been consumed, and we
don't see how it will be possible to overproduce in the future.

The population of America and the world is increasing
very rapidly and consumption of farm products is increasing at an enormous rate. There are no more such large and
fertile areas to open up in our own country nor in Canada.
While there is a great territory in Canada that will produce
wheat (the reports are usually exaggerated), yet it must
come under cultivation very gradually, depending largely on
railroad building. Also, as that territory is developed for
wheat growing the demand in the United States for more
corn and other crops will take up the ground that may not
be profitable for wheat; if this codition ever comes, which
we doubt.

We will deny that Russia will likely be a greater competitor in the future than in the past. If the time comes
when its agricultural resources are much more greatly developed it will be when that country will be advancing to
a higher order of living and the home consumption of good
food will double or triple.

It is also reasonable to suppose, that with profitable
prices for all crops, farmers will not try to put out a whole
township in crops, but that, realizing that a normal crop
brings more than a bumper crop, they will work less, build
up the fertility of their farms and give themselves and their
farms the rest cure which both need badly.

**Q. If a surplus should exist any time, what would be
done with it?**
A.   When farmers control their crops and regulate the
prices they have done a great thing. There are, however,
other uncertainties connected with farming that they cannot control. We refer to the weather. Do the best they
can, they cannot control rainfalls, frosts, heat or cold; also,
insects and blight are uncertain factors in the production
of crops. These factors will make short crops some seasons. If farmers are co-operating they can easily hold the
surplus of good seasons, should they exist, over to the short
years, thus equalizing supplies and prices, and benefiting
both producers and consumers. In case of perishable products, fruit, vegetables, etc., they can be preserved, canned
or manufactured to far better advantage than when each
farmer is for himself.

**Q. How can poor farmers hold their crops to help
maintain the minimum prices?**
A.   We don't think they will need to hold, because the
demand takes an enormous quantity of farm stuff every
day, and if those farmers hold who can, the first markets
can be given to those who cannot hold. But suppose they
should hold. Under the A. S. of E. plan it will be made

profitable to hold because the minimum price will be advanced monthly or quarterly to equal shrinkage, storage, etc., and a slight profit besides. Also the plan makes it **possible** to hold. Organized farmers can pool their crops and borrow money on them which, unorganized, they cannot well do. This is already done to a very great extent for some crops and in some sections.

With the A. S. of E. plan in operation, the demand will be great at the beginning of marketing, because dealers will know they cannot buy for less, and if they delay, the price will be higher.

Q. Is wheat worth $1.00 a bushel?

A. Wheat should not sell for less than $1.00 per bushel on basis of Chicago market any year. But what it is worth will depend on the yield and supply. Farmers go to as much expense and effort to produce a short crop as a full crop, hence should receive as much money for it. After farmers have done the best they can they should have uniform wages and profits in the returns, whether the crops are large or small. From the consumer's standpoint, there is nothing else he can buy of equal intrinsic value to wheat at $1.00.

Q. Have wheat growers been factors in making the prices?

A. They have been. No well-informed person will deny that they have largely changed their plan of marketing. This was particularly noticeable with the 1903 crop, when with a good crop the visible supply was kept smaller than ever known before with the same size crop. In 1904, the price was over $1.00 from the start, and influenced liberal marketing when the price was right, but marketing always slackened as soon as the price declined.

Q. Is it more difficult to get the minimum price for wheat than for other crops?

A. Yes. The reason is that the wheat crop is the first grain crop ready for market, many farmers must have money and they dump their wheat until a great visible supply is built up and this visible supply is a club to beat prices down on the balance. Witness a visible supply of over 50,000,000 bushels of wheat out of a crop of 740,000,-000 bushels against a visible supply of only 15,000,000 bushels of corn out of a crop of 2,700,000,000 bushels. Also there is another reason. Wheat is used exclusively for flour and must be sold off the farm, while the other grains can be converted into meat or other products.

Q. Who are eligible to membership in the A. S. of E.?

A. Farmers (owners, renters and helpers) and friends of farmers who want the A. S. of E. to succeed, with their wives and sons and daughters.

Q. Why do you admit merchants and bankers?

A. Theirs and the farmers' interests are mutual. The success of one class makes it better for other classes. The merchants want the farmers to organize and get good prices, so they can pay good prices for good goods, and not buy the nasty cheap goods, as now they oftentimes do. Bankers want farmers to organize, because it will add stability of value to all property and insure permanent prosperity. Also, the farmers may as well take them into their society if they want to come, as it will be easier to control them on the inside than to shut them out, arouse their antagonism and control them on the outside. Besides, most merchants and bankers are farmers also, therefore we cannot debar all unless we limit a farmer's business to farming. In the A. S. of E., it is hoped all the people in the country and small towns will co-operate to the upbuilding of rural America.

Q. Is the A. S. of E. a secret society?
A. No. Farmers don't need to have any secrets from anybody else. Where equity is given and received, you don't have to have secrets. The farmers co-operating will be so strong that they can go boldly before the world, make their equitable demands and get justice, or take it. Local unions can, however, hold closed meetings any time they wish.

Q. Must a member belong to a local union?
A. No; there are also members-at-large. A member anywhere can get the full benefit of national co-operation without belonging to a local union. The official paper will be the key and guide for action. It will give advice regarding markets, crops, prices, etc., so all can act as one man. Every person should join a local union when possible. Where none, each member-at-large or convert should organize one.

Q. Will farmers stick together?
A. They will when there is something to stick for. In the old attempts they did not get enough benefits, hence the inducement was not present to stick. Former farmers' organizations had for their chief objects **to buy cheaper.** The chief object of the A. S. of E. is to sell at profitable prices. What is buying at lower prices as compared to selling at profitable prices? The A. S. of E. is built for benefits from the ground up. Once let farmers realize some of the benefits of co-operation on this plan, and no influence on earth can drive them apart.

Q. How are members bound to the National Union?
A. By self-interest. There is no binding agreement. It is proposed to make it to their interests to belong to the A. S. of E. If after a fair trial great benefits cannot be obtained, the farmers cannot co-operate. In community, county, district or in department business pledges are made and business agreements entered into that bind the members. Thus members pledge their crops of potatoes, tobacco, etc., to the selling committees, and the courts have held such pledges good.

Q. What is the membership fee?
A. $2.00.

Q. What are the dues?
A. $1.20 a year.

Q. What does the membership fee secure and how is the money used?
A. It makes the person a member of the society, secures membership card full paid for the year, a badge or button, and the official paper for the year. Also literature, bulletins, etc., as issued.
The fees, outside of the cast of the official paper, are used to meet the expenses of state and national unions, employ organizers and to complete the society all over the

country. This last costs money and a lot of it. After the society is completed the fee can be made very small.

Q. How are the dues used?
A. To maintain the local, county, state and national unions and provide the official paper to each member.

Q. Will profitable prices for farmers not make higher prices for consumers?
A. No. When farmers are organized they can cut out the mountains of profits now taken by middlemen or sell directly to consumers. We expect the prices to consumers will be lower. Also consumers are organizing into the A. S. of E., and then the two bodies will regulate the food trusts and middlemen, or deal with each other directly.

Q. How will the farmers' organization affect organized labor?
A. When farmers get profitable prices the labor problem on the farm will be solved, as they can then hire the help neded. It will make a market for a million or more laborers the year round. This movement is the greatest thing for working people that ever was proposed.

Q. How will this movement affect the producer of perishable products?
A. Cold storage houses and warehouses will be provided, where fruit, butter, eggs, vegetables, meat, etc., will be held as the producers' property until the market can use them. In the case of berries, peaches, etc., the markets will be known and supplied to the maximum consumption at good prices, but no more. By knowing the needs of all the markets a much greater volume of products can be directed to them than in the uncertain way as at present, and if an actual surplus exists it will be left to spoil at home, or be preserved by canning or otherwise, and not allowed to break the price on the legitimate supply. The society will be of enormous benefit to producers of perishable crops.

Q. Can this society regulate the price of potatoes?
A. Certainly. This is a crop that frequently sells at ruinously low prices when the production is large. It will be one of the easiest to organize. When the farmers are organized in New York, Michigan and Wisconsin, the trick will be done. A wise distribution of the potato crop, instead of the lack of system, to say nothing about the hindrances thrown about the marketing by exploiters, will afford a good price for the biggest crops this country ever grew. The same illustration will apply to apples and other fruit, also vegetables, melons, etc.

Q. Can the A. S. of E. insure good prices on tobacco?
A. Most certainly. Tobacco growers are now organized in the A. S. of E. and set their prices and get them. The example of co-operation and price making as shown by the tobacco growers is something the country never had before and it is a lesson for all other producers.

Q. Will the minimum (profitable) price limit consumption?
A. No. It will rather stimulate trade and increase consumption because it will remove uncertainties. Under the old system, if the farmer thought prices too low he would not sell. If the buyer thought they were too high

he would not buy. Also the buyer was always fearful the price would go down, therefore he always wanted to buy as low as possible. Under the new system certainty will prevail. There will be no fear or hesitancy. All will sell and buy as much as the market needs, and farm products will go into consumption with greater ease and regularity than by the old system. This plan has beauties and advantages that can not be fully realized or appreciated until it is in working order.

Q. How can farmers store their produce?

A. Several local unions can join together and erect necessary warehouses, cold storage houses or elevators. These will be under their direct control. There will be another class owned by the society in principal cities, where produce can be shipped and stored for account of the owner. Warehouse receipts will be issued on grain and produce, which can be used as credit at banks to secure money.

Q. Is it a fact that the larger the crop the lower the price?

A. It was invariably so before the A. S. of E. came, and there were many cases where the smallest and nastiest crops the country ever raised brought the most money to the farmers, and the largest, finest crops the least money. Hundreds of times farmers saw their efforts crowned with success in producing a crop, only to meet crushing disappointment when marketing.

Q. Will you not need to control production as well as supply?

A. No; we thing not, but this can be done if desirable when farmers are organized. The world will take all the food crops this country will grow and pay a fair price for them if the farmers will regulate the marketing so as to prevent over supply at any time. Consumption is ahead of production now, and we predict will increase faster than production, unless our farmers get better prices to encourage better farming and larger crops.

Q. Do farmers need to market a twelve months' supply in a few months?

A. No. We have referred to this before. Here is the whole secret of failure in the past and success for the future. If the crops ripened an equal portion each day as the demand came there would be no problem. But they don't. Therefore the problem is to control the crops and let them out only as fast as the demand comes.

Suppose a year's supply of coal had to be marketed in three months in the summer; the miners would get a very low price, the middlemen make a mountain of profit, and the consumer would pay more than an equitable price. It is the same way with farm crops.

Q. Will it not be sufficient to have storehouses, get a low rate of freight and cut out the handlers' profits?

A. Never. What profiteth it a farmer if he stores his grain, but lets the speculator, trust or middleman price it at last? Storage charges, commissions and reduced railroad freight combined are not equal to putting a fair price on your own stuff and taking your profit first.

Q. Do you think money can be well spent in marketing farm products?

A. Yes. It is a fact that manufacturers and merchants frequently spend as much money in advertising, traveling representatives and in other ways to find a market as the goods cost in the first place. Farmers have been spending nothing—simply dumping their fine products to let them take their chances on prices, and without any regard to their brother farmer's interests. Through co-operation they can market their goods much cheaper than can any other class, because there is a natural demand for them. Others must create a demand.

Q. On what does the prosperity of our country depend?

A. On the farmers. They constitute about half our population. They are also the greatest consumers. Keep them prosperous by always getting good prices as this society proposes, and the country can not have hard times.

Q. Who will this movement injure?

A. No person doing a legitimate business, but will build them all up.

Q. Can this society prevent adulteration of food products?

A. This is one of the objects of the society, and when established it can effectually prevent adulteration by inspection of food products, by demanding and securing legislation against adulteration and by using a label. Fraud in food must cease. It is injurious to health, besides reduces the farmers' market to an amazing extent.

Q. Why not have a society for each crop? For instance, grain growers, cattle growers, fruit growers, tobacco growers, cotton growers, etc.?

A. Quite unnecessary. One national society, with representatives from all of these special crops on the national board, can act in making prices and fewer officers will be needed; the expenses will be much a less; a better knowledge of crops and markets may be had, and more than all, a mixed producer need not belong to a half dozen societies to represent all his crops.

Q. Do you think the Alliance or the Grange could have succeeded if they had operated on the plan of the A. S. of E?

A. Yes. I am sure if they had made their first object to secure profitable prices for their own goods instead of attempting to put prices on the other party's goods, farmers would be successfully co-operating today.

Q. Are agricultural colleges, experiment stations, farmers' institutes and farm papers doing good for the farmers?

A. Yes. It is well for all classes to be educated and enlightened; but also, no, for they are teaching how to increase production, while we all know the larger the crops the lower the prices. Now, don't think that I am opposed to educating the farmers, but until they are also educated as to how to get a good price for increased crops the efforts and expense of education is wasted. Think about this. Farmers should demand of their institutions a balanced education, at least half on the distributing—marketing—end of their business which is even more important than production. All others are dependent on the farmers. The farmers are less dependent on any other class. Any reasonable price the farmers hold out for must be paid.

Q. How does the food trust operate?
A. It has warehouses in many parts of the country. It buys the farmers' grain, fruit, vegetables, potatoes ,butter, eggs, poultry, etc., soon after harvest or in times of heavy production when prices are low, puts them in elevators, warehouses and cold storage, and deals them out at two or three times the price between seasons. The farmers can attend to all this when organized.

Q. Could the government help the farmers by loaning them money at a low rate of interest?
A. No, not permanently. Besides the farmers don't need help in that way. It would be the most degrading thing that could be offered them to make them the special objects of the country's charity. The farmers' position is the strongest of all. If they will only rise to their true position, they will never need to look to the government for help.

Q. Are not farmers taxed too heavily?
A. Yes; but here again if they will co-operate and get profitable prices they won't need to care how much they are taxed. They can simply add it on the price of their goods.

Q. When the farmers are organized they will likely become a power in politics?
A. They could if they would. We expect them to dictate to political parties, for the interests of consumers and equity to all; but the A. S. of E. is not a political party and never will be. It is for education first and business always.

Q. Could not good prices be made for farmers if your society had a large capital with which to buy the crops?
A. Never. If all the money in the United States treasury was employed for this purpose the scheme would fail. Farmers must individually be responsible for their production as well as their prices. If a company would agree to take all they raise at profitable prices there would would be no check on their production, while the company or society **must find some other person who will take them at an even higher price**; and here would come failure in time.

Q. Why not organize one state and see how the plan would work?
A. This would be useless. It would not work to secure equity on all the crops. The farmers in Indiana can not do much unless the farmers in Illinois, Ohio, etc., will co-operate with them. Also, it would not be possible to make good prices on one crop and let others take their chances, as then the crops that are not controlled would be neglected and the other one would be over-produced.

Q. Can farmers secure profitable prices on their crops regardless of the European farmers?
A. Yes, we claim they can. America has set the price in the past and set it too low. This impoverished the Eu-

ropean farmers until in recent years the foreign countries have placed high tariffs against our farm products to raise the price of their home products. Also, this has operated to reduce our markets. We believe if American farmers will maintain profitable prices, European farmers will raise their prices to meet them. But if the European markets can be retained only at unprofitable prices (and the small export surplus set low prices on all the crop) then it better be abandoned and the American farmers produce only for the American markets.

Q. Is the A. S. of E. a trust?

A. The society is in no sense a trust. It has no capital stock, buys no products nor does it effect or attempt any combination in restraint of trade. It believes that farmers, like all other producers, should price their own products. This they do in national convention, in which the producers of every farm product are represented. The price is in strict accordance with the law of supply and demand, based upon cost of production and the general level of prices of other commodities. The board determines minimum prices for the crops of that year, and farmers everywhere are told to sell freely at the prices, and to hold their stuff when the market is supplied instead of rushing it in upon a glutted market.

Q. Have farmers a moral right to price their products?

A. Somebody prices them. Who has a better right than the first owners? If you would deny the farmers the moral right how can you justify the speculators, gamblers, food trusts, and unfair, scheming middlemen, who rob at both ends and never earned a morally honest dollar in their life? Certainly farmers have a moral right to price the product of their investment, skill and labor. It is a divine right. "The laborer is worthy of his hire."

Q. Have farmers a legal right to combine to price and sell their crops?

A. They have. There is not a state in the country that would deny them this right. In doing this it is not in restraint of trade, but it would be the greatest promotion of trade. Give us equitable, steady prices, with all speculation and gambling ended, and a condition could not be imagined in which business would be of greater volume and more satisfactory.

Following is an act of the Legislature of Kentucky, under date of March 21, 1906:

"It is hereby declared lawful for any number of persons to combine, unite or pool, any or all of the crops of wheat, tobacco, corn, oats, hay or other farm products raised by them, for the purpose of classifying, grading, storing, holding, selling or disposing of same, either in parcels or as a whole, in order or for the purpose of obtaining a greater or higher price therefor than they might or could obtain or receive by selling said crops separately or individually."

Q. Should farmers form a union or should they strive to destroy other trusts and unions?

A. With some people this is the most important question of all. Farmers have been taught to oppose the trusts because they raise the price of goods the farmers buy. They are taught to oppose the unions because the price of

labor is higher than they can pay. They are taught to
fight everything that don't measure down to their standard,
but they never have been taught to raise their standard up
to measure with the highest and the best, until the publisher of Up-to-Date Farming took the field to lead them
out of the wilderness of darkness into the broad light.
Farmers can't overthrow the trusts and the unions, so this
is the end of that. But they can put such prices on their
products as will allow them to meet prices made by others,
increased taxation and pay the market price for labor.
This is the A. S. of E. plan. We will lift agriculture up
until its products are on an equality—for price and profits
—with others.

**Q. Why don't all farm papers help to get profitable
prices for farm crops?**
A. There are various reasons. Some don't understand
the plan. Some want to wait until it is an assured success. Some say that farmers have no right to price their
crops. Some want farmers to wait until Divine Providence
gets good prices for them. Some say prices have been good
enough, and farmers don't need anything better. Some
have other plans to accomplish the same results. Some
are in the hire of the class of people who are now reap-
ing the profit from the farmers' hard work. Some are too
ignorant; some are too smart. Some are jealous, and some
are vindictive. Read this extract from a letter to a person who betrayed his trust:

——————— March 17, 1904.
"Mr. J. A. Everitt, President of the A. S. of E., Indianapolis,
Ind.:
"Dear Sir—I feel it my moral duty to let you know
that a prominent farmers' paper invited me, and made offers to me to take up arms against you. * * * The letter of said prominent editor of a prominent agricultural paper closes in this way: 'I do not know that I care to go
into an open fight with Everitt, but if I could see a chance
to give him a neat stab under the fifth rib I think I would
rather enjoy doing it.'
"Yours truly, _____"

Why don't other farm papers help to teach farmers
how to control marketing and compel a fair price for their
products? The principal reason is that the society must
have an official paper. The plan was originated by the publisher of Up-to-Date Farming. Naturally that paper became
the official organ. They know that the success of the society and the success of the farmers means a large circu-
lation for the official paper. They have been assured that
it was not the intention of the publisher of Up-to-Date
Farming to monopolize the agricultural field, that the
official paper would become strictly a society paper. But
this does not appease them any many of them have done
all they could to injure the movement. They have not the
welfare of the farmer close enough at heart to lay aside
all petty jealousies, excuses and selfish interests and help
the farmers to try this plan.
Farmers should know their friends in a time like this.
Any editor and publisher who opposes this movement is
your enemy, and every editor and publisher who won't help
you to get equitable prices always, by the only plan that
is practicable, is not your friend. When a cowardly edi-

tor says he would enjoy stabbing the author and promoter of this great and good movement that means so much for farmers, he is expressing a wish to stick his dirk into the vitals of the farming industry of the country, and every farmers who loves independence and fair play should stretch out his arm to ward off the blow.

Q. Does the A. S. of E. oppose other farmers' societies?

A. No. The A. S. of E. has the kindliest feeling for all farm organizations. It only asks that all unite to accomplish the first object of this society, viz.: "Profitable Prices for All Farm Products," which should also be the chief object of all. They need not abandon their special forms, but should add this object to their others and make it paramount.

Q. What will be some of the results of co-operation by farmers?

A. The results will be everything the farmers want or should have. Then land will increase in value 25 to 100 per cent. (This prediction has already been fulfilled.) They will beautify their grounds. They will educate their children. They will build good roads all over the country. The farmer and his wife and children will work less and hire more, visit and entertain more. The farmer's wife will furnish her home as well as the city woman does. The farm labor problem will be solved. The boys will want to stay on the farm, because it offers possibilities equal to any other business, and other boys will want to go to the farms. Besides all these things, and many more not necessary to mention, the success of this society will build up the country towns, and through the country merchants the benefit will reach the cities. It will, in short, benefit every legitimate industry, and every man, woman and child in the country. It means more for the world and humanity than anything since the Christian era.

American Farmers
and
The Rise of Agribusiness

Seeds of Struggle

An Arno Press Collection

Allen, Ruth Alice. **The Labor of Women in the Production of Cotton.** 1933

Bailey, L[iberty] H[yde]. **Cyclopedia of American Agriculture.** Vol. II: Crops. 1912

Bankers and Beef. 1975

[Bivins, Frank Jarris]. **The Farmer's Political Economy.** 1913

Blumenthal, Walter Hart. **American Indians Dispossessed.** 1955

Brinton, J. W. **Wheat and Politics.** 1931

Caldwell, Erskine and Margaret Bourke-White. **You Have Seen Their Faces.** 1937

Cannery Captives. 1975

Children in the Fields. 1975

The Commission on Country Life. **Report of the Commission on Country Life.** 1911

The Co-operative Central Exchange. **The Co-operative Pyramid Builder.** three vols. July 1926-January 1931

Dies, Edward Jerome. **The Plunger:** A Tale of the Wheat Pit. 1929

Dunning, N. A. **The Farmers' Alliance History and Agricultural Digest.** 1891

Everitt, J[ames] A. **The Third Power:** Farmers to the Front. 1907

The Farmer-Labor Party—History, Platform and Programs. 1975

Greeley, Horace. **What I Know of Farming.** 1871

Hill, John, Jr. **Gold Bricks of Speculation.** 1904

Howe, Frederic C. **Privilege and Democracy in America.** 1910

James, Will. **Cowboys North and South.** 1924

Kerr, W[illiam] H[enry]. **Farmers' Union and Federation Advocate and Guide.** 1919

King, Clyde L. **Farm Relief.** 1929

Kinney, J. P. **A Continent Lost—A Civilization Won.** 1937

Land Speculation: New England's Old Problem. 1975

Lange, Dorothea and Paul Schuster Taylor. **An American Exodus:** A Record of Human Erosion. 1939

Lord, Russell. **Men of Earth.** 1931

Loucks, H[enry] L. **The Great Conspiracy of the House of Morgan and How to Defeat It.** 1916

Murphy, Jerre C. **The Comical History of Montana.** 1912

The National Nonpartisan League Debate. 1975

Orr, James L. **Grange Melodies.** 1911

Proctor, Thomas H. **The Banker's Dream.** 1895

Rochester, Anna. **Why Farmers Are Poor.** 1940

Russell, Charles Edward. **The Greatest Trust in the World.** 1905

Russell, Charles Edward. **The Story of the Nonpartisan League.** 1920

Simons, A. M. **The American Farmer.** 1902

Simonsen, Sigurd Jay. **The Brush Coyotes.** 1943

Todes, Charlotte. **Labor and Lumber.** 1931

U. S. Department of Labor. **Labor Unionism in American Agriculture.** 1945

U. S. Federal Trade Commission. **Cooperative Marketing.** 1928

U. S. Federal Trade Commission. **Report of the Federal Trade Commission on Agricultural Income Inquiry.** 1938. three vols. in two

U. S. Senate Committee on Education and Labor. **Violations of Free Speech and Rights of Labor.** 1941. three vols. in one

Vincent, Leopold. **The Alliance and Labor Songster.** 1891

Wallace, Henry C. **Our Debt and Duty to the Farmer.** 1925

Watson, Thomas E. **The People's Party Campaign Book.** [1893]

[White, Roland A.]. **Milo Reno, Farmers Union Pioneer.** 1941

Whitney, Caspar. **Hawaiian America.** 1899

Wiest, Edward. **Agricultural Organization in the United States.** 1923